MW00668494

SONGBIRD

Also by Lesley-Ann Jones

Naomi: The Rise and Rise of the Girl from Nowhere
Bohemian Rhapsody: The Definitive Biography of Freddie Mercury
Ride a White Swan: The Lives and Death of Marc Bolan
Imagine
Hero: David Bowie
Tumbling Dice
Who Killed John Lennon?: The Lives, Loves and Deaths of the
Greatest Rock Star
Love of My Life: The Life and Loves of Freddie Mercury
The Stone Age: 60 Years of the Rolling Stones
Fly Away Paul: How McCartney Survived the Beatles,
Found his Wings and Became a Solo Superstar

With David Ambrose, foreword by Mick Fleetwood:
How to Be a Rock Star

With Brian Bennett OBE, foreword by Sir Cliff Richard:
Drummer

SONGBIRD

An Intimate Biography of

CHRISTINE MCVIE

LESLEY-ANN JONES

hachette
BOOKS

New York

Copyright © 2024 by Lesley-Ann Jones

Cover design by Jen Richards
Cover photographs © Getty Images
Author photograph © Daily Express

Cover copyright © 2024 by Hachette Book Group, Inc.

Hachette Book Group supports the right to free expression and the value of copyright. The purpose of copyright is to encourage writers and artists to produce the creative works that enrich our culture.

The scanning, uploading, and distribution of this book without permission is a theft of the author's intellectual property. If you would like permission to use material from the book (other than for review purposes), please contact Permissions@hbgusa.com. Thank you for your support of the author's rights.

Hachette Books
Hachette Book Group
1290 Avenue of the Americas, New York, NY 10104
Twitter.com/HachetteBooks
Instagram.com/HachetteBooks

First published in the UK by John Blake Publishing, an imprint of The Zaffre Publishing Group, a Bonnier Books UK company
First U.S. Edition: November 2024

Published by Hachette Books, an imprint of Hachette Book Group, Inc. The Hachette Books name and logo are trademarks of the Hachette Book Group.

The publisher is not responsible for websites (or their content) that are not owned by the publisher.

The Hachette Speakers Bureau provides a wide range of authors for speaking events. To find out more, visit hachettespeakersbureau.com or email HachetteSpeakers@hbgusa.com.

Books by Hachette Books may be purchased in bulk for business, educational, or promotional use. For information, please contact your local bookseller or email the Hachette Book Group Special Markets Department at Special.Markets@hbgusa.com.

Print book interior design by Envy Design Ltd.

Library of Congress Cataloging-in-Publication Data

Name: Jones, Lesley-Ann, author.
Title: Songbird: an intimate biography of Christine McVie / Lesley-Ann Jones.
Description: First US Edition. | New York: Hachette Books, 2024. | Includes bibliographical references and index.
Identifiers: LCCN 2024040133 | ISBN 9780306836916 (hardcover) | ISBN 9780306836923 (trade paperback) | ISBN 9780306836930 (ebook)
Subjects: LCSH: McVie, Christine. | Singers—England—Biography. | Rock musicians—England—Biography. | Fleetwood Mac (Musical group) | LCGFT: Biographies.
Classification: LCC ML420.M34186 J66 2024 | DDC 782.42166092 [B]—dc23/eng/20240828
LC record available at https://lccn.loc.gov/2024040133

ISBNs: 9780306836916 (hardcover); 9780306836930 (eBook)

Printed in the United States of America

LSC-C

Printing 1, 2024

IN MEMORIAM

Anne Christine Perfect, known as Christine McVie, 1943–2022

Anne Avril "Annie" Nightingale CBE, 1940–2024
Robert "Bob" Brunning, 1943–2011
Dennis Carl Wilson, 1944–1983
Michael Ralph "Mo" Foster, 1944–2023
Eduardo Quintela de Mendonça/Eddy Quintela, 1944–2020
Robert Lawrence Welch Jr./"Bob" Welch, 1945–2012
Peter Allen Greenbaum/Peter Green, 1946–2020
Melanie Anne "Melanie" Safka Schekeryk, 1947–2024
Robert Joseph "Bob" Weston, 1947–2012
Daniel David "Danny" Kirwan, né Langran, 1950–2018
Stephen Malcolm Ronald Nice/Steve Harley, 1951–2024
Steven Richard "Steve" Wright MBE, 1954–2024

The greater the success, the more money, the more opportunities, the bigger our world became, the more I found myself shrinking inside. Reducing. Becoming…less. Less confident. I needed— I thought I needed—a man to validate me. I needed coke and booze to fortify me to go on. It was easier somehow to live in that permanent haze than face reality. Those things made me who I was. Until they made me who I wasn't.

~

You can only mend the vase so many times
before you have to chuck it away.

~

Christine McVie

Such wooing as the ear receives
From zephyr caught in choric leaves
Of aspens when their chattering net
Is flush'd to white with shivers wet;
And such the water-spirit's chime
On mountain heights in morning's prime,
Too freshly sweet to seem excess,
Too animate to need a stress;
But wider over many heads
The starry voice ascending spreads,
Awakening, as it waxes thin,
The best in us to him akin;
And every face to watch him rais'd,
Puts on the light of children prais'd,
So rich our human pleasure ripes
When sweetness on sincereness pipes,
Though nought be promis'd from the seas,
But only a soft-ruffling breeze
Sweep glittering on a still content,
Serenity in ravishment.

From "The Lark Ascending," George Meredith's 1881 poem that inspired
Ralph Vaughan Williams's 1921 masterpiece for solo violin.
It was Christine's favorite piece of music.

For Richard Hughes

CONTENTS

CHAPTER 1

PRELUDE

A white weatherboard mill house leans beside the Little Stour river, keeping watch over the village of Wickhambreaux. Across a picturesque green with its thirteenth-century flint-built church of St. Andrew, green-shuttered manor house and grand Queen Anne rectory lurks an ancient timber-framed ale house known as the Rose. The homely inn, like the medieval Kentish village itself, is a quaintly photogenic refuge. Locals, walkers and occasional sightseers head here to sup and dine. To toast birthdays, weddings and funerals, to rejoice and to mourn, to ponder time both spent and yet to come. Creaking beams, wood floors and spitting log fires heave with fragments of the bygone and the blown. The prevailing mood is cozy, if a little restless. Non-villagers here are en route to somewhere else. Not all of them could tell you where they are heading.

At a time in her life when she had burned bridges and turned her back on her bandmates to make a new home in this tucked-away place, Christine was a frequent visitor to the Rose. She dropped in every day, give or take, at one point, around lunchtime or during the early evening, in need of human contact as well as sustenance, and for want of anything better to do.

I pull up a chair where she used to sit, recalling her silhouette cast by a lamp on the wall beside a corner table. I imagine her there, resting forward on one elbow, bare skin on wood. The thumb of her right hand pressed into her cheekbone. Her palm flattened against her lips, obscuring her mouth. There are pretty, dozing dogs at her feet. She stares, not at you but into the middle distance, through a wax-dripped bottle plugged with a melted stub. Which seems metaphorical. Her life, like the candle in the flask where she once lingered, flared as brilliantly as any in its day but was snuffed out ahead of its time. My late friend the celebrated bassist Mo Foster used to say that when a person dies, it's like a library burning down. So much talent, knowledge, insight and experience, reduced in a flash to ash.[1]

She purchased her property here, The Quaives[2]—a large Tudor house and estate with paddocks, gardens, cottages and barns—in 1990. Several years of renovations ensued, which turned out to be more extensive and expensive than she had anticipated. Had she realized, she said, she probably wouldn't have bought the place. She took up residence in 1998. She had quit Fleetwood Mac, the band that had made her rich and globally famous. At fifty-five her life, to the outsider an endless jet-set whirl of luxury and privilege, was in reality a litany of loss. Of her mother Beatrice when Chris was only twenty-five. Of two husbands, Mac bassist John McVie, whom she married the year her mother died, and Portuguese keyboardist Eddy Quintela, whom she wed when she was forty-three. Both marriages ended in divorce. Of the love of her life, wayward Beach Boy Dennis Wilson, who was her dangerously handsome obsession; who could not help but betray her with her acknowledged best friend, because it was the kind of thing that Dennis did. Of the children she would have adored but never got round to having, mourning motherhood only after her fertility had expired. Of the solo career in which she dabbled, was enriched by and that earned her great acclaim, but to which she could never quite rise to give her all.

There was something of Miss Havisham[3] about Christine, alone in her huge red-brick house on its sprawling nineteen acres, where she planted many trees in memory of lost loved ones so that she could keep them all close by. Her estate was bigger than the whole village, she would joke. She wasn't far wrong. But she was a tragic Dickensian character only in passing. There was no moping about in a rotting wedding gown, no sconces laced with tangling cobwebs, no rat-infested wedding cake and banquet, no clocks stopped at twenty minutes to nine. Having survived catastrophe, although she resisted loneliness she was alone again. Naturally. She would have given anything not to be. She had been "unlucky in love," she admitted sadly. She confessed to having found that a real drag.

Despite which, the romantic in her refused to yield its phantom. Virtually every song she wrote explored, celebrated or mourned passionate love. "I'm good at pathos," she said. "I write about romantic despair a lot. That's my thing, but with a positive spin." The life she built by accident was one of huge creative achievement, but also of deep personal loss. Which was an irony, given that she knew love precisely for all that it wasn't and was: a need, a greed, a paradigm. An excuse, a reason, an illusion. A blessed relief, an apology, a wonder and, ultimately, a curse. She knew love better than anyone, better than love could know her. She had convinced herself that she was better off without it, yet that never stopped her craving it. Like a crushed child suddenly wise to the lie of Father Christmas, yet as determined as ever to await the nocturnal call, she hoped against hope for her One True Love to claim her. Part of her sensed him around every corner. Be careful what you wish for. Truth was, she had already found him. She had blithely worn his ring while he gnawed out her heart.

The next best thing to being loved is being wanted. She tried hard to convince herself. Her needs were met, she agreed, by giving—without ever having to stop to count the cost. With quiet generosity she diminished the hold that money might have had over her, the way it has dominated and destroyed so many of her kind. She could spend without limit, go wherever in the world she chose. Instead, she purchased confinement at a distance from her roots. She immured herself within a chocolate-box backwater, growing lonelier.

*

A life becomes a story only in hindsight. A star becomes a legend only in death. If a legend is someone who makes an unforgettable impression, affecting the lives of millions, and is remembered long after their demise by way of an indelible legacy, Christine McVie was one. Yet her significance was largely unappreciated during her lifetime. When her passing was announced in November 2022, the shock and disbelief that vibrated from continent to continent related less to the tragic end of a remarkable musician who had contributed so much to music, and more to the fact that many who are not of her generation could not be sure exactly which of the women in Fleetwood Mac she was. "I adored her song 'Dreams,'" remarked a household-name musician to me during a phone call after learning that Christine had died. "Her voice on that haunts me, it's sublime." But it was bandmate Stevie Nicks who wrote and who continues to sing the exquisite song that remains one of her signatures, the one that opens with, "Now here you go again, you say you want your freedom." It is of course a track on the band's 1977 twelfth album, the career- and era-defining *Rumours*. Released as a single in May that year, "Dreams" went all the way. Although Chris created many of the Mac's most recognizable and best-loved hits, "Dreams" was not one of them. Nor did Christine care for it the first time she heard it. "When Stevie first played it for me on the piano, it was just three chords and one note in the left hand," she remembered twenty-nine years later in 2005. "I thought, 'This is really boring,' but the Lindsey genius came into play and he fashioned three sections out of identical chords, making each section sound completely different. He created the impression that there's a thread running through the whole thing."[4] By the time the "Dreams" single was released, *Rumours* was already a massive album. The five members of Fleetwood Mac stepped onto the lake.

For days and nights after the sad news came, it was back-to-back Mac all over the airwaves. Most of the national and local radio stations who invited me on to pay tribute to Christine introduced my interview with a Fleetwood Mac hit that was not one of hers. Irritating and lazy, it was to some extent excusable. The mid-seventies, the band's heyday, was after all half a century ago. Few of those researchers and presenters had yet been born. On the other hand, you'd think they would take the time and trouble to check. Credits are nowadays never much effort to research. Music of every genre from every era since the earliest days of recorded sound is freely available at the click of a key. It only takes a minute, girl.

*

Rumours was one of the albums we carried to house parties in supermarket shopping bags. It chafed against our local hero David Bowie's *Low*, Billy Joel's *The Stranger*, Queen's *News of the World* (the one with "We Are the Champions") and Rod Stewart's *Foot Loose & Fancy Free*. Neither old enough nor sophisticated enough for prog presidents Genesis, Yes or Emerson, Lake & Palmer, we hid behind Cat Stevens and Elton John. Carole King's 1971 classic *Tapestry* was over before we hitched a ride on the magic carpet. We got back to it. More or less all the music young teenagers listened to in those days had been recorded by men. Rock, in 1977, was holding its own against the burgeoning swell of disco. Punk was baring its fangs to greet the dawn.

Then *Rumours*, with revelations to make you weep. Not only because the band were an Anglo-American explosion of melody, harmony and in-your-face glamour, with five equally flamboyant stars and an orgy of woo me, screw me, break-me-in-half-and-rip-my-head-off songs. Not only for corduroy-cool Christine's rich, polished contralto or for Stevie's gossamer witchiness and Orson-Wells-on-helium warble; for Fleetwood's crazed drumming, Lindsey Buckingham's deranged shape-throwing and guitar picking and twanging, or for John McVie's insistent bluesy bass. But also because this tantalizing offering with its dainty fairy (Nicks) meets sex-starved, timber-bollocked laird (Fleetwood) in the iconic cover image shot by Herbert Worthington was as thrillingly vicarious as thrills get.[5]

We could not have known, the first few times we heard it, that this addictive collection of hymns to romantic disintegration and disillusion was so personal to its personnel. Interest in intimate ins and outs came later. For now, we were content with virginal voyeurism. We had to be. We had not the foggiest about the real-life boy-girl ducking and diving thing.

I'd been in and out of one or two of those by the time Christine and I began to cross paths. I had relocated to Los Angeles during the mid-1980s, on the payroll of a British newspaper. Her celebrity was low-level. She was a fixture on the West Coast music scene, but was never the kind to draw attention to herself. She tended to avoid celebrity hang-outs and had only a handful of famous friends. A fantastic cook, she'd rather make dinner for folk at home than go out to meet and eat in a restaurant. She couldn't stand the thought of other diners watching her every move and munch. Not that they did. She didn't attract that kind of attention. She had given comparatively few interviews throughout her performing and recording career. Despite her exalted unofficial status as "mother of the band," she had never been Fleetwood Mac's focal point. Stevie Nicks was the undisputed frontwoman, the star, the bobby-dazzler, the golden sex object, slathered over by men and women alike. She and Fleetwood shouldered most of the band's publicity commitments. The majority of journalists were interested only in them. This irritated the life out of guitarist Lindsey Buckingham, who felt deserving of greater fawning and recognition. It suited both Chris and her now ex-husband, John McVie. Neither had ever gone looking for limelight, submitting to press interrogation only when absolutely necessary. In those gentler, pre-personal publicist, pre-full-on-management, pre-saber-toothed-agent times that seem so unlikely today, hacks and turns mingled happily. Interviews were usually what the Americans termed "one-on-one." It would be, "Come up to the house for a swim and some supper." Perhaps the press junket had not yet been invented. If it had, I was NFI.

By then in her forties, Christine was an object of curiosity. She cut a mildly fierce figure in her predominantly masculine attire. She put me in mind of the Celtic queen Boudica. She had legs, as my grandmother used to say, right up to her bum. Endless jeans. Hip-length jackets. A slightly misshapen face and a putty-like complexion framed by cut-and-go hair, with a prominent nose and almond-shaped eyes. She had wonky teeth, which she would one day have straightened. Her smile in later photographs is whiter and better aligned.

Fleetwood Mac's *Tusk*, *Mirage* and *Tango in the Night* albums, the latter their biggest success since *Rumours* a decade earlier, had been and gone. Chris had survived, just, her tempestuous relationship with the Beach Boy, who died three days after Christmas in December 1983, two years after they separated. Out of his skull on drink and drugs, Dennis dropped off a yacht into the cold, cold briny and never came up for air.

She married her second husband, Portuguese singer-songwriter Eddy Quintela, in 1986, and co-wrote with him the song "Little Lies," a hit from the band's fourteenth album, *Tango in the Night*. She later suggested that his co-write credit had been "generous" of her. They are assumed to have divorced in 2003, but the split happened much earlier. He died in 2020. She was "done with men," she insisted, after him. When a woman says this, it's usually reach for the sodium chloride time. I had a hunch that Christine meant it. We do at the time.

We bonded—as far as a humble scribe can bond with a filthy rich international rock superstar—over my single, disturbing encounter with Dennis. During the dinner that British DJ Roger Scott and I had with him in LA, Dennis wept throughout for "his Chrissie." But she made it clear that the love of one's life wields no automatic right to remain welded. Beyond sick of his outrageous behavior, of his lying, cheating, profligate ways, she dumped him and never went back. He went off what was left of the rails, replacing her the year he died with a fourth, or was it fifth, wife Shawn Marie Harris Love (he had married third spouse Karen Lamm twice), who was twenty years his junior.

"Half of him was like a little boy, and the other half was insane," observed Mick Fleetwood, the Mac's leader and drummer, who had introduced Wilson to Christine and never stopped regretting it. "Chris almost went mad trying to keep up with [him]," Mick added. "[He] was already like a man with twenty thyroid glands, not counting the gargantuan amounts of coke and booze he was shoving into himself."

I admired Chris for maintaining her Englishness at a time when it was de rigueur to look and sound American. "What else would I be?" she said. "When you were born in the Lake District, you never quite eradicate the granite. The Midlands [where she grew up], that was never really me. I felt the lure of London early on."

Through her bandmates in blues line-up Chicken Shack, she met and hung with members of Peter Green's Fleetwood Mac. It was Green for whom she initially had the hots. Bassist McVie was casually engaged to someone else at the time. He broke that off to propose to Chris. She loved him, she said. She also longed to divest herself of her maiden name, Perfect, which had been a millstone around her neck since her first day at school. "Christine Anne Perfect" had been scoffed back at her by the odd spiteful teacher as "Pristine and Perfect." They hoped, those tutors sneered, that she had what it took to live up to her name. She divorced McVie, who had relieved her of the millstone. She never reverted, retaining his name even after her second marriage, and thereafter all the way to the grave.

The evolution of Fleetwood Mac features so many twists, turns and convolutions that it is worth pausing to reflect on it here, in order to establish Christine's precise position in the band's history. The line-up made famous by Peter Green but from which he then withdrew consisted of drummer Mick Fleetwood, bassist John McVie, and guitarists Jeremy Spencer and Danny Kirwan: the latter only eighteen years old when he joined in 1968, but already a deft guitarist and gifted songwriter. Christine signed up officially in August 1970. During the band's U.S. tour the following February, Spencer disappeared, and was later found to have been taken in by religious cult the Children of God.[6] Peter Green rejoined the band temporarily, just to help them out of a tight spot and complete the tour. He was replaced by Californian guitarist Bob Welch at its conclusion. In August 1972, Mick sacked Danny Kirwan, ironically for drunken, disorderly behavior. Danny's replacement a month later was Brit Bob Weston. English singer and frontman Dave Walker also came on board. He lasted only around six months. Weston was dumped in October 1973, for his shoot-yourself-in-the-foot affair with Mick's wife Jenny, the younger sister of George Harrison's and Eric Clapton's muse Pattie Boyd. Management and legal issues occupied what was left of the band throughout 1974, following which they regrouped. But before they got to see the New Year in, Bob Welch had quit. Mick happened upon a potential replacement, American guitarist Lindsey Buckingham: a most angst-ridden, introspective and ego-driven man, who said he would consider joining only if his chiffon-draped, pixie-witchy squeeze Stevie Nicks could be in it too, because they recorded and performed as the duo Buckingham Nicks. They came as a package. Another girl in the line-up? Heaven forbid. This could only work if Christine was comfortable with it. A New Year's dinner sealed the deal, and Lindsey and Stevie joined Mick and the McVies. This "classic" Mac line-up was set in stone for the next dozen years, until Lindsey headed for the hills in August 1987. His replacement was a pair of American guitarists, Rick Vito and Billy Burnette. Christine and Stevie both left the band's latest touring incarnation in December 1990. Chris returned five years later to record with them. Rick Vito went his separate way in October 1991. The *Rumours* Five—Mick, the McVies, Stevie and Lindsey—reconvened for a one-off gig in January 1993 to mark Bill Clinton's presidential inauguration. Stevie and Billy Burnette then stepped down from the band, and were replaced by Bekka Bramlett—daughter of American singing-songwriting duo Delaney & Bonnie—and ex-Traffic English guitarist and singer-songwriter Dave Mason. Burnette put in a brief reappearance for one album. In October 1995, the band called the caper a day.

But there was still something intoxicating left in the cauldron. Always something to draw them back and back. Together as Fleetwood Mac, the classic members had always been greater than the sum of their parts. The way they combined, enhanced and fired off each other was far more magical than anything the individuals could achieve by themselves. However hard they resisted, the lure proved too great. In 1996, Mick, John, Chris,

Stevie and Lindsey convened yet again. The following year they were back on the road together, unbelievably, and released their acclaimed live album *The Dance*. After which, in 1998, Chris withdrew again—for absolute good, she said. She insisted that she had retired altogether from music, and that she now wanted to spend her time doing other things.

No spurious past-time could soothe Christine for long. She tip-toed back into solo recording. For sixteen years, she kept her word and avoided the Mac. But the longing was irresistible. Never going back again? In January 2014, she did. Four years later, following a fall-out, the band dumped Lindsey once and for all. Enter New Zealander Neil Finn, formerly of Split Enz and Crowded House, and American guitarist and singer Mike Campbell, once of Tom Petty and the Heartbreakers. The band hit the road again in 2018. They were received like gods, on what turned out to be Christine's farewell tour. Not long after her unexpected death in November 2022, Stevie announced that the party was over.

"We had a really great time and it was a huge tour," she said of that triumphant outing in an interview with New York magazine site *Vulture*. "That (continuing on as Fleetwood Mac) was there in the realm of possibility. But when Christine died, I felt like you can't replace her. You just can't. Without her, what is it? Who am I going to look over to on the right and have them not be there behind that Hammond organ? When she died, I figured we really can't go any further with this. There's no reason to."

Fleetwood agreed. At least, he appeared to: "I truly think the line in the sand has been drawn with the loss of Chris. I'd say we're done, but then we've all said that before…"

*

"Being in the same band as your partner kills a relationship," Christine once told me over a drink, as we sat swapping notes on marriage and men. "Being in a different band from your partner would kill it just as surely. Because the road takes you in different directions, and the temptations of the road are too great. Which is worse? I couldn't say. All I know is that John and I were in each other's faces twenty-four seven. In the end, you get to a point when you want to murder them, if they don't try to kill you first."

For a few years we crossed paths at this and that gathering. She was always warm and welcoming. Dismissive of gossip and rumor, her favorite subject was simply music and musicians. She would never discuss her own songs, neither works in progress nor recorded hits. Those were conversations she had with herself in her head, she said. Though never star-struck in her presence, which she would have loathed, it was the kind of thing that made her squirm, I was always impressed by her.

Shortly before she gave California the boot and moved lock and stock back to England, we met for dinner one night at The Ivy, a crammed, bohemian little place on North Robertson Boulevard. She was sick of the race, she said.

"Rock stars age in dog years in reverse," she said, cryptically. "We are much older than our chronological ages. We are weary and worn. Our skin is thin. We have seen too much. Lived too much. Drugged and drunk too much. We have caused as much damage as we have survived. Looking back on all that, remembering all that, the mere thought of it never sat well with me. It made me loathe myself. I had never been very good at looking myself in the eye anyway.

"All that excess, all that having everything you could want, money no object: it drains you. It numbs you. It ceases to be exciting after a while. All you want is your mother's kitchen with a scrubbed table, old-fashioned crockery and a stool to put your feet up on. Scratchy toilet paper, even. The road, my love, is never a luxury. It is a drudge."

She developed a fear of flying, common among musical artists, many of whom come to dread tempting fate every time they board. David Bowie, Aretha Franklin and Johnny Cash were famously aviophobic. Thom Yorke of Radiohead and Cher shared their fear. Blink 182 drummer Travis Barker survived a real plane crash, so his reluctance was more than a phobia. Killers' frontman Brandon Flowers would never fly on his birthday, while *Tubular Bells* creator Mike Oldfield trained as a pilot to overcome the fear. For Christine, it was the perfect excuse to step off the conveyor belt and settle. During the late 1990s, at her Grade II listed home with its sweeping paddocks, croquet lawn, lavender beds and rambling outhouses, one of which she converted into a low-level recording studio so that she could work with ease on her songs, we sat at either end of an eight-seater solid oak dining table and shared a pass-the-marmalade moment. I was there to discuss a book idea. She had shown initial interest, hence the invitation. But by the time I arrived, she had gone cold.

"Nothing to see here," she said.

Really?

"You heard."

I sensed that she couldn't bear to retread it all. As for the nightmares, no to those. Never going back again. Nevertheless, during interviews she gave during what turned out to be the final months of her life, she started talking again about writing a memoir.

I had looked forward to seeing more of her in the Garden of England, where we both now lived. My house was only nine miles north of hers. But work necessitated a move back to London, where I was ragged with deadlines and kids. She was immersed in her dogs and her music. The years evaporated. We ran into each other after a lengthy gap, at an awards ceremony and lunch at the Savoy. Now peering into her seventies, Christine was still upright. She still towered. She remained proudly stylish and youthful, there was no little old lady in there. We chewed cud as I took a turn around the room with her. She stopped here and there, proffering her program for signature and posing for pictures. She was having the "best day," she said. To me, she seemed detached. She later admitted that she was bored.

Living in the sticks?

"That."

Although she refused everything but water that day she was, she confided, drinking heavily again. She was also swallowing codeine like Smarties, for back pain. She would eat lunch or early supper on her own in the Rose: "Talking to yourself over a plate of bangers and mash is not a good look." Apart from her brother, who lived only half an hour away, she knew virtually no one locally. She would pause in the street, pass the time of day, admire the odd mutt and chit-chat with the neighbors, she said. But there was never more than that. She had not made any real friends. She had staff—assistants, cleaners, gardeners, a handyman—most of them hired word-of-mouth or through agencies, and drawn from nearby towns. It occurred to me how removed she must have felt in her ivory tower on the outskirts of that village, and how alienated from the locals—some of whom would have resented her, others who may have been fascinated by her but perhaps assumed that because of who she was, she would be unapproachable. You don't just invite a rock superstar you don't know personally into your kitchen for a bowl of soup; if only because it is humiliating to be turned down.

"There is always something interesting about a pop star living in a small community," observes clinical psychotherapist Richard Hughes. "Everyone in the village wants a part of them. They are constantly having to let people down. There's always a neighbor who plays the guitar who wants them to listen to their latest song. It gets complicated. The superstar hides. They have no choice."

Chris had little in common with most of the residents of Wickhambreaux. Her own tribe were often inaccessible. Friends would promise to come down but got round to it only rarely, because "things" always happen last-minute. More often than not, her musician pals would be on the road. She needed to be among her people. By which, she meant the freaks, the dreamers and the misfits. The conjurors of magic. The likeminded folk who felt, as she did, the tickle of lyrics at the back of her throat, the prickle under the skin on her arms when she found the right notes to accompany them.

"You talk about this stuff with non-musicians and there's always a sense that they think you're slightly bonkers," she said. "There's a language that musicians speak. Across the genres, I mean. We get it. Our job is to deliver our musical take on life to the fans who absorb and, in many cases, live their lives by it. So we have to try to understand them. We have to dissect emotions, strip them down, make them digestible. This is hard. Emotions are hard. They are no easier for the likes of us because we can write about them. If anything, they are even more difficult. Write a song like 'Songbird' and people assume you have all the answers. If only they knew. They probably do. They don't want to."

Where do the songs, the magic, come from?

"You're asking the wrong person. But if you ever come across someone who can explain it to you in a way that makes sense, give me a call."

With that she was away. Me too. I had an O'Hare-bound flight out of Heathrow to catch. We cheeked goodbye as I legged it for a cab. It was the last time I ever saw her.

CHAPTER 2

THE SHEEP BOY
WHISTLED LOUD*

That the unborn child is capable of absorbing external influences, experiencing a broad sweep of emotions and even storing information for later, is widely accepted today. The very suggestion would have been scoffed at during the 1940s. There was a war on. Most people were preoccupied with death, not birth. With the real threat of Nazi invasion. With the terrifying possibility hanging over their heads that Britain could fall at any moment to German rule. Bringing babies into that disrupted, dangerous, all but doomed world must have caused their mothers great anguish. Even if their children were born alive, there was every chance that they would not survive. What hope?

Yet babies will come. Christine's mother Beatrice was delivered of her second-born on Monday, 12 July 1943. Terrible things were going on in the world that day. Two thousand miles east near the Soviet city of Kursk, one of the largest tank battles in history commenced. Its long-disputed losses are now reckoned to have been as many as 800,000 Soviets and 200,000 Germans. The Battle of Prokhorovka involved 6,000 tanks, 2 million

---

* From *Elegiac Verses in Memory of My Brother, John Wordsworth* by William Wordsworth, 1805.

troops and 4,000 aircraft. It marked the end of the German offensive on the Eastern Front, the main front of the war, and of course dominated British newspapers that week; as did the Allies' hold on a hundred miles of coastline when 2,000 allied vessels poured men into Sicily. Researching news pages from the period is fascinating. Daily battle updates were interspersed with quaint ads for such must-haves as Monk & Glass custard —"It isn't plentiful but it *is* good"—Bournville Cocoa, Milk of Magnesia and Phosferine tablets, the latter a tonic to perk up the run down and for everything from "maternity weakness" to "decay" and "nervous debility."[1]

Christine almost got to share a birthday with her elder brother, John, born on 13 July a few years earlier. Those inclined to connect invisible dots, to enthuse over the "coincidence" of siblings sharing a star sign (Cancer), might conclude that this explained why they were always so close. The qualities they had in common, insist those of a mind to, were "written in the stars." Both intelligent, highly creative, precise payers of attention to detail. Both calm, careful, modest and unexcitable types, unfazed by dilemma or obstacle. Apparently. I have never met her brother, so I cannot vouch for him. Christine, however, was all of those things. She was also unmoved by astrology. "Reading horoscopes is a bit pointless," she said. "I'd rather go for a walk." It is notable that in this regard, she and bandmate Stevie Nicks would fail to align. Stevie, a "triple Gemini," lived by the Tarot (there are whole decks inspired by her), her copious crystals, lucky necklaces and other talismans, her superstitions, her angels, her fanciful poems and prayers, and by whatever was or wasn't "in the stars" that day. "Pluto had just crossed into her house of love and Saturn was on her Neptune, squaring her Capricorn Moon and Midheaven and Cancerian Venus" being a typical observation of her. Verily. The kind of thing at which, despite her love and respect for Stevie, her talent and her friendship—to a point—Christine would almost imperceptibly roll her eyes, as if to say, "Bollocks." She was, however, inclined to mention here and there that she was "a Cancer." As if that explained anything.

Fetal medicine did not exist until the late 1940s. It would not be established until after the war, post-1945. Even then, procedures were limited to the use of penicillin to treat syphilis in pregnant women in order to prevent, in their offspring, congenital effects of the disease.

Only after her death did I begin to wonder about Christine's prenatal life.

Given the vast amount of research in the field of pre-natal science since the 1950s; given the complex, complicated, contradictory, introspective, self-effacing, epicene and enigmatic woman that Chris became; and given, further, the unusual characters, occupations and preoccupations to which she was exposed both pre- and postnatally, I cannot help but visualize a voracious, restless, needy little fetus who was troubled by her mother, soothed by her father, unsettled by her boisterous brother and impatient to get out into the world and join in. A team player. As in utero, so in life.

"That is what makes Chris so great," said Mick Fleetwood years later. "She's a band player, not a solo act."

In 1982, years before I became a mother, I read a startling book entitled *The Secret Life of the Unborn Child*. Its author, Dr. Thomas R. Verny, the pioneering physician recognized today as the godfather of prenatal psychology, is one of the world's leading authorities on the effect of the pre-birth and early postnatal environment on the psychological development of the human child. Decades of research led to his conclusions that the unborn baby is hugely capable of learning; that she is able to hear and respond to voices and sounds, we now know from sixteen weeks and perhaps even earlier; that she is sensitive to her parents' feelings about her; that she can react to love, can even warn us about as yet undiagnosed medical problems and potential hazards, and is already an active, feeling, responsive human being.

Babies, explains Dr. Verny, don't simply hear music in the womb. They can recognize the same tunes after their birth. They can remember melodies. They are also affected profoundly by unpleasant, disturbing and threatening sounds. The latter have been shown to interrupt and even stunt their development.

I was blown away by this book. It changed my habits and behavior during my own pregnancies. I played my entire record collection to my unborn children, and attended countless concerts and gigs. All three of them are musical, two professionally.

Although I had read it several times, I had not reached for Dr. Verny's masterpiece for years when I began to research Christine's life. I knew that she hailed from a musical family; that her paternal grandfather William Henry Perfect had been a pipe organist, allegedly at Westminster Abbey (although unlisted, often queried), and may have been an organ scholar there. Her father, Cyril Percy Absell Perfect,[2] was a violinist and music teacher. Her elder brother played the saxophone. Her mother, Beatrice, known as "Tee," had never been musical. Christine remarked that her mum was "left out," given that the rest of the family could both play and read music. She also made a point of saying that her mother was possessed of a "decent" singing voice, possibly embracing and including her out of kindness.

Beatrice Edith Maud Reece was born on 28 May 1915 in Kingston-Upon-Thames, south-west London.[3] We do not know how twenty-four-year-old Beatrice first encountered her future husband. Middle-class Edwardians tended to meet their future spouses through family and friends, or in the workplace. Professional Edwardian men not of independent means needed to work and save to provide for a wife and family. Hence, they tended to marry later in life, often taking as brides women younger than themselves. Christine's parents were no exception. Cyril was a decade his sweetheart's senior. In 1939, when he was thirty-four and as Europe stood on the brink of war, he married Beatrice in Merton, a neighboring borough to Kingston. Given that Christine's elder brother was born that year, their mother would appear to have been pregnant with him on their wedding day. Neither here nor there today, pre-marital pregnancy was considered scandalous back then. The whispered word on the street would be, "But they *had* to get married."[4]

In years to come, Christine would say that all she had wanted as a child was what "everybody else" had: "an ordinary mother." Her own was a loving, caring, spirited soul—in more ways than one. For Beatrice, twenty-eight years old and mother of a four-year-old when she gave birth to her only daughter, was a medium, faith healer and psychic.

Declining to reveal whether she had inherited anything of her mother's clairvoyant ability, or whether Beatrice had traded professionally in that field, Christine could not have been more supportive of her mum's vocation and gifts.

"Well, *I* believe they were real," she said. "She was a healer."

She proceeded to explain how Beatrice apparently cured the terminal illness of a family friend. "There was an old friend of my dad's, in Newcastle—this rich old lady who lived in a run-down castle. She had terminal cancer," said Chris. "She sent a pair of her kid gloves to my mother, who wore one during the night, and a couple of weeks later there was a phone call: the doctors were amazed that all the cancer was completely gone."[5]

Years later, Stevie Nicks would endorse the claims about Beatrice's abilities, referring back to a prediction that Chris's mum had made about Fleetwood Mac. The first two albums released by the band after guitarist Lindsey Buckingham and singer-songwriter Stevie Nicks had been brought onboard sent them soaring. "We knew immediately that Fleetwood Mac was going to be huge," Stevie said. "We knew, almost like we could just look into the crystal ball. Christine's mom was a medium—like, a psychic medium, right? And her mom had a lot to say about it, like, 'It's gonna be huge.'"[6]

Did Beatrice make those predictions from beyond the grave? Because she died on 23 September 1968: six years before Stevie and Lindsey joined the band. Christine and Stevie had not yet met. The first two albums by the new line-up featuring Mick Fleetwood, John McVie, Christine, Stevie and Lindsey— *Fleetwood Mac* and *Rumours*—were released in 1975 and 1977 respectively.

Whether or not Christine was blessed with psychic ability of her own, she was convinced that her signature composition was the result of a night-time visitation that sent her flying to the keyboard to play it.

*

It seems likely that the less quantifiable, more mysterious aspects of her mother's personality and behavior must have influenced Christine before her birth. How could she not have been affected? If only to the extent that some degree of spiritual intervention always seemed totally natural to her, which does appear to have been the case. Very few of us could lay claim to the same.

When she was about eleven, Chris recalled, she had a wart under her nose that was making her fretful. She complained to her mum about it, who focused on it one evening, then reassured her daughter that it would be gone by morning. Sure enough. How much of that could have been down to Christine's unquestioning acceptance that when her mother insisted that something would happen, it would surely come to pass? Could the power of belief have been the primary force at play here? The little girl must have witnessed some out-of-the-ordinary things, to have been prompted to remark that all she had longed for during her childhood was "an ordinary mother." Even before she was born, all that summoning of spirits real or imagined, the focus on perceived inhabitants of supernatural realms and obscure dimensions, the pain-wracked howls of the more severely afflicted among her patients, and the routine hummings, chantings, mutterings and spell-like supplications that are the stock in trade of the medium, psychic and faith healer could have stirred bewildering energies.

To such rhythms, as to the incessant fingering of piano keys and the sad, comforting saw of the violin bow had tiny, unborn Christine been jolted and lulled. At least it wasn't to the point-blank boom of exploding bombs, collapsing buildings and the screams of wounded civilians. This war baby gasped herself from the womb not into some stale, moonless, sandbagged inner-city shelter but into fragrant air and light, in the comfort of home. Compared to the birth that she could have endured, Christine landed in relative paradise, in the Lake District. In the bucolic northwest corner of England so close to the Scottish border that accents there are sometimes barely distinguishable. For many during those years of upheaval, it was a shelter from danger and conflict. Most of the time.

Following the Government Order given on the morning of 31 August 1939, Operation Pied Piper began the next day, two days before war broke out. Areas considered to be at great risk of being bombed or turned into battlefields were largely evacuated, of mothers with infants, the pregnant, the elderly and most children of school age. Torn from the arms of stricken parents, kids flooded into the Lake District and other rural areas all over the country. A second wave of evacuees followed in 1940, when the air raids stepped up: 1,600 school children were delivered from the North East to escape the Luftwaffe bombs falling on Newcastle's shipyards and buildings; still more were transported directly from London. Children were required to be equipped with "kit," outlined in a Ministry of Health leaflet:

"a handbag or case containing the child's gas mask, a change of under-clothing, night clothes, house shoes or plimsolls, spare stockings or socks, a toothbrush, a comb, towel, soap and face cloth, handkerchiefs; and, if possible, a warm coat or mackintosh. Each child should bring a packet of food for the day." Each wore a brown luggage label pinned to their coat, on which had been written their name, school and evacuation authority. Taken from their parents and sometimes separated from siblings, they were accompanied on their journey by guardians, most of them teachers or volunteers from the Women's Voluntary Service. On arrival, each was handed a carrier bag containing his personal rations: a can of meat, two tins of milk, two packets of biscuits and a quarter-pound of chocolate.

In June 1944, when Hitler aimed his V1 "vengeance" weapons at London, a third wave of evacuees was dispatched to Cumbria. School records show that they remained there until the autumn. Plenty of families had no contact with their children for months or even years, beyond handwritten letters sent and received. When they returned home, most of the evacuees were four or five years older than when they had left. Everything about them had changed. So, too, had the personalities and lives of those who had been forced to part with them. In some cases, tragically none too rare, their families no longer wanted them.

Why were Christine's family, who were from south London, in the Lake District during the war years? At first, I assumed it must have been because her mother had a small child, and that they had been evacuated. But Beatrice and her son did not relocate there without Cyril. The couple conceived their second child there in late 1942. The day after Beatrice gave birth at home in Greenodd the following July, it was her husband who went to the medieval market town of Ulverston[7] (locally, pronounced "Oostan") just northwest of Morecambe Bay to register their daughter's safe arrival—probably on foot, as few people had cars in those days—

making the almost-seven-mile round trip along unmade tracks, over bridges and stiles, through woodland, cutting across open farmland and proceeding parallel to the estuary to reach the register office in the Town Hall near the Market Place.

Had school master Cyril been transferred to the Lakes by the Board of Education to teach, accompanied by his wife and son—there being, thanks to the evacuation program into the region that commenced in 1939, a huge influx of school-age children? Or did the Perfect family relocate there under their own steam in anticipation of threat? That is possible, given that they were middle-class suburban Londoners of relative means.

Christine's father may well have visited the region before, during his childhood. His own father, Christine's paternal grandfather William Henry Perfect—the aforementioned organist—was born in 1876, only a hundred or so miles southeast of the Lakes in Huddersfield, West Yorkshire. During the Industrial Revolution, the prosperous wool-trade town choked under a blanket of smog from factory and domestic coal fires. Its buildings were blackened, its fetid rivers and canals devoid of life. William himself could have been taken on family holidays to the Lake District, a popular destination during the Victorian era if only for a breath of fresh air. The railways reached Windermere in 1847, affording people of all classes the opportunity to escape the grime and gasp of sprawling cities such as Manchester, Liverpool, Newcastle and Leeds. Steamer boats also served the larger lakes. Could memories of that idyllic destination have lingered in William's mind? Might he have taken his own sons there in turn, seeking to inspire them with his own affection for the place?

On 15 August 1904, when he was twenty-eight, William married southerner Rose Prockter in Balham, south London. He became Assistant Master at the Rutlish School on Rutlish Road, Merton, less than five miles away. The school had been founded with the wealth of William Rutlish, official embroiderer to King Charles II in 1661. Formerly a grammar school, latterly a state comprehensive, the establishment would relocate to nearby Watery Lane, Merton Park in 1957. William and Rose's eldest son Cyril, Christine's father, was born in Balham on 23 June 1905. He was christened on 29 March 1908 at St. Saviour's Anglican church in Raynes Park, in what was then Surrey. At the time of his christening, the family were living at 11 Rutlish Terrace, Shelton Road, Merton. Why did they wait until their eldest son was nearly three years old before having him baptized, during the same year that his brother Bernard Leslie was born? No reason is recorded.

By 1917, according to the records of the National Census, the family appear to have been living in Cambridge, probably due to a professional posting of William's. The youngest of his three boys, Richard William, was born there that same year. In 1925, when Richard was only eight and Cyril just twenty, their forty-nine-year-old father died suddenly. Cyril was now head of the family, obliged to work to provide for his mother and brothers. His long-held dream of becoming a first violinist in a symphony orchestra, or even a solo concert violinist, was dashed. At least for the moment, while he did his duty. Following in his late father's footsteps, Cyril became a schoolteacher.

As such, he avoided being called up. This was by no means a case of duty-shirking. According to Parliament UK, plans for limited conscription applying to single men aged twenty to twenty-two were approved in the Military Training Act of May 1939. This required able men to submit to six months' military training. Some 240,000 registered for service. On 3 September 1939, when Britain declared war on Germany, an extended measure was passed. The National Service (Armed Forces) Act imposed conscription of all males aged eighteen to forty-one. The medically unfit were exempted, as were clergymen, teachers and certain classes of industrial worker, such as bakers, farmers and those engaged in medicine and engineering. All were needed to keep the country running. Conscientious objectors faced tribunals to argue their cases. If not dismissed, they were given alternative, uniformed, forces-related jobs. In December 1941, a second National Service Act was passed to make all men up to age sixty, and all unmarried women and childless widows aged twenty to thirty, liable for call-up.

Compared to south London's drab sprawl, the fells and dales of the Lakes are heavenly.

The small village of Greenodd in what was once known as Egton-with-Newland, later Egton cum Newland, sits on the northern bank of the River Levens Estuary within the Crake Valley, on the edge of the Lake District National Park. It was once a small port on the highest navigable point on the estuary, handling exports of copper ore from Coniston, gunpowder from Backbarrow, limestone from local quarries, raw cotton, sugar and coal. As such, it enjoyed considerable status during the late eighteenth and early nineteenth centuries.

Because both Greenodd and nearby Ulverston were ports with bonded warehouses,[8] banks flourished in both village and town to service their financial needs. All local banks were thus closely linked with shipping. Some of the banks merged over time. The arrival of the Furness railway in 1844 led to the decline of local shipping activities. Becoming surplus to requirements, most of the banks closed down. Greenodd's sub-branch of Martins Bank Limited on Main Street, which opened for business in 1898, was mothballed during World War II along with many other tiny sub-branches because there were not enough staff to man them. It reopened after the war, but closed for good in 1970. The buildings that had once belonged to and housed the banks were sold off or let as residential properties. In one of these, Holme Bank on Main Street, a detached, slate-roofed stone property divided into apartments, Christine was born.

`Her birth certificate, issued on the day after her arrival, states the family's place of residence in two sections. The first of these entries featured an error, which was crossed out and corrected. Her father gives his occupation as "School Master (Elementary)." His child's name is written clearly as "Anne Christine"; not, as so often referenced, the other way around.

It is likely that Christine's mother was cared for and assisted during the birth by a midwife, or at least by wives and mothers from the local community. Until 1939, most British women gave birth at home, attended by a midwife. But the war presented new challenges. Bombing had destroyed many urban hospitals. Midwifery services were relocated to emergency maternity homes outside the major cities. The more than 12,000 women uprooted from hearth and home and obliged to have their babies remotely were expected to remain in their rural billets until the conclusion of conflict. Despite general disorganization and other problems, 10,500 babies filled those emergency maternity homes in 1940 alone. The following year, the number almost tripled. In 1943, when Beatrice gave birth to her daughter, hers was one of more than 810,000 live births across the whole country. The figure would peak in 1947, post-war, to over a million babies. The second wave that would follow it during the early 1960s would establish the demographic known as "baby boomers." Showing that babies can be relied upon. They keep coming.

It still stands, the house in which Christine was born more than eighty years ago. It is, today, a private abode, close to the Ship Inn and Greenodd Brewery on a Main Street that has seen better days. The narrow thoroughfare is lined with two-up, two-downers, and some two- and some three-story terraced stone houses. A few are cemented and pebble-dash clad. Most have sash windows, some have small loft extensions, and one or two have permanent Christmas decorations affixed to exterior front walls. The plaster molding above a number of the doors is said to be more common in the county of Lancashire, of which Greenodd was once part. The village's inhabitants are rural residents and tenants, many of them elderly. Some of the older houses still bear signs of yore: a Constabulary Station here, a traditional butcher's shop there. A village bakery, a tiny post office with an integrated shop and a petrol station are the extent of the local amenities.

There are two pubs, although at the time of writing one of them appears to have closed down. Several homes offer bed and breakfast. Other houses, some of them historic, are offered in their entirety as holiday lets. Visitors come to Greenodd because it is ideally placed for exploration of the Lake District National Park. At the entrance to Main Street, elevated from the road, sits a stone and cement-clad village hall dating back to the 1870s. Latterly renovated and extended, it once served as the headquarters of the local detachment of the Home Guard, a battalion of unpaid, part-time soldiers. The local church, St. Mary's, presides over the village. Penny Bridge Church of England School, opened in 1869, sits tight on the hillside beneath the church between the villages of Penny Bridge and Greenodd, enjoying spectacular views across the Leven Estuary and all the way up the Crake Valley to Coniston Fells.

We are not far, here, from the Roudsea Wood and Mosses National Nature Reserve. At pebble's-throw pace are places that might have inspired J. K. Rowling: Orrest Head, Wild Boar Fell, Eskdale, Sea Toller, Fairies Cave, Buttermere Tunnel. Red squirrels abound here. Rare carnivorous plants such as rootless bladderworts, sundew and butterwort inhabit the bogs, peatlands and wetlands, feeding on insects and invertebrates. Golden eagles were once prevalent, though none has been seen here since 2015. Ospreys, red kites, buzzards, peregrines and several endangered species of fish are often sighted. Wild fell ponies are as synonymous with the Lakes as are their hardy Dartmoor counterparts with southern Devon, or the Shetland pònaidh with the northern

Scottish Isles whose name they share. And everywhere you look, sheep and more sheep: the farming of which has been a dominant industry here since Roman times.

It would be comforting to imagine that the Lakes were immune to the ravages of war; that this far-flung corner opened its arms to Christine's family with the offer of peaceful refuge, a haven in which to keep their heads down while devastation raged. They could then re-emerge when normality resumed. There is a misleading sense of timelessness about the place; a sense that it wants us to believe no clock has ticked here since the days of the Lake Poets—Samuel Taylor Coleridge, Robert Southey, William Wordsworth—who honored and preserved its boundless beauty in words. Having been born in Cockermouth, Wordsworth spent sixty of his eighty years here, from his schooldays at Hawkshead to lengthy spells in Grasmere and Rydal Mount. "I Wandered Lonely as a Cloud," prompted by the vision of daffodils at Ullswater, is one of the nation's best-loved poems. Many other writers and poets sought inspiration in the Lakes, not least Percy Bysshe Shelley, John Keats and Alfred, Lord Tennyson. Jane Austen recalled the region in *Pride and Prejudice*. Beatrix Potter, born in London, moved to Hill Top Farm near Hawkshead in 1905, the year that Christine's father was born. Her *Peter Rabbit* stories, celebrating locations and creatures familiar to her there, earned her lasting global fame.[9]

Where nothing is expected to happen, everything can and does. The Lakes were never immune to war. Jutting west into the Irish Sea with a straggling 150-mile coastline stretching from tiny Haverigg in the south all the way to the Solway Coast in the north with several estuaries and historic harbors in between, the region was always vulnerable. Bombs were dropped on Barrow only fifteen miles south-west of Greenodd in September 1940. In April and May the following year, it came under fire again during the Barrow Blitz, when 91 people were killed and 531 injured.

Barrow was targeted because of its steelworks, previously the largest in the world. The works and its shipyard were badly bombed, and the fallout was deadly. Many residential neighborhoods were destroyed, and more than 10,000 homes were flattened. Neighboring towns and villages were also bombarded. Barrow was able to provide air raid shelters for only about 5 percent of its population. Conishead Priory five miles south of Greenodd was taken over as a military hospital.

It fell to the Home Guard to patrol and protect the coastline, lakes and primary mountain passes. They guarded in shifts around the clock, laid mines and constructed extensive barriers. Working at their regular jobs during the day, they trained in the evening and at weekends. The Westmorland Home Guard were one such outfit, charged with protecting Windermere against the risk of German flying boats landing there. Not only in case of potential invasion, but also because an aircraft factory near Ambleside used the lake to test their planes. The fells were used for troop training exercises, particularly for tank crews, and for the development of anti-tank weapons. Elsewhere in this remote location, extensive War Office camps housed thousands of prisoners of war. Throughout Britain, more than 400,000 German and Italian prisoners were held in such camps. The Lake District was favored in this regard, for its remoteness.

Uniformed like the men, members of the Women's Land Army undertook strenuous forestry work, earning themselves the nickname "Lumberjills" and the formal title the Women's Timber Corps. The timber produced was used on the railways, in mining, for aircraft manufacture and to make charcoal gas mask filters. They also took on farm work, often moving in with farming families because the work was arduous and long. They created allotments out of disused plots for the cultivation of fruit and vegetables, as part of the national "Dig for Victory" drive. Many helped the war effort via the voluntary Women's Institute, part of whose remit was to "knit for victory," making socks, scarves, sweaters and blankets for servicemen, evacuated children and hospital patients. Hand-knitted socks were prized for their durability over the machine-manufactured equivalent, while homemade contributions cost the forces nothing. For women, many of whose husbands were away fighting, knitting for the war effort provided a much-needed psychological boost via the belief that they were contributing something. WI members also cared for evacuees, helping to billet the children, many of whom were inner-city kids who had never previously been away from home. Settling into rural communities was hard for them. The ladies organized tea parties and country walks, and kept the bairns entertained. They also engaged in fundraising, grew vegetables and ran market stalls, where they sold surplus produce. They made jam in vast quantities to preserve the fruit, and collected rosehips for pharmacists to make vitamin C supplies for the children. And they assisted the Women's Voluntary Service, aiding the fire service, St. John's Ambulance, the Air Training Corps and the police. It seems likely, given the community-minded woman she certainly appears to have been, that Christine's mother would have been part of the Women's Institute, and would have stepped up and done her bit.

*

Christine scraped into the so-called "Silent Generation." Born between 1928 and 1945 and preceding the baby boomers, these were the children raised to obey authority, to "do as you're told," and to be seen and not heard. Some may protest that she was arguably a boomer: born during the final years of war, devoid of personal memories of that period but with a head filled with vivid, detailed, second-hand recollections handed down to her by her parents. Because adults in those days talked about the war for years and years afterward. Those of Christine's age group are often considered default and cultural boomers if not technically demographic ones. Raised on rationed food, at least until 1954, baby boomers were healthier than many today. They could expect to remain at school longer, not only because the school-leaving age was raised to fifteen but also because of increased opportunity. By the time Christine turned ten in 1953, the modern teenager was on the move toward center stage. Adolescents were driving their own trends in music, fashion and film, refusing to conform to parental expectation, challenging authority and breaking rules. While youthful rebellion was no new phenomenon, the fifties teen was fueled by a soundtrack more powerful and all-pervading than anything heard before. Turning eighteen in 1961, and getting the key of the door in 1964, Christine was there for the Beatles but had already got the blues.

She never said much about the Lake District. Barely anything about her birthplace remained in her memory. If she did recall more in private, she kept it to herself and discussed it only with her loved ones. She had but a single flashback, she said: to the time when she dropped into a river and almost drowned.

"I was born in Greenodd and we lived there for three of four years before moving to Birmingham, where my father was a music teacher," she recalled in 2022, only months before her death. "Cumbria is a beautiful part of the world and we had a good time"—suggesting that she was oblivious of war-related activity. She had been too little. "But my distinct memory is of nearly drowning. I slipped in the mud and fell in the river, and they had to get me out using a fishing net."[10]

There is paradox in the recollection. To have been born in the Lakes, far from the epicenter of enemy action, may well have saved her life. Yet the only thing she could recall about her few years ensconced there was that her fledgling existence had almost ended in tragedy. Did she relive, years later in 1983, her personal moment of terror as a toddler upon hearing that Dennis Wilson, the love of her life, had drowned?

CHAPTER 3

BEARWOOD

"Cumbria is a beautiful part of the world and we had a good time."

Her words nagged me. What a peculiar remark to make. Blissfully unaware of the war and all its upheaval though Christine must have been while she and her family lived in the Lake District —she was under five, after all, and an oblivious infant—she would have been well aware of war history and its wider impact by the time she said that. She was neither insensitive nor indifferent, which is why the statement surprises me. The ability to gloss over uncomfortable matters, to rise above and move swiftly on appears to have been a feature of her personality from an early age. She had never been, she admitted, one to dwell on things. Perhaps not outwardly, but so much was simmering inside.

Christine was three or four years old and of preschool age when the Perfects relocated to Birmingham. Specifically, to Bearwood, southern Smethwick in the West Midlands, often described as the historic heart of England. Densely forested in ancient times, the region was primarily rural until the nineteenth century, when it developed and expanded rapidly. Bearwood has a landmark tavern called the Bear at the junction of Bearwood

Road and Three Shire Oak Road, where the likes of Thin Lizzy and Judas Priest gigged in the early seventies. Its original William Mitchell pen factory later became a nursing home.[1] Smethwick's most desirable residential areas, Lightwoods Hill and Warley Woods, would feature prominently in the Perfect family's future. Cyril Perfect took up a post as a music teacher at St. Peter's College, Saltley, less than twenty minutes away on the other side of Birmingham, and taught violin at St. Philip's Grammar School.

St. Peter's, an Anglican school and teacher training college, was founded in 1852. Its wonderful Tudor revival architecture gives the building the appearance of a University of Oxford college. Hit by a Luftwaffe bomb during the war, it was shut down in 1941 but later re-opened, closing for good as an educational establishment in 1978 long after Cyril had retired. St. Philip's, a Roman Catholic Boys' state grammar school,[2] was a fine red brick and stone edifice built between 1859 and 1861. The grammar school closed in 1976, after which it was maintained as a sixth form college until 1995. Thereafter until 2005, it housed South Birmingham College.

There are people from Smethwick who claim to hail from the "Black Country." The term evokes, in viewers of television's multi-series crime drama *Peaky Blinders*, which commences during the aftermath of World War I, grim and violent scenes of hardship, deprivation and gang warfare. Understood today to comprise the metropolitan boroughs of Dudley, Sandwell, Walsall and the city of Wolverhampton, you won't find the "Black Country" on any map. Some who live there or are from there insist that the area has no defined border; that it is less a physical place, more an imaginary realm blending memories of its past with their own historical association with it. The thousands of factories and forges that punctuated its landscape during the nineteenth century, choking the air with smoke, are one explanation for the term. Another is the thick seam of coal known as the South Staffordshire Coal

Seam. Extending from the southern boundaries of Bentley, Walsall to Coseley in the west and West Bromwich in the south, it appeared above ground at various points designated by purists as the "only true Black Country: where you could actually see the coal." Smethwick was no such place. More than a few of its inhabitants maintain that geography has nothing to do with it. It seems to be all about perception and opinion. If people feel that they are from the Black Country, then they are.

In the eloquent words of Professor Carl Chinn MBE, an historian specializing in Birmingham and Black Country history, "The digging of coal from the South Staffordshire Coalfield scarred and blackened the ground and its burning blackened both the air and the faces of working folk." Smethwick, he explains, lies technically outside the Black Country, along with places such as Bearwood and Warley. But, he adds, "whatever its boundaries, the Black Country was and is more than a place defined by minerals and work. For a place is nothing without its people.

"Carved out by their landscape—as much as they carved it out in the digging of coal, limestone, fire clay and iron ore—and forged by their manufacturing, as much as they forged the metals crucial to their industries. So, then, are the folk of the Black Country tied by their sense of place, their understanding of their past, their awareness of their culture and their pride in their language. Because of these strong characteristics, the Black Country is a place that becomes more than a geographical entity, infused as it is with a spirit that reaches out from those who have gone to those yet unborn.

"The survival of that spirit is entrusted to the living. Let not the bond be broken."[3]

Black Country-born drumming superstar Don Powell of Slade puts it more bluntly. "Awlroight, ow bist?!" ("All right? How are you?!") he greets you tongue-in-cheek, with a bear hug. "It's a working-class thing," reflects the Bilston, Wolverhampton-born six-foot pounding powerhouse who, alongside singer and songwriter Noddy Holder, co-writer and multi-instrumentalist Jim Lea, and lead guitarist Dave Hill, achieved six UK number ones and twenty-four Top 40 hits with gimmicky misspelt titles such as "Mama Weer All Crazee Now" and "Coz I Luv You." Slade, one of the most popular British groups of the seventies, plugged the gap left by the Beatles. Their droves of fans dressed in copies of their idols' eccentric garb. Often credited with having kick-started the glitter-stomp revolution, Slade captured the nation's imagination to a degree that is almost impossible to imagine today. Their rowdy exuberance, thudding beat and wall-of-sound blare rendered them the new working-class heroes.

"It's 'working-class' because if you're not working, you don't eat," says Don. "My dad, Walter, slaved in a foundry all his life. Mum, Dora, had a job in an electrical components company. Where we lived was called the Black Country because of all the smoke. I was always driven to find a way out."

Bearwood is rich in musical history. Before their breakthrough, the Beatles performed at Smethwick Baths, known locally as "Thimblemill Baths," on 19 November 1962. Nineteen years old at the time, local student Christine may well have attended the gig, given that the venue was a little over a mile from her home. The grand Grade II-listed Art Deco building on Thimblemill Road opened in March 1933. It was requisitioned as an air raid shelter during the war. Local children like Christine later learned to swim there. Referred to in the press as "the Black Country swimming baths" when the facility marked its 75th birthday in 2008, it doubled during the sixties as one of Britain's top music venues. The wooden boards that were used to cover the pool during the winter months were trodden not only by the Beatles, but by the Kinks in February 1965 and the Who a year later. The Rolling Stones and the Small Faces also shook a leg there. Chances are that young Christine was present for those gigs, too.

Smethwick Baths, which closed to the public in July 2023 ahead of the launch of a new aquatic center, has been infamous for years for its apparent high level of paranormal activity. The center's reinforced concrete tunnels in the bowels of the building, used as a storage facility during the winter season for stage equipment and sets, were renowned as the most haunted destination in the region. During its construction in the 1930s on what was once open fields and farmland, excavators uncovered a medieval plague pit a dozen feet below what became the building's main reception. The mass grave, containing some 300 bodies, was left untouched and filled in again. Directly above the grave was the location of the World War II air raid shelter, said to be haunted by the ghost of a young boy drenched in white powder. Many staff members and contractors reported sightings of him. Investigation revealed that the corpses of plague victims were routinely doused in lime powder to dehydrate them and reduce the spread of infection. A wooden store at the tunnels' far end was said to contain an angry, misogynistic male entity who would appear from time to time as a mist that moved from chamber to chamber. He once allegedly terrorized a group of female ghost hunters by hurling a heavy wooden table at them. There was also, it is claimed, the ghostly presence of a sweet-natured child, who not only showed herself to many paranormal experts but also whispered in people's ears and would hold their hands. Apparently communicating through mediums, she is said to have explained that she once lived close to the building and that she was taken by a disease. Tradesmen often found themselves conversing with a red-headed male in a boiler suit, though no such staff member existed. Gangs of children tearing through the tunnels, the yapping, mewling spirits of dogs, cats and even a galloping horse were seen. The building also housed a war-time morgue for local bombing victims, where orbs, shady figures and terrifying groans were often seen and heard, and where visitors frequently felt nauseous. Elsewhere, the scent of lavender, a lady in RAF uniform, footsteps and puddles, slammed doors and all manner of handles and switches operating themselves were experienced. While things went bump in the night, a phantom tea lady wheeled her squeaking trolley the length of otherwise silent corridors.

Who knows? Christine's mother didn't. Despite the fact that she was one of the locals who led regular ghost walks. By 1954, when her daughter was nearly eleven and preparing for her 11-plus exam,[4] Beatrice Perfect had become something of a celebrity in their community as a psychic, medium, hypnotist and faith healer. She not only conducted popular ghost walks, but claimed to be guided by an "Indian spiritual controller" whom she called "White Eagle." I found a cutting from that year in a now-defunct newspaper, the *Birmingham Gazette*[5] in which Beatrice is billed as "a ghost hunter who doesn't believe in ghosts." The piece announced that she was to lead a walk on Saturday, 9 January 1954 to a Handsworth, Birmingham house, to investigate "knockings and footsteps."

"All the other ghost hunts I have been on have been wash-outs but good fun," she said. "I expect this will be the same. I have never seen a ghost, and until I do, really clearly, I shan't really believe in them."

Beatrice was thirty-eight years old at the time, and working as a secretary at a local girls' secondary school. She was also Secretary, probably voluntarily and in her spare time, of the Birmingham Psychic Research Society, an organization that no longer exists. The unnamed reporter must have interviewed her at the family home, because they describe Mrs. Perfect pointing to a painting on the piano at her home, and give the address as 52 Monmouth Road, Smethwick. The house is still there: a terraced, red-brick abode on a residential street, with a small, low-walled front garden and space enough to park a family saloon.

"That's White Eagle," said Beatrice of the figure in the painting. "He's my spiritual controller." The "Red Indian," she said, helped her to cure people living miles away. She would sit down and ask for White Eagle, she explained, and she would feel a "cold band" pressing across her forehead. "Then the image of the patient appears in my mind. I see beams of light going to the image and back."

She claimed to have cured her own sister of leukemia ("a disease of the blood cells"), after doctors had declared that there was no hope. But she admitted that she had never seen White Eagle "in the flesh," while other mediums insisted that they had. One night, she confided, she had felt compelled to try and paint the native American. "She is a hopeless painter," said her "artist husband" Cyril (not a mention of his musical virtuosity). The result bore a strong resemblance, agreed her fellow mediums, to the White Eagle they had encountered. "He must have guided me," insisted Mrs. Perfect, who added that she had "visions" of people who had been dead for years, and that she passed on messages for them. It was great fun, she said: "…just like going to the pictures." She informed the reporter that she had enabled a young schoolboy to play better cricket by hypnotizing him into sleeping more soundly, thus helping to relieve him of his inhibitions.

It is easy to understand why Christine would have felt alienated by all this; why she had longed, in her own words, for "an ordinary mother." Whether we believe in psychic phenomena or dismiss such obsessions as nonsense, these things preoccupied Beatrice and made her less available to her daughter. Christine was, she herself said, "confused by all the weird stuff. Whether beings from the other side were there or they weren't, I didn't want to know about it. It definitely put some sort of barrier between Mum and me. Possibly as a result of that, but who knows—I'm not the sort of person to analyze things that much—I always felt much closer to my pop."

"She must have felt distant from her mum," comments clinical psychotherapist Richard Hughes. "Her mother's involvement in such things would have been really othering. To be 'othered' is to feel different and shamed. To have a mother who was a bit 'woo woo' and interested in esoteric things could have been especially difficult at that time. The fifties were still very much the post-war period. People tended to be fearful of the supernatural, the spirit world and so on because of the Nazis' preoccupation with occultism.[6] If you were not part of the orthodoxy, people were likely to avoid or even attack you. Someone like Beatrice Perfect would have been regarded as an outsider. We can see why that would have been alienating for Christine. Growing up with such a mother, with that kind of thing going on at home, she would have been teased for it at school. She would have been ridiculed and ostracized."

Which is ironic, given that many mothers and perhaps also fathers would have turned to people like Beatrice in their hours of grief and bereavement, having lost sons in action during the wars; who would have beseeched mediums and psychics for "signs" that their loved ones lived on in spirit; who would perhaps have begged for "evidence" of their continued existence, or would have asked to be connected with them. Christine said she was well aware, as a child, of her mother's paranormal activities. While she believed wholeheartedly in Beatrice's abilities, these may well have troubled her daughter and made her feel insecure. It could account for why she grew into a low-key and withdrawn young woman who was always reluctant to draw attention to herself.

Christine fed herself, literally, as though to compensate for what was lacking emotionally. She was "a podgy child in love with food, especially chocolate," she admitted. Could fattening herself up have been a deliberate ploy to render herself "*im*perfect"? The heart bleeds for the little girl if it was. Pediatric psychologists now regard any relationship that leads to food issues in a child as neglectful, and the child as being developmentally traumatized. I had a dream about zipping back in time, taking Christine by the hand, seeing her home and cooking her a big, hot dinner with chocolate pudding and chocolate sauce for afters.

*

"The Midlands was a curious place during the war and post-war years," reflects Richard Hughes. The grandson of a former Midlands armaments factory owner, his fascination for the region while he was growing up led him to study its history.

"Beyond the factories were huge airfields, lots of American GIs, and of course prisoner of war camps. With so many incomers flooding the place, an air of fear and paranoia prevailed. The war years had seen the exodus of large numbers of people from cities to more rural areas like Shopshire and the Lakes. People were still on the move throughout the rest of the 1940s and into the early 1950s. Folk felt unsettled. People were suspicious, in particular of psychics: because it was believed that they were spies. There was a public announcement campaign warning people about the dangers of witchcraft and psychics. It was feared that they were communicating with psychics in Germany."

Preoccupation with witchcraft rose in Germany after World War II. By the time West Germany was founded in 1949, obsession with witches, faith healers and *hexenbanner* (practitioners of "un-bewitching") had risen to near-hysterical proportions: 80 percent of witchcraft cases in Germany from the 1920s through the late 1950s are said to have occurred post-war. After twelve years of Nazi rule, fledgling West Germany was a place enveloped in fear. Thousands of ethnically German refugees surged into a land where their acquired culture, customs and language were alien, making integration difficult. Paralyzed with fear, people were suspicious and defensive. The economic miracle of 1950s Germany "reduced the fear of exposure of potential wrongs committed during the

Third Reich," explains author Monica Black. "In turn, claims of witchcraft dwindled."[7]

Beatrice Perfect's activities caused her family anxiety because communing with the dead was regarded as witchcraft. As late as the 1950s, witches in Britain were still being punished by law. Their medieval predecessors had cast long shadows. Acts of Parliament passed over hundreds of years had resulted in the execution of around 500 witches. A further Act in 1736 repealed certain laws but imposed fines on those claiming to have magical powers. This was repealed in 1951 by the Fraudulent Mediums Act, which prohibited a person from claiming to be a psychic, medium or other spiritualist while attempting to deceive and to make money from the deception (other than solely for the purpose of entertainment). This in turn was repealed in 2008. Another, the 1824 Vagrancy Act, had made punishable offenses of spiritualism, astrology, fortune-telling and related practices.

Helen Duncan (1897–1956) was the last British woman to be jailed for witchcraft. The Scots-born psychic medium held séances from the 1920s. During one that she performed in Portsmouth in 1941, she claimed that the spirit of a sailor told her the HMS *Barham* had been sunk.[8] Wartime censorship prevented public announcement of such catastrophes. Only the next of kin of deceased servicemen were informed. The authorities were allegedly alarmed by her "insider knowledge." Duncan posed a threat, not because they feared her perceived connection to "the other side," but because she might reveal military secrets to the enemy. She was charged with fraudulent activity under section four of the 1735 Witchcraft Act, and also under the Larceny Act for accepting money under false pretenses. Her Old Bailey trial caused a sensation in wartime Britain, during which she was denied the opportunity to prove her powers before judge and jury. She was found guilty of witchcraft, though innocent of larceny, and was sentenced to nine months in Holloway women's prison.

Released the year the war ended in 1945, she undertook never to hold another séance. But she was caught red-handed in 1956. She died soon afterward in Edinburgh, at the age of fifty-nine. Her family and friends have since campaigned for her posthumous pardon. Every application has been denied. Consider that Beatrice Perfect was practicing the "dark arts" openly by the early 1950s. Though the occult was in demand, she skated on thin ice.

"The effect on Christine, even if it was subliminal, would have been profound," observes Richard Hughes. "Freud's view on people who believe they are psychic is that they are sensitive to a narcissistic parent, usually the mother, who has mood swings. Who is sometimes very loving, at other times very cold. These extremes are incredibly confusing to a child, who is on alert at all times anyway. The child grows up believing they have almost a second sight. That they can read and work people. So Beatrice would have had her own mother, Christine's grandmother, as the narcissistically wounded person. Beatrice grew up sensitive. So not only did she believe herself to be psychic but she—just as her mother must have been—was narcissistic."

Those who think they have psychic abilities, Hughes adds, believe they are special in some way. "It's incredibly difficult growing up with someone like that. It goes through the generations. And it's chronic. There can be a grandiosity to such individuals that is very hard to penetrate. Imagine if such a person were your mother, and how Christine must have felt. Within the family unit, Beatrice's psychic energy would have been the dominant force. It's possible that they explored this among themselves. But given the period of time we are concerned with—post-war—it probably wasn't explored. It may have been posited that Beatrice had a special gift but her daughter didn't, which would have left Christine feeling inadequate and insecure, and that she was lacking in some way. It's also entirely possible that the mother could have recognized equivalent ability in her daughter, but dampened it down. I find it fascinating that Christine later unwittingly aligned herself with another 'witchy woman,' one who even identified as a 'Welsh witch,' and who presented as in tune with all things mystic and spiritual: Stevie Nicks. And, of course, Fleetwood Mac were witchy themselves, very folky, mysterious and unfathomable. But in the meantime, rejected by her mother in subtle, subconscious, unarticulated ways, Christine had to find her own specialness. Which eventually she did."

The way that narcissism plays out, explains the psychotherapist, is all about specialness. If a mother feels that her child has it, that specialness, she can choose to nurture that in her offspring and try to make it a positive. On the other hand, she can ignore it, and ensure that her child doesn't get a look-in. Either way, the consequences can be damaging.

"Because a psychic is super special," Hughes explains. "Your level of specialness is off the scale. You have access to a whole other realm that most people are denied. Even if that realm exists only in your head, you find that you can easily convince others of it, especially the vulnerable, the needy and the grief-stricken. Is it real? It doesn't matter. *They* believe it. If they are able to convince themselves, they have no problem convincing others. Thinking about the dynamic of that family all these years later, there must have been resentment in the mother against the father-daughter bond. To make matters worse, Cyril and his two children had music in common—and music is the realm of the real. It is visceral. It's about instruments, skill, precision and intricacy as well as about creativity. Crucially, it involves working closely with other people. Beatrice's world was ethereal. A spirit world. She worked with dead people. Those two realms are worlds apart. Having worked with people in the psychical world, I can tell you that they do have a sense of specialness about them. They do believe that they have a gift. What else can a gift do but alienate others?"

Her growing awareness of the fact that her mother was seen as an outsider, and that some people were suspicious of her, had a lasting effect on young Christine's development. "I don't remember feeling that at the time," she said, "but it's possible I didn't allow myself to acknowledge it. All these years later, I get it." It contributed, she agreed, to her own sense of being an outsider. Which musicians always are.

*

The majority of upper working-class and lower middle-class homes in England from the late 1940s and into the 1950s had a piano. A musical family, the Perfects were no exception. Christine would recall having been introduced to the instrument at the age of around four, but could not remember showing much interest. It was not until she was eleven years old that her parents committed her to regular lessons. She reached Grade 7, falling short of the full eight grades, because she suddenly lost interest in classical music. She was also taught Theory, enabling her to sight-read.

"We weren't rich but we were an educated family, academically speaking," she told writer Robin Eggar in 2004.[9] "I studied classical piano. I went to lessons for a good many years until I discovered Fats Domino in my piano stool at home. It [the sheet music] was my brother's. I blame him for everything. He is four years older than me and a sax player, really good. It was after that I gave up classical music, and started to learn to try to play the blues. I wrote my first song when I was sixteen. It was rubbish, but probably better than some of the ones I have written recently. I skirmished with writing, then I stopped."

In 1956, at the age of thirteen, she transferred from her local secondary to the progressive Moseley Junior Art School on Moseley Road, Balsall Heath, five miles southeast of Smethwick. According to the National Archives, "a Junior Art Department for boys was set up in the Birmingham Central School of Art in 1900. A Girls Department was added in 1921. In 1924 a second Junior Department (for boys) of Arts and Crafts opened in Vittoria Street. These two departments later amalgamated. In 1945 it became known as Moseley Road Art School, and control was transferred from the College of Art Sub-committee to the Secondary Schools Sub-committee. In 1975 the school amalgamated with Mount Pleasant School to form Highgate School." The fine building, designed by W. H. Bidlake, an acclaimed exponent of Birmingham's arts and crafts movement, still stands, and is Grade II listed. It fell into disrepair in later years.[10]

The school, like many art schools, would produce internationally acclaimed musicians—Roy Wood of the Move, Electric Light Orchestra and Wizzard, Brian Travers and Ali Campbell of UB40, Christine McVie—and a number of notable artists: not least pop art movement co-founder Peter Phillips, abstract painter John Walker, later based in New York, and David Prentice, artist and co-founder of sixties Birmingham Ikon Gallery. It offered three-year courses to secondary age children, with entry at twelve/thirteen giving a second bite of the cherry to children who had failed their 11-plus.

"It's really interesting when kids who should be academic are not," muses Richard Hughes. "The failing of exams should never be taken at face value. It can be a trauma response. There can be cognitive dissonance. The brain can be in survival mode, unable to connect with academic ideas. Christine was, as she said herself, from an academic family. But there came a point at which she wasn't academic. Perhaps she showed earlier promise, but that fell away at the crucial point. There could well have been something traumatic going on in that household, to do with her parents. She may not have had the psychological space to be fully academic. Some people throw themselves into study to escape whatever the trauma is. But people who are more right-brained—more emotional, intuitive and creative, the kind who grow up to be writers, artists or musicians, working in fields that require creative expression and free thinking—can disconnect from academic learning. Because Christine moved to this particular school, with its emphasis on artistic pursuits, it is safe to assume that something like this happened."

As well as basic, standard subjects, pupils were taught a wide range of artistic disciplines beyond drawing and painting, including modeling, technical drawing, metalwork, stencil work and sculpture, for which Christine had a particular talent. She "came alive at that school," she remembered. "I was so lucky to go there." Not least because the establishment was co-educational. The presence of boys caused her to take a long, hard look at herself in the mirror and decide to do something about her appearance. Which is a particularly challenging, self-aware thing for a pubescent girl, effectively still a child, to do. Because, at the age of thirteen, Christine weighed more than 13 stone.

"I was a monster," she said. "Mammoth. Huge. A mound of blubber. I had a face like a pumpkin. I hated myself. I couldn't bring myself to look in the mirror. I had no interest in fashion, not that there was much of that going on at the time, it was all variations on what your mother was wearing and some of the time her actual clothes. The Swinging Sixties were yet to come."

As she told Robin Eggar, "When I went to art college, I suddenly realized how cute guys were, and I wanted one. I did eat a lot of chocolate when I was at school. Then I started eating salads, and it melted off me. I don't consciously eat mountains of chocolate anymore."

Within two years, thanks to that Fats Domino songbook lurking inside her piano stool, Chris had the rock'n'roll bug. Fats, the outsized American singer-songwriter and pianist born Antoine Domino Jr. in New Orleans, Louisiana, in 1928 had kicked off the fifties as a leading R&B hitmaker and fine purveyor of piano-based jump blues, the origins of which could be found in Creole blues, Dixieland jazz and boogie-woogie.[11]

He sang in a seemingly distant, almost mumbled style, pounding his piano as though in competition with the heavy percussion he favored. His 1950 single "The Fat Man" is widely hailed as "the first rock'n'roll single," as if anybody could ever prove such a thing. In any case, it was probably the first record to shift a million copies. "Ain't That a Shame" was a major hit in 1955, and established him as a rock'n'roll star. Fellow "Noo Orlins" natives Lloyd Price, Clarence "Frogman" Henry, Smiley Lewis and Little Richard followed. Fats's well-padded frame, kind nature and resistance of blatant sexuality in his act rendered him a safe bet for television exposure. He conformed to an unspoken subtext of the time, that black music needed to be acceptable to more reserved white audiences in order to hold its own in America's musical mainstream. Adaptability was essential, which Fats seemed to sense. No, Little Richard never compromised, nor diluted his outrageousness, but broke through anyway. There's always one. But hindsight reevaluates him to some extent as a comedy act, the first great showman in music rather than first and foremost a musician.

For Christine, Fats would remain an enduring influence. As she would later tell the *New York Times*, if it hadn't been for the blues, she would never have developed her music-writing skills. Her love of and appreciation for classical music never receded. She would always be grateful for her early classical training, which helped her create some of rock's most legendary songs. This was reflected in her choices for the BBC Radio 4 program *Desert Island Discs*. Appearing on the show in 2017, she offered the following as her selections:

"Concerto No. 4 in F Minor," Antonio Vivaldi: "This one always reminded me of my father," she said. "He was often playing Vivaldi."

"Ain't That a Shame," Fats Domino: the blues/rock'n'roll star who switched her on.

"Roll Over Beethoven," the Beatles: the 1956 hit written and recorded by Chuck Berry, with its indelible prediction that rhythm and blues would one day be as respected as Beethoven or Tchaikovsky. It is one of the most covered numbers in rock'n'roll, the most famous renditions being by Jerry Lee Lewis, Carl Perkins, the Beatles and the Electric Light Orchestra. The record had been one of Paul, John and George's favorites before they became the Beatles. They recorded their cover on 30 July 1963 for their second British LP, *With the Beatles*. George Harrison plays and sings lead.

"Man of the World," Fleetwood Mac: written by the band's founder, original lead singer and guitarist Peter Green in 1969. It made number two in the UK in June that year, and languished in the chart for some fourteen weeks. It would have various subsequent outings. The song reflected Green's mental health, already in turmoil. "A beautiful song. A poignant song," said Mick Fleetwood. The perfect tribute to the man who started it all.

"Cathy's Clown," the Everly Brothers: written by Don and recorded by the brothers in 1960, about a man betrayed and shamed by his sweetheart. From personal experience? Their bestselling single and a worldwide smash, it is also a masterclass in how to swerve from the well-beaten track of classic songwriting structure. It influenced the Beatles hugely, who re-created the harmonies for what became their first UK number one, "Please Please Me."

"Angel Come Home," The Beach Boys: from their 1979 album *L.A. (Light Album)* featuring solo recordings by the band members during an episode when they were barely speaking. Co-written by Carl with an outside songwriter, it is sung by Dennis Wilson. It's a clumsy number, but maybe Chris heard in it a direct plea from Dennis. "I'll be in heaven when my angel comes home."

"The Lark Ascending," Ralph Vaughan Williams: a short work inspired by a poem, written for violin and piano. It must have reminded her so much of her violinist father. It was, she said, her favorite piece of music.[12]

"I'd Rather Go Blind," Etta James: the classic blues number written by Ellington "Fugi" Jordan with Etta and released in 1967. Christine covered it two years later and earned Chicken Shack a hit.

*

She also had the hots for Phil and Don, the Everlys: a pair of singing brothers from a Brownie, Muhlenberg County, Kentucky family with country music origins. They had been regulars on local radio since their early teens, and made their debut at the Grand Ole Opry, Nashville's home of country music, in 1957, just ahead of their national breakthrough. Their first hits were written by husband-and-wife team Boudleaux and Felice Bryant. Their records were produced in Nashville by guitarist, multi-instrumentalist and all-round legend Chet Atkins, who created "the Nashville Sound" by discarding the traditional fiddle and steel guitar accompaniments hitherto synonymous with country in favor of piano, percussion and rhythm guitar. The Everly Brothers' "Bye Bye Love" was one of the first to showcase this. The boys could also rock. They covered Little Richard's

"Lucille" and Roy Orbison's "Claudette" as if to prove it. But their stock-in-trade was the sweet, melodic, harmonious, country-infused teen ballad. Although the Bryants set the ball rolling with "Bye Bye Love," the naughty "Wake Up Little Susie" and the self-indulgent (if you know what I mean) "All I Have to Do is Dream," the boys more than matched them with "When Will I be Loved," "So Sad" and others while adhering closely to the formula. The subject matter was universal: problems at home, problems at school, problems with girlfriends; conforming to the expectations of the era, maintaining respectability and quelling the sexual urge, at least appearing to, all wrapped up in a cute, sentimental, deliciously intimate way.

Their recordings reflected the way things were done in small-town America. They enchanted audiences abroad with a taste of the culture that was set to dominate the world. When they were all but displaced by the Beatles, those all-too-similar harmonies must have stuck in the craw. There was something about those voices, those songs. Tender, teenaged, bewildered Christine, like everyone else, was hooked.

CHAPTER 4

STATE OF THE ART

Perked-up, slimmed-down, freshly enamored of the opposite sex and with the blues on her fingers and tongue, Christine was on a mission. Her new obsession, the music that dated back to the Delta bluesmen and which echoed remote, distant misery, was never going to get a fifteen-year-old Smethwick schoolgirl to the Mississippi Delta. But it could get her to London. Fobbing off her mum and dad with the half-truth that she'd be staying the night at her friend's house, she and classmate Theresa Gilbert boarded a Euston-bound train at Birmingham New Street, took the tube to Leicester Square and traced their way into the depths of Soho.

The hub of Britain's music and film industries, late 1950s Soho heaved with celebrity and sex. It was where songwriter and composer Lionel Bart first heard the American R&B brought in off the ships by Merchant Navy seamen, and was inspired to write the first British rock'n'roll songs for Denmark Street's music publishers. Bart had played a part in the discovery of teen heartthrobs Tommy Steele, for whom he wrote "Little White Bull," and Marty Wilde; had penned "Living Doll" for Cliff Richard, Britain's answer to Elvis Presley; and by 1960 would have earned no fewer than nine Ivor Novello Awards. His musical *Oliver!* generated the hit "As Long as He Needs Me" for Shirley Bassey; and he created the proto-musical *Fings Ain't Wot They Used T'Be* about fifties lowlife London, the very underbelly in which Christine now found herself.

She probably knew next to nothing about its seamier side, or of the red-light reputation that had given Soho a bad name. Despite which, most visitors flocked there not for cheap titillation or off-grid sex but to experience live jazz performed by professional musicians in small, sweaty dives where they could get up close and personal with them. Of which Club Eleven had been one of the first when it opened on Great Windmill Street in 1948, later relocating to Carnaby Street. Johnny Dankworth and Ronnie Scott fronted house bands there. Skiffle sprang to life at the Jazz Club, 34 Bryanston Street, and new venues mushroomed by the week. Soho became the domain of the beatniks: cool copycats of America's Beat generation, the disaffected intellectual youth and downtrodden hipsters first identified in New York, popularized by writers Jack Kerouac and Allen Ginsberg, and who would soon be credited with foreshadowing the worldwide hippie movement.

Beatniks had a penchant for coffee bars. They gathered there to pose and pout, drape themselves artfully over chairs and tables while they recited poetry, discussed Italian and French art films and swapped records. They plundered style magazines for fashion tips, and jived together, both to records played on jukeboxes and to live singers and backing bands. Such bars remained open into the early hours, giving them the edge over pubs that sold alcohol and were therefore obliged by law to close at 11 p.m.

The 2i's at 59 Old Compton Street was the go-to coffee bar. Opened in 1956 and named for the Irani brothers who ran it— "the two Is"—it would be hailed as "Europe's first jazz club" and "the birthplace of British rock'n'roll and the popular music industry."

A plaque on the street wall at that location commemorates it, though the bar closed for good in 1970.

The other must-visit was an obscure little record store on South Molton Street, technically beyond Soho on the other side of Regent Street. "Stock Records was the place to be in the fifties," remembered archivist and radio producer Phil "The Collector" Swern. "They stocked all the imports. R&B, blues, rock'n'roll. Little Milton, 'Queen of the Blues' Koko Taylor, Chuck Berry, Bo Diddley, Fats Domino, John Lee Hooker, Elvis Presley. We were like kids in a sweet shop in there."

How had respectably raised, provincial schoolgirl Christine come to hear about Soho's throbbing music scene and the 2i's? It was thanks to the once dominant music papers that delivered news about releases, tours and interviews with artists to the furthest corners of the land. The *New Musical Express* (*NME*) was the first to launch a singles chart, in November 1952. By the early 1970s, it would be the UK's best-selling music paper. Its main rival the *Melody Maker* had launched some twenty-six years earlier, building a solid reputation as a jazz journal for musicians in dance bands. It debuted its weekly singles chart in 1956. The *Record Mirror* was the first to publish an album chart, in 1954, and also majored in Chris's hot love, rhythm and blues. By the mid-1960s, the dawn of a heyday for music journalism, Chris was immersing herself weekly in the reportage and reflections of now legendary wordsmiths Ray Coleman, Chris Welch, Richard Williams and Michael Watts.[1]

That debut excursion to the capital by two clueless but determined young teens seeking an agent, a break, anything, turned out to be Christine's first public performance. At the 2i's, she and Theresa swapped their school uniforms for matching stage outfits—black skirts, tiny red jumpers (it was the fifties) —and managed to get a turn on stage ahead of the Shadows, no less, delivering their tentative take on the instrumental "Walk,

Don't Run"[2] and a couple of Everly Brothers numbers they had practiced to death on acoustic guitars. Years later, Chris couldn't remember how they got home that night, nor whether they even did. "There must have been hell to pay," she reflected when we discussed it. There usually was, for infinitely less than absconding to London. Teenage girls were kept on the tightest leash by their parents in those days. That daring act of defiance afforded them a taste of another world; one to which Christine felt strangely drawn, but could never, at that point, have dared to imagine herself part of.

*

She had planned to become a teacher, she said. While she was competent at drawing and painting, taking after her father Cyril as an artist just as she did as a musician, it was sculpture that became her passion. Random, you might think. Could she teach that? She hoped to. Inspired by the ancient Egyptian, Assyrian and Greek friezes and figures held up as examples, by the Romans, by Michelangelo, by Picasso's radical pieces, by Rodin's "Kiss," Henry Moore's "Recumbent Figure" and Barbara Hepworth's "Mother and Child," Christine admired the three-dimensional artform for its "completeness, its subtle qualities." While the assumption prevails that 3D reveals everything, the real beauty of sculpture is its scope to contain and conceal. Christine never expected, she said, to be able to create fabulous and unique works of art herself, to the point that she would become "collectable." But she felt such passion for the discipline that she believed she could enthuse and convey it to students, teaching them its history as well as guiding them through the practical elements: drawing, form, osteology and myology, the rudiments of stone and wood carving, and modeling in clay. There was an added attraction: that of prospective employment. Tutors of sculpture were not exactly thick on the ground. "There was this idea in the back of my mind that if I chose a relatively unusual subject, I would always work," she said, "even though I assumed I'd be a housewife and mother at some point, like everybody else. I didn't have big ambitions."

The art form having long been a male domain, historians are inclined to pontificate: about the *sexuality* of sculpture, about attitudes toward getting one's hands dirty, about such aspects rendering it no world for the respectable woman. It was more subtle than that. According to art historian Professor Pauline Rose, it was widely believed in the late nineteenth century that women could not be sculptors "given their supposed preference for color, and thus for painting. It was also assumed they were at a disadvantage in terms of physical strength. If they did manage to produce sculpture, this was assumed to be derivative since they were believed to be incapable of originality." Potential sculptresses were also discriminated against for more mundane reasons. "They were not usually expected to follow a career," Professor Rose reminds us. "…it was taken as a given that any creative impulses would be fulfilled through marriage and family responsibilities." Despite which, a number came to the fore and made their name, not least Mary Spencer Watson, Ruby Levick, Margaret Giles, Lilian Maud Wade and Rosamund Praeger, of whom Christine was aware.[3]

The Festival of Britain in 1951, showcasing recovery, strength and the best of British to the world, wielded lasting influence in the fields of art and design. Billed as a "tonic" for a nation still getting over rationing and frugality, the celebration ushered in a new design aesthetic and launched the careers of many new designers, particularly in graphic design, furniture and textiles. Fifties sculptors began experimenting with alternative materials such as steel and glass, and undertook the sort of large-scale projects that led to the 1970s rise in landscape art. While surrealism held its own, juggling a rational view of life with an acknowledgment of the dream world and the subconscious, enthusiasm for abstract expressionism was in decline.

The pop art that emerged in Britain during the mid-1950s and reached the U.S. by the end of that decade had begun as a revolt against traditional views of what art should actually be. The movement would swell during the 1960s and '70s with influences from other cultures and countries. Young artists had begun to question what they were being taught at art school, as well as the methods used to teach it. There was growing realization among students that the art they saw in galleries and museums reflected nothing of their own lives or the material things they saw and used every day. They began casting their nets more widely for inspiration: to Hollywood, comic books, the advertising industry, pop music and even the packaging of consumer goods, for its imagery and symbolism. Pop art, according to purveyor of the form Richard Hamilton, had to be popular—designed for a mass audience; transient—a short-term solution; expendable—easily forgotten; low cost, mass-produced, young (aimed at youth), witty, sexy, gimmicky, glamorous and big business.[4]

"Modernist critics were horrified by the pop artists' use of such 'low' subject matter and by their apparently uncritical treatment of it," explains Tate Modern. "In fact pop both took art into new areas of subject matter and developed new ways of presenting it in art and can be seen as one of the first manifestations of postmodernism." Most early British pop art was heavily influenced by American culture filtered through the post-war lens of "there'll always be an England." Hallmarked by parody, disruptive and facetious elements, the movement would produce the likes of Andy Warhol, Roy Lichtenstein, Jasper Johns, James Rosenquist and Peter Blake. Had Christine ever imagined herself as one of their number? Never in a million, she said.

"But she obviously had a talent for making things with her hands," observes psychotherapist Richard Hughes. "It is significant. Immersing yourself in clay or plaster of Paris seems messy and disorganized, but there is a precise discipline to it all. You need to have that, and Christine clearly did. She wouldn't have been studying it otherwise."

What kind of sculpture did she create? Had I ever seen any of it? I didn't think so. My mind revolved back to my visits to her Kentish home, The Quaives. That fabulously cluttered, love-infused home had seemed faintly old-ladyish, not in the least rockstarish, and was not unlike my parents' home in the same county. It offered few clues that I could recall. She didn't draw my attention to anything she might have made, painted or drawn. I examined again the estate agent's sales brochure, lavishly photographed to showcase her house when she resolved that it was time to move on. In the sitting room, in pride of place on her mantelpiece, stood a silver-framed black and white photograph of a lady I now know to have been her mother. High on the wall beside the overmantel mirror, there was a framed Elisabeth Frink-style torso, back and rump. Could that have been Christine's? There were a few unusual abstract paintings among the more traditional pictures, and small pieces of pottery on her oak and glass coffee table. What else? An amazing, handmade-looking screen in her dining room, with a 1920s vibe but also an air of 1960s Biba. Tapestry-upholstered dining chairs, which I recognized as identical to those in the dining room of my uncle and aunt. A collection of lead crystal objets. A typically cluttered though pristine kitchen with a profusion of chopping boards—French, Provence-style, pieces she had perhaps picked up on her travels in Tuscany or the Far East. Those boards were perhaps the equivalent of collectable souvenir spoons, every one of them with a backstory. There was a low-ceilinged music room in an outhouse with drum kits, a shawl-draped grand piano, framed photos and abstract art on the walls. But no obvious pieces that could have been sculpted by Christine. Perhaps there had only ever been the work that she created and exhibited during her college years. Maybe she never made another thing after she graduated. Many students destroy their undergraduate work, or give away their creations to parents or other family members.

As in her house in Los Angeles, there was an abundance of books and possessions. She was evidently into filling her abodes with things that gave her joy and made her feel at home. Some may have been presents. She loved her nicknacks, her bits and bobs, her antiques. She was fond of going to galleries, art shops and antique fairs, picking up finds that would sit well with what she already owned. She was given, she said, to moving things around to accommodate new purchases and show them off. Rotating belongings and refreshing rooms, the sign of a good homemaker, was clearly a preoccupation.

"Every possession would have had meaning, signifying a specific time in her life, or could have been associated with a loved one or a cherished friend," remarks Richard Hughes. "The sense of that in her rooms was very strong."

But there was no indication of her being a random, for-the-sake-of-it collector of anything and everything, as she confirmed to James Halbert in 2004. "The only thing I collect is antique perfume bottles," she said. "Art deco and cut-glass stuff, or any other odd ones that catch my eye as I hobble past antique shops or antique fairs. I try to get up to London a couple of days a week for a bit of retail therapy, and that usually has the desired effect."[5]

Her most prized possession, she said, was an oil painting of St. Cecilia, the patron saint of music. "It's hanging up in my hall landing, and it was painted by a guy called Peter Frampton—not the rock musician but a turn-of-the-century painter from 1904 or thereabouts. St. Cecilia is playing the organ, and she's surrounded by beautiful spring flowers. I don't know if many people have even heard of Frampton, but he's becoming quite collectable."[6]

She was mistaken about the artist, who was in fact the celebrated late Pre-Raphaelite painter Edward Reginald Frampton (1872–1923). He painted "Saint Cecilia with Angels" in 1898. She acknowledged the error much later, and joked about the spinet at which Cecilia is seated in the painting. "It looks like she's playing a Hammond B3," she said, harking back to her own early playing days.[7]

*

I hadn't given much thought to sculpture since my own lame attempts with wire and papier-mâché in school art classes; nor since my year out as a student in Paris, where I got into the habit of taking my lunch into the sculpture garden of the Musée Rodin on the Boulevard des Invalides near where I lived. What I knew about sculpture—about most art—could be etched on a button. Only now that I come to think of it does it occur to me that all art forms have something in common, if only that they must be about filling the void. Artists explore and exploit the void in very personal and unique ways. Sometimes avoiding it altogether, illustrating their denial. Sometimes confronting and engaging with it. Creating music out of silence or modeling a statue from a shapeless lump of clay are, in this context, the same thing. They are both about making something out of nothing. As American trumpeter and jazz musician Miles Davis said, "It's not the notes you play, it's the notes you don't play." In Shodo or Japanese calligraphy, dating back to sixth-century China, the spaces are as integral to the work as the brush strokes. It is also said that the "negative" (blank) space can only be created by the writer's "spirit of life." The result represents simplicity, beauty and a connection between mind and body. The concept of "ma," or empty space, creates a fine balance between brush strokes and emptiness. In other art forms, the space, the silence, the void similarly become as important as what the artist fills and surrounds them with.

It matters. Because to look at or listen to art, something created by another human or humans, is to step outside ourselves; to escape the confines of our existence; to stop thinking about and prioritizing self. Because art can be a means by which to "hold back death," or at least to kid oneself that such a thing might be possible. Because to create is to remain relevant, and to survive. Wealth, property and possessions become immaterial. It's the reason why Paul McCartney, the Rolling Stones and other musicians of their generation appear to be working harder than ever into their ninth decade, continuing to create, tour and perform way beyond a financial need to. It is why Pablo Picasso strove fervently during his final four years, until his death in April 1973 at the age of ninety-one, to create more art than at any other time in his life.

"Making things with your hands exists on two levels," observes Richard Hughes. "There is the creation of utilitarian objects —bowls, vases, plates, things that you can use, and also break without worrying too much, and about which there is something very authentic. Clay comes from the ground, we mold it with our palms and fingers. The things we make with it need to be touched and used. There is also the making of something simply as an object of art, about which there is something quite pretentious. All sculpture exudes a quality that makes you want to touch it. You stand looking at one of Michelangelo's figures and you want to run your hands over those sinews and muscles, to bring the statue to life if you could. Which is all very resonant of Pygmalion."[8]

*

Whether or not she was aware of the educational history of her predecessors, Christine had joined hallowed ranks. From the late 1950s onwards, British art colleges had been the breeding and training ground for rock musicians. John Lennon studied at Liverpool College of Art, but was ejected after failing his exams. Ealing Art College produced several of note, not least Pete Townshend, Ronnie Wood and Freddie Mercury. Roger Waters, Nick Mason and Rick Wright attended Regent Street Polytechnic, while Dave Gilmour and Syd Barrett went to Cambridgeshire College of Arts and Technology before they united as Pink Floyd. Keith Richards, as he would, described his alma mater, Sidcup Art College, as "a kind of guitar workshop." Brian Eno left Winchester School of Art with a Diploma in Fine Arts. Cat Stevens went to Hammersmith College of Art, Ray Davies to Hornsey and Ian Dury to Walthamstow. Eric Clapton could have graduated as a designer of stained-glass windows had he stuck at his course at Kingston Art College. David Bowie, meanwhile, insisted that he did stick it, but didn't. At his secondary school, Bromley Technical High School, the then David Jones's art teacher was Owen Frampton, father of guitarist Peter. But after David left school, that was it as far as study was concerned. There was never any establishment of tertiary education, no art school, for the future Ziggy Stardust.

*

Her keyboard playing and hesitant singing, her interest in guitar music and the blues drew Christine inevitably into the orbit of other like-minded musicians during her art college years. But how did the blues hook a teenage white girl in the Midlands who had never been out of the country, let alone to the U.S.? What made her eschew pop and rock'n'roll in favor of it? The answer might lurk in a line by late guitarist and singer songwriter B. B. King, who described the blues as "the mother of American music. That's what it is—the Source."

The blues, we know, evolved out of the suffering of African Americans, primarily in the south of North America at the turn of the last century. Its influence expanded during the 1950s and '60s, embracing musicians from all ethnicities and even crossing the Atlantic. Post-rock'n'roll, musicians seeking the roots of rock found the blues. The so-called Blues Revival of the 1960s in territories where there had not been blues in the first place led to an influx of still-living legends. The most significant figure in the British Blues Revival, it is claimed, was John Mayall, whose Bluesbreakers boasted Peter Green, Eric Clapton, Mick Taylor and Jack Bruce, though not all at once. They forget Alexis Korner, the French-born multiracial "founding father of British blues," who landed in London aged twelve in 1940 and discovered American blues in, of all places, an air raid shelter.

Every musician is inspired by someone who came before. Alexis's call to arms came from Chicago-born boogie-woogie pianist and songwriter Jimmy Yancey. The son of a vaudeville entertainer who became a child prodigy, Yancey toured America and Europe, and started his recording career in 1939. It was one such recording that young Alexis heard one night purely by chance during a German air raid. It changed his life. "From then on," he said, "all I wanted to do was play the blues."

Post-war, Korner learned to play piano before lifting a guitar. He attempted electric guitar, but couldn't get on with it at first. He went back to acoustic, and two years later joined Chris Barber's Jazz Band. In 1952 that outfit merged with Ken Colyer's Jazz Group, and Korner found himself a member of that. On the scene, he met guitarist and harmonica player Cyril Davies. Within two years they were touring the jazz clubs as an electric blues duo. They launched the London Blues and Barrelhouse Club at the Round House pub in Soho, where they would perform and also welcome visiting American bluesmen. They started recording their music in 1957, and in 1962 formed Blues Incorporated, an early supergroup of the best of British blues players of the early 1960s. The line-up, a moveable feast, at times included future Stones drummer Charlie Watts, future Cream lead singer and bassist Jack Bruce, lanky vocalist Long John Baldry and eventual Stone Ronnie Wood's older brother Art.

That same year, Alexis and Cyril then launched the Ealing Blues Club. This move would later be regarded as pivotal; the moment when British blues came into its own. Young blues enthusiasts flocked there from all over London and the southeast. Among them were Stones-to-be Brian Jones, Keith Richards and Mick Jagger, singer and harmonica player Paul Pond, who would rise to fame as Paul Jones, and South African keyboardist Manfred Sepse Lubowitz, later acclaimed as Manfred Mann. Blues Incorporated landed themselves a residency at Harold Pendleton's Marquee Club, in those days on Oxford Street, where the Stones would make their debut on 12 July 1962, Christine's nineteenth birthday. The venue moved to Wardour Street, Soho, in March 1964, and for the next quarter of a century would host virtually every artist of significance.

The Marquee was the jewel of the London clubs, said Mick Fleetwood. "All the musicians wanted to play there. It was a jazz club until the brilliant, groundbreaking management of John Gee, who guided its metamorphosis into the seminal rock and roll/rhythm and blues club whose influence is still relevant today." He harbors a memory of playing there with his pre-Fleetwood Mac band the Cheynes that he describes as "stomach-churning."

"We had no following and it was a miracle to have been asked to back the legendary blues star Sonny Boy Williamson," Mick remembered. "This giant of a man played a tiny harmonica and dressed in the coolest suits, all mismatched fabrics in wild designs. We had studied his albums and learned his every note by heart to prepare for this honor. On the night, Sonny Boy went totally off-book, dropping into the middle eight at different places. We just didn't get it, and kept trying to play the song the way we had learned it. We even tried to correct him by corralling him back to the way the song was supposed to go. This did not go over well. He stopped playing in mid-song and bawled us out in front of the audience for not following his lead, not listening or watching for his signals."[9] They would know better next time. Peter Green's Fleetwood Mac made their first appearance there in 1967.

All of which sounds eye-wateringly boys-club and testosterone-driven; certainly no place for a beautifully raised and perfectly poised English rose.

When England's first experience of American blues was occurring during the 1950s, courtesy of visits by acoustic country bluesmen Sonny Terry, Big Bill Broonzy and Brownie McGhee, Christine was in her early teens. She was fifteen when Muddy Waters introduced his amplified electric guitar sound here in 1958. As an avid reader of the music papers, she would have read Big Bill's claims in British press interviews that he was the only living American bluesman. She would also have been fascinated by Willie Dixon's contradictions. The Chess Records artist, songwriter and arranger got together with German promoters to create the American Folk Blues Festival, and proved Bill Broonzy wrong. Because most of the great bluesmen were still with us.

For ten years from 1962 and for five years from 1980 when the festival was revived, the greats turned out for it in droves: Muddy Waters, Buddy Guy, Sonny Boy Williamson, John Lee Hooker, Son House, Lightnin' Hopkins and Howlin' Wolf. Staged annually, the festival brought the blues to a whole new audience. Most of the artists had never performed beyond the U.S. The first British outing was held in Manchester in 1962. Among the audience lurked the usual suspects, Jagger, Richards and Jones; and somewhere in the back there, future Led Zeppelin guitarist Jimmy Page. At the early London outings, Erics Burdon and Clapton (an Animal and a Yardbird) and fourteen-year-old Steve Winwood, soon to be of the Spencer Davis Group, are fabled to have been in attendance. These excursions were almost exclusively male, with notable exceptions: Big Mama Thornton, "Queen" Victoria Spivey, "Queen of the Blues" Koko Taylor, teenage Helen Humes, a singer with Count Basie's band, and Sugar Pie DeSanto, aka Peylia Marsema Balinton, who toured with the James Brown Revue and whose childhood best friend was Etta James. A wild dancer and back-flipper as well as a singer, Sugar Pie recorded her song "Do I Make Myself Clear" as a duet with Etta, Christine's future inspiration, in 1965. They got themselves a hit.

Almost every artist of the British Invasion started out playing the blues. Enthusiastic fans of what they heard and saw, young British artists set about re-creating it. Peter Green's Fleetwood Mac cut their teeth on traditional blues, but then diversified. As did others, such as the Moody Blues, whose debut album comprised exclusively blues tracks. Conceding to their own inauthenticity, they stirred a mellotron into the mix and stepped back a little. The precise emergence of "rock" out of the blues has proved impossible to pinpoint. Not even Peter Green's definition explained it. "If it's a slow song it's the blues, if it's a fast one it's rock" doesn't quite cut it.

The irony was that at that time, back home in the U.S., the blues were falling on deaf ears. It wasn't simply a case of white audiences being reluctant to show enthusiasm for the traditional music of the black man, either, while jazz, Motown funk and Stax soul were gaining in popularity. Over there, even Howlin' Wolf and Muddy Waters were being ignored. Over here, they were hailed as gods. When British groups such as the Stones went directly to those originals for inspiration, over the head of Elvis Presley—who had plundered the genre and made his name as the white boy who sang and played black music—what they were really doing was carting coals to Newcastle. But despite their greatest efforts and enthusiasm, they never truly nailed the essence of the blues.

Why didn't they? Couldn't they? They hadn't lived it. Although the best of the Brits sounded brilliant, their efforts lacked the requisite despair. There was no pain. They had never experienced true misery. This lot had had it easy, compared. They gave it their best, but could never truly emulate it. Because their early lives had never been black and blue. Neither had Christine's. Which made her focused, plaintive, arresting voice and her natural affinity for the blues all the more remarkable.

CHAPTER 5

BLUE MOON

There was nothing contrived about it. No masterplan. Hers was just one of those extraordinary careers that a person sometimes stumbles into quite by accident. The idea that she may have set out to carve a path as a professional musician was something she found laughable. To Christine, it was simply a hobby; something that she did for fun, on the side. She enjoyed hearing and playing the blues. It made her feel good, hanging with others who felt the same. Beyond that, during those early days, she gave it barely a thought. Did the fact that "the blues" was a predominantly male domain lend it an added frisson of allure? Chances are. But those who sing and play, who reveal a modicum of aptitude, copious enthusiasm and a hint of eccentricity often drift naturally into the orbit of like-minded others. Musicians are bound to attract each other's attention sooner or later, particularly within the confines of a college campus and its locale. Bob Dylan wrote in his autobiography *Chronicles*[1] that once he'd begun to perform live in small venues, he was consumed by a sense that he was now part of an "invisible nation" of shared culture, songs and stories dating way back. The now ubiquitous casual performance culture known as "open mic" dates back to New York's early sixties Greenwich

Village folk scene, when amateurs showcased their talent at "basket houses." In cafés offering the opportunity to perform live, a basket or "hat" would be passed around to collect currency for the musician or the comic, in lieu of a fee paid by the venue. Greenwich Village in that sense is acknowledged as the crucible. Modern open mic embraces much more than the standard singer-songwriter strumming a few covers on an acoustic guitar.

Christine's first experience of playing in a band was pounding the keys in a skiffle group called the Bobcats. Their guitarist Chuck Botfield went on to found sixties beat group the Rockin' Berries. After she graduated, Christine met the broodingly handsome Spencer Davis from Swansea, south Wales. Davis had started life with an "e" in his surname, but dropped it in anticipation of a career in the U.S., where he would undoubtedly have been mispronounced. He was four years Christine's senior, had learned to play harmonica and accordion at the age of six, and had discovered the blues while living in London where he worked as a bank clerk and then for HM Customs & Excise. The crushingly dull work sent him back to the drawing board at the age of twenty: at the University of Birmingham, where he read Modern Languages, namely French, Spanish and German. Among musicians, he would come to be known as "Professor." His degree led to employment as a teacher at Yardley's Whittington Oval junior school. He'd sing the blues around town of an evening, accompanying himself on his trusty twelve-string. Spencer and Christine fell in together. Just good friends, yeh? A couple of people I interviewed insist it was more than that. "How do they know? They were not there!" was a typical Christine retort to speculation. She contradicted herself in a May 2022 interview with *Uncut*: "I was seeing him, and we used to go around to all these clubs. That's how I got to know Steve Winwood. There were lots of good people around like Black Sabbath, Savoy Brown…"

Boyfriend and girlfriend, whatever, they launched a short-lived vocal duo, busking hither and thither and, for what turned out to be the briefest of interludes, becoming fixtures on the folk and blues circuit. At the Golden Eagle[2] on Hill Street in Birmingham city center, a popular destination for blues enthusiasts and followers of R&B, they came across the Muff Woody Jazz Band featuring Muff (Mervyn) Winwood and his little brother, the aforementioned Steve, fifteen years old and "...playing piano like Oscar Peterson and singing like Ray Charles," as Davis recounted to the *Guardian* in 2014. Spencer bagged little Stevie for his band, allowing Muff to join too so that he could drive his kid brother to their gigs. Calling themselves the Rhythm & Blues Quartette, they performed R&B covers in local clubs before moving to London to take up residence at the Marquee. They changed their name to the Spencer Davis Group in 1964. Island Records founder Chris Blackwell signed them, and released *Their First LP* (actually the title) the following year. Come New Year 1966 they were celebrating their first number one, "Keep on Running": a cover of Jackie Edwards's Jamaican ska number souped up as a riot of Motown-flavored R&B. Their biggest hits "Gimme Some Lovin'" and "I'm a Man" precipitated the departure of the Winwood brothers in 1967. Spencer kept the band going, and eventually became an executive at Island.[3]

Christine, meanwhile, caught the eye of Andy Silvester and Stan Webb. Stan, from Fulham in London, had moved to Kidderminster with his family after leaving school. Seduced by the skiffle craze that swept Britain during the 1950s, he formed his first group in 1952 when he was only sixteen. The Strangers Dance Band performed in youth clubs and pubs all over the area. Webb then launched another band, Shades Five. He turned pro, and moved to Birmingham. The line-up toured a West Midlands circuit well-established by husband-and-wife promoters Joe and Mary Regan, who ran, among others, the famous Ritz Ballroom in Kings Heath. The couple had turned the old cinema into a successful live music venue. Several of the acts they staged there advanced to international stardom, including the Beatles, the Stones and Pink Floyd. "Shades Five was my first crack at being a professional musician, working for Mrs. Regan in Birmingham doing the Old Hill Plaza, the Plaza in Handsworth, and The Brumbeat Cavern," Webb later recalled. "If you didn't do those, you weren't anyone!"

It was a visit to a Hurst Street record store that prompted a change in Stan's musical direction. "I started hearing all the blues stuff at this record shop called The Diskery that was wonderful. Went up there on a Saturday, they had all these American records playing, covers all over the ceiling. And that's when I first got *Freddie King Sings*. I took it home and listened and thought, I don't believe this!" Immersing himself in American blues and R&B, Stan began casting about for like-minded musos. He bumped into local blues singer David Yeates, and in a heartbeat was talked into Yeates's own band, the Sounds of Blue. His sidekicks were Stourbridge Art College flutist turned saxophonist Chris Wood[4] and rhythm guitarist Andy Silvester.

"We did some of the Shades Five circuit, but the main thing was this one gig on a Sunday at Dudley Liberal Club, every Sunday for a year and it was absolutely packed," Stan remembered. "On bass and harmonica sometimes was Christine Perfect, and Andy Silvester played rhythm guitar. Then Phil Lawless took over on bass and Christine switched to piano. Chris Wood played sax." It was Silvester who invited Christine to join the Sounds of Blue. When a new bassist landed, she beelined back to the keyboard. "Strict blues, no songwriting," she said, when asked what kind of music she and that band used to play. "Andy was a blues freak and had tons of 45s. We just dragged up some lovely old blues no one had ever heard.[5]

"Andy...used to give me all kinds of records, African American blues artists, and I got hooked," Christine said. "I ripped off a lot of licks from some of those records...It was quite punchy, back in those days. A lot of kick-ass music. We were all very underground. People would get their pints and pay half a pound [ten British shillings, the equivalent of just under £10 sterling now] to watch these bands sweating it out in these big halls above pubs. It was an amazing time. Then we'd travel to places like Eel Pie Island."

The small island in the River Thames at Twickenham, west London, was the site of the Eel Pie Island Hotel, an important fixture on the live circuit. Built in 1830 and name-checked by Charles Dickens in *Nicholas Nickleby*, it became a music venue in 1956, presenting local trad jazz bands. Progressing from jazz to become a hub for blues and rock'n'roll, it hosted many future household names, the Who, the Stones and Eric Clapton among them. The venue closed in 1970, and was destroyed by fire during demolition the following year.

"I didn't have a clue as to what to do on piano," Christine would later admit. "Stan bought me a Freddie King album [the same copy he'd purchased for himself?] and that was the beginning of my absolute love for the blues."[6] Texan-born King, revered today as one of the "Three Kings of the blues guitar,"[7] partied as hard as he played. Subsisting on a diet of morn-to-dawn Bloody Marys, he toured 300/365, thrashing his audiences with his distinctive wild blues sound. It wasn't only his music Christine was turned on by. The girl couldn't help it. She was warming to the risk-taking theme. Because fans expect a bit of over-the-top from musicians.

The band joined the ranks at the Seven Stars pub in Stourbridge, where one of their regulars, the future frontman of Led Zeppelin, would plead to get up with them and squawk a few blues numbers. Young Robert Plant was now and again indulged. When the Sounds of Blue disintegrated, Christine shrugged, cut her losses and moseyed on down to London, where she rolled up her sleeves, looped a pin cushion over one wrist and set about dressing windows for the Regent Street department store

Dickins & Jones. Andy and Stan pushed on reluctantly without her, reinventing their outfit as Chicken Shack. The clumsy name could surely have been improved upon. It's an old American blues term meaning "roadhouse," an inn or a bar serving food on the road out of town. They must have hoped it evoked something of the essence of true blues. In truth, it smacked more of the fried and pungent fast food for sale at Colonel Sanders' roadside motel in Corbin, Kentucky. Andy kept in touch with Chris, penning imploring letters that lured her eventually back to Birmingham.

"In 1966 we talked Christine into joining Chicken Shack," remembered Stan Webb. "She didn't want to for ages, and at that time there weren't really any female band members on the British blues scene. I think she only joined to shut us up."

Following in the footsteps of the Beatles, who completed five tough residences in the German port on the Elbe River before establishing global fame, Chicken Shack found their way to Hamburg and performed at the fabled Star-Club on the Große Freiheit. There was perhaps no harder environment for a well-raised young Englishwoman accustomed to home comforts. In that male-dominated cesspool of sailors, sauce and sex, the emphasis was on profit. Desperate to keep their establishments packed with sloshed mariners knocking back the beer, club owners laid on live entertainment to detain them. Germany boasted few rock and pop performers in those days, so the turns were drawn mostly from England. Keen but as yet unsigned bands flocked to Hamburg's Reeperbahn red light district, particularly from Liverpool and the Midlands. Billeted in unsavory accommodation, retained on minimum wages and banging out several short shows a day and three-and-a-half-hour long shows a night, they were slaves to the rhythm. They wouldn't find any lucky breaks there, either. But they would get to tighten their sound, hone their stagecraft, face the toughest imaginable crowds, be ignored and at times have to brawl their way out again.

Only a couple of females of note ever performed at the Star-Club: Brenda Mae Tarpley aka Brenda Lee, the American "Little Miss Dynamite" famous for "Rockin' Around the Christmas Tree" who would go on to sell 100 million records; and Beryl Marsden from Liverpool, who played the venue from 1963 when she was just-seventeen jailbait, and was banned from wandering the streets after 10:30 p.m. Ballsy Beryl, who took no prisoners, would support the Beatles in 1965 on their final UK tour. She went on to perform with Shotgun Express alongside Rod Stewart, Peter Green and Mick Fleetwood.

But where were the Lulus, the Cillas, the Dustys? Petula Clark, Sandie Shaw and Marianne Faithfull? Where was Lynn Annette Ripley, known as Twinkle, or Helen Shapiro—a star at fourteen, who would also tour with the Beatles? According to Frank Allen, bassist with the Searchers, Hamburg was no place for a female who was not a waitress, a stripper or a hooker. There were so few exceptions to this rule that the arrival on the scene of "Cora und Carin," the identical-twin hard-butter sisters from Munich, otherwise known as "das schlagerduo" on account of the music they sang—a light folk-pop known as "schlager" (essentially German country music) that surged in popularity throughout Germany and Austria during the 1960s—caused a phenomenon. Cora and Carin on a Hamburg stage? One of the all-time ultimate musical paradoxes.

Frank Allen's own sojourns there were an eye-opener. "The Star-Club, owned by Manfred Weissleder and managed by Horst Fascher, was a converted church nestling among a string of bars and sex clubs," he told me, unaware that it had originally been converted into a cinema. "During our several stints there, we shared the stage with such legends as Bill Haley and His Comets, Joey Dee and the Starliters, the Everly Brothers, Bo Diddley, Gene Vincent, Vince Taylor, Ray Charles, Fats Domino, Jerry Lee Lewis and many more." He also met, and felt the sharp edge of the tongue of, John Lennon, during the Beatles' final stretch when they were on the threshold of superstardom.

But Christine was no pouting popsy seeking solo stardom. She wasn't there to put herself above any parapet. She wasn't seeking to emulate the famous ladies who sang the blues in old America. She was the keyboard player and one of the singers in an otherwise run-of-the-mill male British blues band. She wasn't "the token bird," she was one of them. But that in itself placed her in a category of one. Because there were no other British female blues artists to speak of. Some will point at Julie Driscoll, who sang with Brian Auger's Trinity and gained fame via a cover of Bob Dylan's and Rick Danko's (The Band) "This Wheel's on Fire." But their brand of blues veered more toward the psychedelic. That sub-genre would be consolidated by Janis Joplin at the 1967 Monterey Pop Festival. Music had yet to be enhanced by the brilliance of blues queen Bonnie Raitt.

So there Christine stood, at some of the most basic bars Hamburg had to offer in 1966, necking beers with the boys either side of her. She lined up with them to cadge "Prellies" from the waitresses and toilet attendants. Those Preludin pills were what kept the performers awake. If she had no choice, the choice was always hers.

What Chris had been exposed to as a fifteen-year-old schoolgirl in Soho was nothing compared to Tor zur Welt, the "Gateway to the World." Located close to the sprawling docks, Hamburg's day-and-nightly influx of rampaging sailors seeking beer, bands, babes and brawls in its bars, brothels, strip clubs and nightspots was a living hell. But the members of Chicken Shack threw themselves into it. They delivered for around six or seven hours day and night, drew huge crowds and became an instant hit. Their reward was an extension to their residency.

"We did about a six-week stint at the Star-Club in Hamburg. That was brilliant, some of the best times I've ever had," said

Stan Webb. "Tony Ashton (Liverpool rock musician then with the Remo Four) and Ritchie Blackmore (guitarist and future co-founder of Deep Purple) were there, and we all used to meet up at Kurt's Beer Shop. We were the only band doing the sort of stuff we were doing. The Star-Club at that time wasn't getting many people in. Inside a week we started packing them in, and they were so pleased with what was happening they put the money up and cut the hours. We couldn't do any wrong."

Christine mentioned in interviews that she had been "nineteen or twenty" when the band played Hamburg. But she and Chicken Shack worked there during 1967. She turned twenty-four that July. Then again, as she also said, "I was pissed all the time. It was a rave! The nightlife was amazing, but to be honest, we had to do three or four sets a day on rotation, so the music got a bit stale after a while. It was an experience, though."

When the band returned from Germany, they signed a contract with Mike Vernon's record label Blue Horizon, toured Britain, and began their rise to fame as part of the British blues boom.

Veteran music critic Ken Hunt saw them live at a pub in south London in 1968, and was blown away. "I stood about two yards from Christine, who was playing the piano and singing into the microphone," he mentioned in a *Guardian* feature in 2014. "She was some sort of divine. I was too shy to talk to her. When *40 Blue Fingers, Freshly Packed and Ready to Serve* came out soon afterward, she was the main reason to buy the album."

Chicken Shack also put in an appearance at the Seventh National Jazz and Blues Festival, a three-day outdoor event staged on 11, 12 and 13 August 1967 at Balloon Meadow, Royal Windsor Racecourse. The acts were shared across two stages, the main one a precarious open-air structure that offered little protection from the elements and looked as though it might blow away at the slightest gust. The other was within a marquee nearby. Although plagued by technical problems—outdoor PAs were as yet in their infancy, and there was a lot of bored lingering by bands waiting for the sound system to be fixed—some 40,000 fans attended over the whole weekend. "A host of guitarists...had their sound reduced to a near pathetic level," reported *Melody Maker* at the time. "Peter Green's Fleetwood Mac made an impressive debut (on the fragile main stage) while John Mayall was received with fervent enthusiasm. But Eric Clapton is still 240 [sic] miles ahead of the other guitarists in his field."

As well as for performances by Amen Corner, Arthur Brown, Jeff Beck, the Small Faces, the Move, Marmalade, Zoot Money, Cream, Paul Jones, Ten Years After, the Nice, P. P. Arnold and John Mayall, this festival would be remembered for that first-ever appearance by Fleetwood Mac. Launched only the month before, the Mac's original line-up consisted of lead guitarist and singer Peter Green, who was freshly out of John Mayall's Bluesbreakers, slide guitarist and singer Jeremy Spencer, drummer Mick Fleetwood and bass player Bob Brunning. Green had named his band after the dream rhythm section he didn't quite have yet—because although Fleetwood was on board, Green hadn't succeeded in persuading bassist John McVie out of the Bluesbreakers who kept him reined in with a steady wage. Christine admitted openly that her head was turned by charismatic Peter Green. Chicken Shack performed after Alan Bown and before Fleetwood Mac, who were followed by Donovan and then future Wings-man Denny Laine. Stevie Winwood, Eric Clapton, and Beatles and Stones guru Andrew Loog Oldham lurked on the sidelines to hear Hurdy Gurdy Man Donovan singing songs of love. "Chicken Shack—featuring Stan Webb, Christine Perfect, Dave Bidwell and Andy Sylvester [sic] made their UK debut with their new line up..." reported *Melody Maker*. "Previously they had been performing a residency at the Star-Club at Hamburg, which must have developed their performing chops to a high degree." Loitering within tent, on the marquee stage instead of on the ramshackle open-air one, they gave the Mac a run for their dough.

As both Fleetwood Mac and Chicken Shack were managed and produced by Mike Vernon, and were also using the same recording studios, opportunities to cross paths occurred frequently. When Chicken Shack were not playing, they tended to follow their Mac mates around. Christine soon found herself contributing piano parts on *Mr. Wonderful*, the band's 1968 second album. Her enthusiastic accompaniment really lifts the track "Rollin' Man."

"As her presence increases she brings, if you can say it today, an increasingly feminine spirit to the blokey set-up," reflects music business executive Jonathan Morrish, who would make his name in the industry as the personal publicist and confidant of George Michael and Michael Jackson. She also contributed, uncredited, to their follow-up, *Then Play On*. Many in the know including Morrish name this as their favorite Fleetwood Mac album. It is "an extraordinary record," as Jonathan says, recorded "as they leave the blues behind them, and the drugs take them into new places. It's fabulous. And Peter Green, Jeremy Spencer and Danny Kirwan are magnificent."

Chicken Shack's 1968 debut single "It's OK with Me Baby" backed by "When My Left Eye Jumps" featured Christine's voice on the A-side and Stan's on the B-side. Neither song appeared on their first LP, the curiously titled *40 Blues Fingers, Freshly Packed and Ready to Serve*. Both single and LP made considerable impact, the latter even climbing to number 12 on the album charts. The follow-up single "Worried About My Woman"/"Six Nights in Heaven" later that year featured Stan on both tracks. It did nothing.

The all-important second album, *O.K. Ken?*, released in February 1969 made it to number nine. It about-turned soon enough because there was no single available for airplay to support and promote it. The decision to release a track from the previous album as a single was a curious one. "When the Train Comes Back"/"Hey Baby" showcased Christine on both sides, but reception was lukewarm. The same could not be said for their live performances, which continued to attract enthusiastic audiences. Realizing that they had to do something to promote the second album on the radio, they recorded a quick cover of a song made famous by American blues artist Etta James, "I'd Rather Go Blind."[8]

That same month, Christine, Stan Webb, Andy Silvester and drummer Dave Bidwell convened at the CBS studio on London's New Bond Street presided over by engineer Mike Ross, who not only recorded Fleetwood Mac's earliest albums but also, their groundbreaking single "Albatross," and "Happy Jack" and "I Can See for Miles" for the Who. Terry Noonan, who wrote the incredible string arrangement for the Fleetwood Mac single "Need Your Love So Bad," arranged a horn section for Chicken Shack's rendition of Etta's signature.

Now they were talking. Etta girl. Christine's haunting lead vocal put the band on the map and the single at number 17. It also earned her 1969's Female Vocalist of the Year award in the 1969 *Melody Maker* Readers' Poll.

"I remember when she won," former *Melody Maker* journalist and later deputy editor Richard Williams told me. "A few of us went to a pub for a drink afterward, and she came along. [She was] very unaffected, and [she had] an interesting un-Hollywood, un-rockstar, un-superficial, very attractive kind of sexiness."

As Mac's new bassist already knew. Reader, he had married her.

*

"I'd Rather Go Blind" turned out to be Chicken Shack's only hit. It was also supposed to be Christine's swansong. She had decided to leave the band before it was released. Her wifely future, as far as she could then see, did not include recording or touring with a band. Given her experiences as a jobbing musician, it can come as no surprise to learn that the novelty of being a woman in a man's world soon wore thin, and that she badly wanted to escape it. The world knows now how that worked out. A certain significant other sadly never got over it.

Although he hailed from the same era and genre as the likes of Eric Clapton, Jimmy Page and Jeff Beck, Chicken Shack's Stan Webb never became a household name alongside them. Which is nothing unusual. Of the millions of musicians who strive for fame and fortune via their craft, the merest handful make it. Almost forty years after he watched Christine walk away from his band after securing them the only hit they would ever celebrate, Webb was still servicing the same circuit he had pounded during the good old days, and still playing the stale old dives. A professional musician for four decades when interviewed in January 2006 by writer and author Trevor Hodgett ahead of the reissue of the first four Chicken Shack albums as a triple CD, Webb believed he was at the top of his game. "I like what I play now," he insisted. "It's more fluent, more creative and more individualistic. I was a late developer. I never liked much of what I did in the sixties and through the seventies and eighties, but from the nineties onwards I started to enjoy much more what I was doing."

Did he feel betrayed by Christine? How long have you got? She had insisted to Stan and the rest of the band that she was turning her back on music to become a housewife and mother. Her solo album was the first hoof in the incisors. The second was her solo British tour.

Geoff Docherty remembers it well. The man who put rock'n'roll on the map in the north-east of England during the sixties and seventies, luring the likes of Led Zeppelin, the Who, Pink Floyd, T. Rex and David Bowie to the venues of Sunderland and South Tyneside, still refers to the occasion when he promoted Christine Perfect as a solo artist as his "saddest ever gig." Docherty, the motherless son of a miner and an orphanage child who fisticuffed his way to a gig as a hotel doorman before becoming a concert promoter in his own right, put Chris on at the Fillmore North. Her manager at the time was Harry Simmonds, who also managed Chicken Shack. Harry and Geoff were chums. They agreed between them that Chris would open her tour at the Fillmore on 14 November 1969. "I was ecstatic at such a major scoop," Docherty remembered, excited at the prospect of presenting this recent winner of the *Melody Maker*'s prestigious female artist of the year award. "[I] eagerly set about promoting her appearance in the belief that I had one of the biggest draws in the country."

A few months earlier, Docherty had moved location from the Bay Hotel to the Locarno Ballroom, a large Mecca Organisation venue that could accommodate a 3,000-strong crowd, on Newcastle Road, Sunderland. He named his Locarno Ballroom promotions after infamous U.S. promoter Bill Graham's legendary pair of venues in New York and San Francisco, the Fillmore East and the Fillmore West. On specific nights of the week, Sunderland's Locarno transformed as though by magic into the "Fillmore North."

When at last the date of the gig arrived and Christine was en route north, the venue was deluged by bouquets, telegrams and other tributes for the artist, and the phone was ringing off the hook. "Everything was ready for Christine's arrival, and when she finally walked in and saw the flowers, she was absolutely thrilled," Geoff recalled. "On meeting her, my initial impression was that she was a lovely lady, whose manners, dignity and friendly nature were beyond reproach." He was excited for the gig, anticipating the usual healthy turnout at the venue that never welcomed fewer than 1,000 punters on a Friday. "About an hour after opening, I casually looked out, and was visibly shaken to see that the place was still virtually empty," he said. "I quickly returned to the dressing room and put on a brave face."

Docherty was well aware of how important this gig was to Christine. Not only was it the opening night of her debut solo tour, but she was now well known throughout the land thanks to her success with the Chicken Shack hit "I'd Rather Go Blind." That piled the pressure on. He didn't want to project that onto Chris, however, so he assumed a positive demeanor, only stealing a final glimpse at the crowd just before Christine was due to walk out there. "On doing so, I froze, as there were only about two dozen people standing in front of the stage," he said. "The attendance was a disaster, and there was nothing I could do." The reason? Chris was touring as a solo artist with just a single hit record to her name. She had established neither reputation nor following. The venue's audiences were accustomed to bands, to whom they could dance, let rip and rock out. There was something too proper, too sedate and well-behaved, about a one-woman musical entertainer. Whoever's fault the booking was, bad call.

"How many people are in?" Christine asked him when he popped back in. Docherty waffled a response. "Her piercing eyes seemed to have sensed something was wrong. I squirmed uneasily as she walked from the dressing room to peep out into the ballroom," he said. "My heart sank as the shock immediately registered over her distraught face. She ran back to the dressing room and began sobbing. It was the saddest sight I was ever to see at the Fillmore, especially after so many triumphs."

He stood watching helplessly as she sat and cried. What to do? Should he leave her to it until she calmed down? Attempt to console her, and reassure her that the numbers didn't matter, it was the quality of the music that counted? Geoff decided that she deserved his moral support, which he proceeded to give her. "I felt an overwhelming urge to put a comforting arm around her in the hope it would give her strength," he said, "but to do so seemed inappropriate and futile. The dressing room seemed like a morgue, and I'd never felt so helpless in my life."

Christine pulled herself together. She got up, brushed herself down and prepared to meet her modest crowd. "With her face drained and her pride shattered," said Geoff, "she braced herself for the oncoming ordeal. On nearing the stage, her faltering steps took her closer to what seemed like impending disaster." Her promoter looked on admiringly as brave Christine stepped out and greeted her audience. "The tension was unbearable," he recalls, "but to our amazement, she was magnificent. Upon hearing her sweet, soulful voice, people from the upstairs balcony came down to listen, while others emerged from the shadowy corners of its vast, empty spaces. Christine glanced at me as people gathered round to hear her. I smiled encouragingly from the side of the stage with admiration at her resolve and determination to succeed."

It was when she played what he referred to as her "pièce de resistance," "I'd Rather Go Blind," that the night really turned a corner. Her audience rewarded her with real appreciation. Their reaction even earned her an encore. In the dressing room afterward, Geoff congratulated her on her brave, inspired performance. He then accompanied her to Tiffany's, the late-night club next door, where he bought her a bottle of wine and sat down for a heart-to-heart. "We conversed about all sorts of things," he remembers. "She had totally relaxed and was marvelous company. Meeting Christine proved to be an enriching experience, and never once did she complain. From that day on, whenever the going got tough, her display of triumph over adversity was an example I always sought to follow."

*

After Chris was accepted as a permanent member of Fleetwood Mac, bitterness got the better of Chicken Shack's Stan Webb. "At the time of 'I'd Rather Go Blind,' we were still doing blues clubs, but we should have been doing the Albert Hall," he said. "That's where my frustration lies." He also blamed management, or rather their greed and incompetence. During a seven-week tour of the U.S. with Deep Purple when they even performed at the hallowed Madison Square Garden, their management extended the duration of the tour by a month and a half, and the band nearly collapsed under the strain. Then, lamented Webb, they were informed that money had been lost: "And that's when a little light went on, on top of my head!"

It was nothing compared to the betrayal that he blamed on Christine. "She's never acknowledged Chicken Shack at all, which is ridiculous, because we were the whole stepping stone for her," Webb complained. "I'm afraid it's a trait in the entertainment world: people forget where they came from and the people who help kick them off."

It wasn't true.

Christine was always talking about her former bandmates. She often mentioned them and paid tribute to them in interviews. She did so throughout her long career, right up until the year she died. She expressed enormous gratitude toward them—not only for having persuaded her back to Birmingham and into their line-up at a time when she had decided to call it a day, but also for the ways in which they had raised her game, put her at ease and helped her to feel more confident. She acknowledged them endlessly, with obvious love in her heart. Stan Webb, seventy-seven at the time of writing, wasn't listening. Either that, or maybe he doesn't want to hear.

CHAPTER 6

HORIZON

Because they are the foundation stones of Christine's own story, it is important to set Fleetwood Mac's founding fathers in context, before reminding ourselves how she came to join their number.

Every history of the band recounts that Bob Brunning was the band's original bassist, and that John McVie came on board soon afterward to replace him. Mick Fleetwood himself begged to differ, but then neglected to straighten the story in his autobiography. Through carelessness and forgetfulness, myths persist. It was his "lifelong friend" David Ambrose, Fleetwood explains, who was the band's first choice as bass player.

"In those early years, not long after we met, [Dave and I] were driven by the music that brought us together," he relayed to me in 2020, when he contributed a very personal, loving foreword to Ambrose's memoir that I was ghost-writing. "It all started with our rhythm-section work in the band the Peter B's, which morphed into Shotgun Express with Rod Stewart and Beryl Marsden on vocals," Mick said. "Those were groundbreaking bands for me as a drummer. In truth, many lessons were learned playing alongside Dave which would stand me in good stead for all my playing years ahead. One of the most important lessons that I learned from him was, and still is, that 'it has to swing, no matter what!'"

Reflecting on the first bands he worked with, Mick said, it was possible to see "trace elements of the embryonic beginnings of the core of Fleetwood Mac. That core was Peter Green, myself and Dave Ambrose.

"Dave was asked to be the bass player in Fleetwood Mac. Hold that thought. It was at that moment in time that he made a decision to seek out other musical opportunities…However, one thing was for sure: it was a decision that would lead him to many different creative endeavors in the music world. Later on, he would start working in the record industry."

Due to his passion as a player, Mick remembered, Ambrose rapidly excelled. "His incredible knowledge and understanding of musicians helped him to sign some major acts and to nurture the very best talent. While working as the director of A&R at EMI, he also looked after the likes of Queen and Pink Floyd. This truly shows the groundbreaking vision he had for music. Although the drummer and the bass player took different paths, we each found our way into this crazy industry. We were both blessed with great success, which I for one attribute without question to those early, formative years."[1]

David Ambrose realized early on that rock'n'roll would eat him alive if he stuck with it. "You're off your head if you want to be a rock star," he told me. "It'll render you bankrupt and drive you over the side sooner than make you rich and famous. How do I know? I was there. I climbed the charts, did the drugs, pulled the birds, and strummed with the best of them: Mick Fleetwood, Rod Stewart, Ray Davies, Jeff Beck. I teetered on the brink of superstardom. I had it all, lost the lot, hit rock-bottom and almost succumbed to the inevitable, depression setting in and almost finishing me. I jacked it all in for steady jobs, only to be sucked right back into the music business for a second coming, discovering and breaking some of the most fantastic artists this country has ever produced: the Sex Pistols, Duran Duran, the Pet Shop Boys and more. I had a fine time making them rich and famous instead."

He can tell us from bitter experience, Ambrose says, that it's a game that takes more than it gives. "It sucks you dry and spits you out. It never makes a better person of anybody. It demands infinitely more than musical talent. You can be the most incredible prodigy—Elton John, say, who was teaching himself at the age of four, was having piano lessons at seven and won a scholarship to the Royal Academy of Music when he was eleven. Or Keith Emerson, who used to walk around with Beethoven sonatas under his arm, but could also play like Jerry Lee Lewis and Little Richard, so the school bullies left him alone. Or Rick Wakeman, taught formally from infancy, who played in school bands and progressed to the Royal College of Music before becoming a session guy for David Bowie, Cat Stevens and T. Rex. You've been playing better than them since you were in the womb, and you reckon it's your moment to make the leap? *Pause*."

The first thing you need to do, as Christine also discovered, is to unlearn it all. "Classical training is the most massive hindrance," Ambrose warns. "It'll do you no favors. Punk was conjured by artists without musical talent who wanted to make music. Why not? It was different, and rock'n'roll is nothing if not about being different. Punk proved that what you need above all else is attitude. You've got to have vision. You need to speak for the times you're living in, reflect what's going on down on the streets. You'd better do it with more pluck, spunk, style, elan and perseverance than the countless thousands of other wannabes," he says. "You have then got to grow a hide thicker than a pachyderm's, because you are going to get beaten."

What else?

"You've got to be cool. Most musicians are. They have to be, to survive. You can't learn to be cool, you either are or you're not, which is the problem. You have to know your market and be au fait with the latest trends. You need to know your licks inside out and keep updating them. The drummer who plays old-fashioned licks soon dates. The same goes for guitarists, vocalists, keyboardists and brass." It's vital, he says, that you write your own songs: "Because it's what gives you identity. It's the skill that lends meaning to everything else you do. It's the point of doing it. A rock'n'roll poet like Bob Dylan is really no different from the guy in tights with a lute, wandering from village to hamlet in days of old, centuries before newspapers. The task of the minstrel is to think hard about the message, to couch it in compelling and memorable terms, to deliver it artfully, and to keep coming back with more and more ideas. You think that's easy?"

Then there's the dark side. The back-biting, back-stabbing, back-beating dark side. The betrayal, the isolation, the exploitation, the emotional upheaval. Psychological damage. Booze, drugs, women, men, sex. Rock'n'roll and sex are indivisible. They always have been.

"Sexuality is important, as an artist, to embrace and use as ammunition in your creative life," Ambrose affirms, adding that it's essential to understand that part of your life and how it makes you feel. "Any time I approach writing a song," he says, "I think about the fact that since I started having sex, my creative life changed dramatically, as did my ability to write a song with more genuine depth, more reality."

Is this what happened to Christine? "Oh, undoubtedly. It's just that her cauldron was being stirred by the wrong person. Imagine how explosive things could have been, the creative heights to which she might have soared, had she coupled with Peter Green. Who adored her just as she adored him, but it wasn't to be. John McVie got in first."

Ambrose was still a student at art school in London when he got to know the man who would change Christine's life. "I was hanging on at art school by a thread, playing my bass in and out of a number of semi-pro line-ups and combos that seemed to be going nowhere fast. Surrounded by fellow-musician friends who were getting ahead, I began to fear that I was doomed to failure," he says. "Cut loose from my family, forever anxious about where the next fiver was coming from, I admit that it irked me to see Mick Fleetwood, Pete Bardens and the Cheynes touring, playing the Marquee Club and supporting some of the top acts of the day, such as the Yardbirds, the Zombies, and John Mayall's Bluesbreakers, and jamming with Sonny Boy Williamson. Mick was forging a friendship with the Bluesbreakers' bass player, a tax office worker called John McVie. If only any of us could have known what those two were heading for."

But the record-buying public weren't as enamored of Mick Fleetwood's Cheynes as their enthusiastic live following suggested, as David Ambrose feared. "By January 1965, it was all over," Ambrose recalls. "They went their separate ways. Pete was snapped up immediately to replace keyboard player Jackie McAuley in Belfast group Them with a mad, moody frontman by the name of Van Morrison. Mick moved out of the Bayswater flat he'd been sharing with Roger Peacock at about the same time as Roger split up with his girlfriend, Pattie Boyd's younger sister Jenny. Mick and Jenny got together at long last—and if ever a couple was made for each other, it was those two. Mick responded to an ad in the *Melody Maker* from the Bo Street Runners, an R&B outfit from Harrow whose name was inspired by bluesman Bo Diddley, and joined them as their drummer. And then Pete Bardens launched another new band, Looners Ltd, and invited me on board to be their bass player. Our drummer, of course, was Mick Fleetwood."

They began a weekly residency at the fabled Flamingo on Wardour Street, changed their name apparently by the week— the Looners, the Pete Bardens Quartet, the Peter B's, Peter B's

Looners—and became everybody's favorite opening act. When their guitarist Mick Parker quit, nobody wept: guitarists then (as now) were ten a penny.

"Pete soon found us a credible replacement," recalls Ambrose. "Confusingly, also called Pete. He didn't exactly blow us away at first, but I could see that there was something about him. Whatever it was, Pete Bardens had perceived it, and we just had to trust him that this guy was the one for us. The new guy looked a bit weird and wonderful, and would certainly prove to be a talking point, but I was yet to be convinced by his musicianship. I soon got what Pete Bardens saw in Peter Green."

Born Peter Allen Greenbaum on 29 October 1946, Green hailed from a poor Jewish family in Whitechapel in London's East End. The youngest of his family's four children, he took up the guitar when he was eleven, and started teaching himself to play. The instrument, a cheap Spanish model, belonged to his brother Len. Peter had been in and out of a few bands, such as Bobby Dennis and the Dominoes and the Muskrats, before Bardens found him. He had played bass for the Tridents, the group from which the Yardbirds had poached Jeff Beck to replace Eric Clapton. And, significantly, he had also played with the Bluesbreakers, standing in for Eric when Clapton absconded with a bunch of gypsy minstrels for a summer in Greece. Peter had then started pestering John Mayall for a break. "It struck me as odd that he would do such a presumptuous thing," remembered Ambrose. "But Peter had not yet shown us his true colors."

Green played a Gibson Les Paul because Eric Clapton had one. He reproduced Clapton's riffs faithfully. "If at first I was inclined to dismiss him as just another copycat, I would soon be eating my words," says Ambrose. "He grew on me. I enjoyed his company. We honed our act as the ultimate instrumental outfit. We found ourselves opening for Bo Diddley at the Flamingo. I started hanging with Peter socially. I confess to having been taken aback when we were sitting on the top deck of a bus one day and Peter interrupted himself mid-sentence to turn and stare deeply into my eyes. For a moment I feared he was going to confess undying love for me. What he actually said was, 'Dave, you've got the blues. And so have I.'"

What was that supposed to mean? David couldn't help wondering. Was this some cack-handed way of telling David that he'd written a new song, and that he wanted to try it out on him? Or could he have been casting aspersions on David's character, telling him to his face what everyone else must be whispering behind his back: "…that I was a miserable sod and unbearable to be around?" said David during our interviews for his memoir. I was so taken aback that I could find nothing to say in response. I looked away and changed the subject, embarrassed and unnerved. He never said it again. I put his words right out of my mind. "It was only much later that I'd would remember what he'd said that day, and would understand what Peter Green had he'd been trying to tell me. I had *the blues*. I was a true musician. In my heart and in my soul, deep down. The syllables reverberated, articulating both salvation and condemnation. Peter recognized me because I was like him. This is how musicians are: drawn to each other, we cling on for dear life, because we are simply not like other people. As it happens, in different ways, Peter Green and I were as doomed as each other."

By February 1966, Peter B's Looners had a record deal with Columbia. Their debut single was a cover of American artist Jimmy Soul's Calypso-esque "If You Want to Be Happy." The B-side was a Pete Bardens' original, "Jodrell Blues," inspired by the Cockney rhyming slang "Jodrell Bank." Oh, boys. "This moreish up-beat number featured Pete [Bardens] swaggering away on blues piano," says Ambrose, "which I secretly preferred to his organ-playing. Peter Green had a searing, insistent guitar solo mid-way through 'Jodrell Blues' that sent shivers down my spine. It still does.

I have never grown tired of listening to it. Watching him play, it was as though Peter and his instrument had become one; that the guitar had assumed his voice and that Peter himself was actually singing through it. It was extraordinary. I remember glancing at Mick Fleetwood in disbelief the first time Peter played it, and Mick staring back at me as if to say, 'Christ, where did *that* come from?' There was something almost spiritual about it, as if it had come from a higher plane. This was guitar-playing on a level that none of us had heard before. He clearly had a gift for cutting right to the meaning of things. His playing was so brilliant that he eclipsed Pete on keys.

"Shortly afterward, we were performing one of our regular all-nighters at The Flamingo when Pete's organ expired mid-song. What happened next was truly astonishing. Without even a flicker of panic, Peter Green simply stepped forward and casually took over where Pete had left off, bridging the gap with inspired, sensational guitar-playing. It left the audience gasping. Yet again, Mick and I stared at each other. What wizardry was among us?"

There were plenty of other such occasions when Peter Green outplayed everybody. "Mick and I knew we were witnessing something that had never been seen before," says David. "He had at last emerged from his dusty chrysalis to reveal himself as the rarest of specimens: a guitarist with a unique tone. This was a fantasy, and something that is impossible to achieve in the real world. And yet, there was Peter making magic before our very eyes. It was like watching him turn into a Les Paul, is the only way I can describe it. Convulsive, vibrato-heavy and groaning with emotion, with true blues, it was a sound from another world.

"I thought back to the side-burned, bad-shirted Peter Green, who had underwhelmed me with both his presence and his playing when he'd first appeared on the scene. Was it physically possible to improve this much, this fast, to the point at which you had completely reinvented yourself? I doubted it, and yet was confounded by the point-blank proof. Unless my eyes and my ears were deceiving me, which couldn't be the case because Mick Fleetwood was seeing and hearing all this too."

But mind-blowing virtuosity never came cheap. The price was Peter Green's dark side. Deep dysfunction in his background had not only driven him to musical virtuosity, it had also made him weird and insecure. "He was wracked by envy and despair," remembers Ambrose. "Although he played easily as well as his hero Clapton, he didn't sing. Couldn't? Who knew? Inferiority consumed him. He bemoaned the fact that he had such a long way to go."

Their band fell apart, as bands do. Mick Fleetwood replaced Aynsley Dunbar in John Mayall's Bluesbreakers, but lasted only six weeks. The Bluesbreakers' bassist John McVie and Mick had become deadly drinking partners. An incident on tour in Ireland prompted John Mayall to kick Fleetwood out and replace him with Keith Hartley. Peter Green left of his own accord, explaining that the chemistry wasn't there without Mick Fleetwood. "As a parting shot of goodwill," says Ambrose, "John Mayall gifted Mick, Peter and John McVie some studio time at Decca in West Hampstead. They emerged with a number of good tracks, the most distinctive of which was a twelve-bar Chicago blues piece onto which Peter had overdubbed a miraculous whimpering harmonica part. They called it 'Fleetwood Mac.' The name crystallized in my head the moment I heard it."

Peter Green was playing better than ever. His magnum opus "Albatross" and the Fleetwood Mac album *Then Play On* showcase Green's sensitive and original interpretation of the blues, which overshadowed the competition. "He wasn't Clapton, nor was he Beck," muses Ambrose. "Peter was in a class of his own, the realization of which must have absolutely terrified him. Not only that, but those around him, all too aware of his brilliance, now wanted to exploit him and make him a star. The rottweilers were throwing themselves in his face. Clifford Davis, a booker at the Gunnell agency, tried to make Peter go solo so that he could manage him. Mike Vernon, at the time a staff producer at Decca Studios who had overseen the Bluesbreakers sessions, sought to sign Peter's latest project to his independent blues label, Blue Horizon. All Peter wanted to do was play his guitar."

But it was never, David laments to this day, that simple. "Because of the way that Peter Green's sad story unfolded down the years, a litany of schizophrenia and drug abuse, we were all seduced by the notion of a puzzling individual who perhaps never truly existed. The self-effacing musician burdened by unbearable talent that he resisted exploiting for money or fame was for all the reasons irresistible. But it wasn't quite like that. Most of the best artists I've encountered or worked with have one thing in common: they are the ultimate contradiction of extreme self-belief and crippling self-doubt. Peter was like that. The paradox lent majesty to his musicianship. That majesty was overshadowed by human weakness, condemning him to a life of bleak despair."

*

John Graham McVie, the only child of Reg and Dorothy—he'd had a sister, he has said, but she died in early childhood—arrived on 26 November 1945 in the municipal borough of Ealing, then Middlesex, less than three months after the war ended. Ealing, which lies west of the capital, would become part of Greater London twenty years later. Like Paul McCartney he began his musical life on the trumpet as a little boy, and switched to the guitar at fourteen. He honed his craft copying numbers by the Shadows, later swearing allegiance to the bass. His first bass guitar was a pink Fender identical to that used by the Shadows' Jet Harris, purchased by his father on credit. "He brought it home one day as a present, and I went mad," John later recalled. "I stood in front of the mirror in my room and dreamed I was Jet Harris."[2]

He made music with kids at his school, Walpole Grammar, from which he withdrew in 1962 when he was seventeen. His first group was called the Strangers. As one of the Krewsaders, his first professional line-up formed with boys from the street where he lived, he won his first professional engagements. The boys performed mostly at weddings, delivering faithfully rehearsed renditions of the sounds of their beloved Shadows. John embarked on a nine-month course with the Civil Service as a trainee tax inspector, and stuck with it for the duration even after he'd auditioned for and joined John Mayall's Bluesbreakers. He remained with the band for nearly five years, despite numerous hirings and firings for drunken and disorderly behavior. By Christmas 1967, John had taken his rightful place in the band that already bore his name.

A little over seven months later, when he was going on twenty-three and she was already twenty-five, he started going out with, as they said in those days, the lovely Christine Perfect of Chicken Shack. "One night we were at the Thames Hotel [near] Windsor, and I was sitting with Chris, and I asked if she would care to go out to dinner some evening. She said she would, and it was quite romantic," said John. His ex-fiancée-in-passing, an unnamed temporary sweetheart, couldn't have been too charmed to see the beautiful blonde keyboard player from Chicken Shack hanging around at every Mac gig she could get to when she wasn't playing somewhere else herself. John then disappeared for a while, on Fleetwood Mac's first American tour.

"By this time I was really crazy about him," Chris told American music writer Cameron Crowe for *Rolling Stone* in March 1977. "But I didn't know what was happening with him. Chicken Shack did a ten-day stint at the Blow-Up Club in Munich [named after Antonioni's legendary 1966 film] and I had this strange relationship with a crazy German DJ who wanted to whisk me off and marry me. I turned him down…and wrote John a big letter." Explaining exactly how she felt about him.

Fleetwood Mac and Chicken Shack duly returned. John proposed to Chris one night at Soho nightclub and live music venue the Bag O'Nails.[3] The many rumors that they had married only a fortnight after meeting were erroneous. Christine reckoned it was actually about seven weeks. Still tight. Why the rush? "I loved him. He loved me. Good reason," she told *Rolling Stone*. But *did* they? The trend during the 1960s followed that which had dominated the 1950s. It was dictated by the parents. Young couples tended to marry in haste then repent at leisure because "living in sin" was as yet wholly unacceptable. That tide would not turn until the 1970s. Domestic disapproval coupled with stern refusal on the part of landladies to rent rooms to twosomes unshackled by bands of gold often left them with no choice.

At which, a little bio-mischief kicks in. You may say I'm a cynic, but I'm not the only one. Because we know a bit more about "love" today than they did back then. We have the advantage of neuroscience to guide us. Some believe it to be little more than searing affection prompted by sexual desire. They point to evolution, which favors monogamy because it increases the chances of survival of the offspring. We are told it was when the human brain grew larger that its capacity for emotion kicked in. The ability to "love" relies on a part of the brain known as the "angular gyrus," which is found only in humans and great apes. "Romantic love" mimics the mother-child bond. It is conceivable, scientists note, that William Shakespeare's angular gyrus was hyperactive. Not only did he "get love," he gave us the language through which to express it. He may be love's most celebrated purveyor, but he was not the first. Ancient love poems prove that it had existed for thousands of years before the Bard; poems such as "The Love Song of Shu-Sin," dating back 4,000 years B.C.E. and discovered during excavations in the Mesopotamian region. There is also "The Song of Solomon" in the Old Testament, which celebrates erotic love; while Arab poet Ibn al-Rumi of Baghdad penned love poetry during the thirteenth century A.D.

Why do we become addicted, as Christine surely did, to "romantic love"? Because it releases the feel-good chemical dopamine and the hormone oxytocin. This blend binds lovers until "companionship" and "familiarity" set in, encouraging us to remain with our partner. If we stay, we avoid the pain of separation. John and Christine shared an "epic romance," didn't they? Does anyone?

She found John "endearing," Christine said, explaining that she had "fallen" for his sense of humor. She was also, it had to be said, in love with his band. "I absolutely worshipped them," she told *Goldmine* magazine in 1992. "To me they were the ultimate music that was going around at the time." And, "We were the hugest fans. They were so red-hot, they were killer." And as she explained to *Rolling Stone*, "They just had tremendous charisma—especially Peter Green—and Jeremy Spencer was such an outrageous little guy onstage. I used to go and see them when I wasn't working." The brilliance, the fantasy of Peter Green was what she probably fell for.

John and Christine were married on Saturday, 3 August 1968 at the register office in Oldbury near Birmingham. There was no coverage in the press, neither bride nor groom having yet hit the big time. But a small, formal announcement by Christine's parents of their daughter's forthcoming marriage had been published, as was then the custom, in the local paper: on Thursday, 1 August in the *Birmingham Post*. Peter Green was the couple's best man. Awks. Because Chris had had a crush on McVie's bandmate for as long as she could remember. "Peter was very, very cute," she admitted. "He was a cocky bugger and disarmingly charming. He was the one that really attracted me first. You couldn't take your eyes off him. But I saw John. There he was."

The night before the ceremony, Peter phoned Chris and begged her not to go through with it. "It was Peter I really liked in the beginning," she confirmed to Mark Ellen, editor of *The Word* magazine in July 2004. "When John and I decided to get married, Peter rang me the night before and said, 'Don't do it, you hardly know the guy.'"

"Yes, Peter Green really didn't want her to marry John," confirms music writer, broadcaster and podcaster Mark Ellen. "So whether he had feelings for her too, I don't know. I got the impression she was entranced by him early on. For whatever reason," he elaborates, "she was powerfully attracted to either supremely talented but frail and complicated men like Peter Green—it seems she was totally in love with him when she used to see Fleetwood Mac, and first joined the band—or highly dangerous, charismatic hell-raisers like Dennis [Wilson, of the Beach Boys]. I think she came from a fairly low-key home, and had a massive appetite for excitement and adventure. And she did seem maternal, to John McVie and [later] to Stevie [Nicks] too."

Did Green have any inkling that Christine really had the hots for him, not John? Or was he madly in love with her himself? She couldn't say. Green never said. Christine said that they had never discussed it. "I never told him I fancied him, I'm not that kind of girl!" she told Mark Ellen. "And he never said if he fancied *me*. You'd have to ask him." Misgivings notwithstanding, Peter stepped up to do his duty. No other Fleetwood Mac member attended the wedding.

Their low-key nuptials, bare-essential guest list and modest celebration had more to do with sad circumstances than casual neglect. "We just got married locally because my mother was sick," Christine told the *Guardian* in 2022. "Oddly enough, there was that famously husky-voiced singer…Joe Cocker! He was staying at the same hotel, and he got plastered with us, on our wedding night! Until we kicked him out."

Beatrice was in fact gravely ill. Most mothers long to see their daughters settled, and Beatrice appears to have clung on for that. Seven weeks later, on 23 September, she died at the family home on Monmouth Road, Warley Woods. She was fifty-three. Her widower, Christine's father Cyril, by then aged sixty-three and a retired training college lecturer, registered her death himself that day. The cause, medically certified, was given as "Carcinoma of pelvic colon with multiple secondaries." Colorectal cancer had spread to the extent that nothing more could be done for her. Beatrice was, in the parlance of the day, riddled with it. Thus did a young woman embark upon married life grieving for a beloved mother taken too soon.

Far be it from me to intrude upon the private lives of this clearly close-knit and private family. They are not public figures. Christine's talent, fame and influence are not theirs. They are entirely incidental to her story. My invitations to them to talk to me for my tribute to the family superstar were unwelcome. I understood this, as any professional writer would, and stepped back.

It is worth remembering that if a statement is true, it is not defamatory. Opinions are permitted, provided that they are not expressed as fact. The disclosure of private information about living, identifiable people sometimes leads to legal action. Had any of them agreed to talk to me, I could tell you their stories. As things stand, I can share only what the law allows.

The facts are blurred. After Christine's mother Beatrice died in September 1968, her father Cyril either remarried or entered into a further cohabitational relationship (the record states "Spouse: implied," but Cyril referred to his new partner as his "wife") that same year. A child born two years earlier, in June 1966 before Christine's mother had died, was brought into that relationship. The child's parents had been married to each other at the time when her birth was registered. A second child arrived six years later in 1974, making Christine's father a dad again at the age of almost seventy, and a father of four overall. Both of his "new" children—the first Christine's step-sister, the second her half-brother—were children of the marriage. Suffice it to say that Christine remained close to her beloved "Pop" until he died—and to her step-mother, who was not dissimilar in age to Christine, for the rest of her life. And that she loved, and was deeply loved and cared-for by, decent, hard-working people who continue to live worthwhile lives.

*

"John McVie told us all that he was going to be Christine's road manager and not play anymore," reveals David Ambrose. "Which was quite the statement. Though I couldn't help interpreting that as to my advantage. I thought John was going to quit Fleetwood Mac and I could sneak back in. Because I belonged there. I had seen the error of my ways, I could play the arse off anybody, and I wanted to be in that band. But John stayed put. I was forced to come to terms with the fact that my Fleetwood Mac dream was over."

Ambrose thought Christine was wonderful. "How someone with such a classical background could get involved in blues music to the extent that she did, I found remarkable. I understood her need. It was the same as mine. I had been desperate for something to ease my soul, and so had she. The Christine I knew was a very sad person. She looked tired of life, even in her mid-twenties.

"I did actually try to chat her up once, when I was a bit over the limit," he admits. "It was at the Royal Garden Hotel in London. She looked bloody tired that night, I can tell you. I remember saying to her, 'Come on: I'm a painter, you're a painter. I bet you're a wonderful painter. Why don't you do one for me?' Obvious euphemism. Needless to say, she didn't take me up on it."

Was he attracted to her? "It depended on how much I'd drunk, frankly. I can say now, not in a cruel way, that Christine was not pretty in the conventional sense. Her rather fruity nose did her otherwise quite lovely face no favors, though she did have the most striking sapphire blue eyes that seemed to peer right into your very soul after the fourth or fifth drink. She was deep, but not at all flirtatious. She acted very demurely, in fact, which I found rather gorgeous. She wasn't a sexy woman, in that she didn't flaunt it. She didn't dolly herself up, she never wore much makeup... and she was exactly the sort of girl I liked. She played the English Rose rather well, but at the same time she was funky. That was very attractive to me. She had a middle-class demeanor. She was not a flash dresser. She mainly wore jeans, and dressed to be one of the lads. I couldn't understand what she saw in John McVie, who was a mess. I didn't really get their relationship. He was a big drinker and a bit of a hell-raiser when he hit the Scotch. While no goody-two-shoes, she was the opposite.

"John Mayall fired him twice for drunk and disorderly behavior, and he never changed. Why couldn't Chris see what she was letting herself in for? I could talk to her for hours, and I did. Though John had green eyes, he was never jealous of me. She was a loyal wife. They were together."

But for how much longer?

*

John and Christine didn't see much of each other. Both bands toured often and when she left Chicken Shack, she tried a disastrously unprepared solo tour and LP. Christine gladly retired to be John McVie's old lady. "I thought it was extremely romantic," she said. "Obviously a little bit of the glamour of what Fleetwood Mac was in those days rubbed off. It was almost like someone marrying a Beatle. You married one of the locks in the chain and you were part of them."

CHAPTER 7

IMPERFECT

Christine had made her bed. She now had to lie on it. Many a young wife would hot-foot it home to Mother whenever new married life grew challenging; when the last shreds of confetti had blown away on the breeze, and once the apparent idyll had revealed itself for what it was. My own ridiculously young mother walked out on my father and wailed all the way home to my grandmother several times during their tenderfoot first year together, whenever something he did or said or didn't displeased her. Her mum would always pack her off home to her husband. But Chris never had that luxury. Her mother was gone. Her dad had committed himself quickly to another, much younger woman, who had also come to the relationship with a tiny child. If she had ever been so, Christine was no longer Cyril Perfect's blue-eyed priority. Though never estranged from her newly extended, blended family by this development, she was on her own now.

At twenty-five, she wore a simple wedding band behind her unconventional flat-stoned black onyx engagement ring, the stone said to symbolize support, stamina and determination and to help the wearer to persevere, as well as being the classic birthstone of the month of July, Christine's birth month. She was a reluctant professional musician who had already had enough of it. She just wanted to get off the road, stay at home and be the model housewife. What did global superstar Chris make of her earlier incarnation, I asked her in 1999, after she had quit the band. "I barely recognize her," she said. "We can never know what life has in store, can we, or how things will turn out. The pieces of the puzzle only fit together in hindsight. I sometimes wonder whether I would have been happier if I'd stuck to the plan. Become a mum. Supported John in his career, and kept in the background. Would our marriage have survived? I signed up for the duration. I think he did too. Divorce, in those days, was a dirty word. People felt ashamed if anyone in their family had been through it. But the boozing got in the way, and the boozing was because of the road. John drank to cope, with both who he was and who he wasn't. You find yourself wondering who you are in the end. That state of mind is also highly contagious."

She had said similar to *Rolling Stone* two years earlier: "I dare say, if I hadn't joined Fleetwood Mac, [John and I] might still be together. I just think it's impossible to work in the band with your spouse. Imagine the tension of living with someone twenty-four hours a day, on the road, in an already stressful situation, with the added negativity of too much alcohol." Added Stevie Nicks, who was sitting in with Chris during that interview, "And John knows that he needs to quit, but you know none of us are going to go over there and nail him to the wall."

John and Chris were married for six years. By the time their split was made absolute, they had been a couple for nearly eight. "We were very happy," she later said. "Very happy for probably three years, and then the strain of me being in the same band as him started to take its toll. When you're in the same band as somebody, you're seeing them almost more than twenty-four hours a day. You start to see an awful lot of the bad side 'cause touring is no easy thing. There's a lot of drinking...John is not the most pleasant of people when he's drunk. Very belligerent. I was seeing more Hyde than Jekyll."

*

Christine left Chicken Shack in 1969, a year after she and John had tied the knot. She did so, she said, because they had become ships that passed in the night. With both on the road in separate bands, one would be arriving home with a suitcase crammed with dirty clothes just as the other was leaving. How was she supposed to keep up with their laundry, the shopping, the cooking and cleaning and be out there playing in a band, too? They both needed a wife. Not that it was ever a question of her having to be the one to quit so that the husband could hang onto his job and carry on fulfilling himself creatively. As David Ambrose revealed, John at one point suggested that *he* should be the one to give up playing in a band, and become his wife's road manager. Everyone involved would have found that unusual and challenging, not least because John's tenure in the band preceded hers. Chris later said that she would never have entertained the idea. Because her inclination to be a traditional spouse was so strong? She thought so. Her wifely, motherly instinct compelled her to care for her man, and to make a comfortable home for them to share and a refuge for him to return to. It was, she agreed, the way she had been brought up. Her maternal inclination was strong. She mothered John naturally. She saw no reason why they would not have children. But it was not to be. One little chance remark of Chris's said it all: "We didn't try. We didn't not try. It just didn't happen."

Whatever the cause, Chris and John never had children. By 1970 she was an unofficial member of Fleetwood Mac, and joined at the hip twenty-four seven to her husband. Their inability to spend sufficient time apart was the primary killer of their relationship.

Between Chicken Shack and Fleetwood Mac, Christine recorded and released her debut solo album. Entitled *Christine Perfect*, it came out on Mike Vernon's Blue Horizon label, and featured custom backing group the Christine Perfect Band made up of Yorkshireman Rick Hayward—a Blue Horizon session man who had played with many artists including Freddie King, Eric Clapton and Jack Bruce, and who was a good all-round guitarist and a professional astrologer on the side; Top Topham—another Blue Horizon session guy, who had been the Yardbirds first guitarist and who played alongside Marc Bolan; drummer and percussionist Chris Harding; and Martin Dunsford on bass. The collection features a groovy, confident cover of American blues artist/harmonica player Little Walter's "Crazy 'bout You Baby," and a punchily defiant interpretation of swamp-rocker Tony Joe White's "I Want You."[1] John McVie and Danny Kirwan from Fleetwood Mac appear on "When You Say," Chris's cover of Kirwan's own composition for the Mac's September 1969 album *Then Play On*. Inevitably, there is Christine's Chicken Shack hit, the Etta James cover "I'd Rather Go Blind." The recording is redeployed on this album exactly as she and her former band had made it, which was allowed because her solo album was released on the same label as Chicken Shack's.

As far as Christine was concerned, her solo debut did not age well. Interviewed by *Contemporary Keyboard* magazine a decade after the twelve-tracker had first appeared, she seemed almost apologetic: "When I made that record, I wasn't really sure about my talent, or about what direction I wanted to go in musically," she reflected. "There were people all around who were trying to make me into this kind of a singer or that kind of a singer. Mike Vernon was a great help in many ways—I'm playing music now partly because of what he did to get me started—but even he was pushing me into becoming sort of a black-style English singer. I didn't really feel artistically together until I joined Fleetwood Mac."

Consider the span of the band that made Christine famous. What of its convoluted incarnations? How did it evolve from Peter Green's quirkily English anachronism of an all-male, square-don't-care-cos-we're-underground blues outfit to a California-based, mixed-gender, Anglo-American, globally dominant soft-rock-meets-pop quintet?

The British blues boom was short-lived. Bands who had cut their teeth on rhythm and blues—the Stones, the Animals—were now receding from pure blues to pursue other influences. They reinvented themselves constantly. Pop music was dominant, tastes were changing rapidly, and today's sensation was soon yesterday's news. Who could keep up? Not stuck-in-the-mud Peter Green, who was the most unfathomable of blues purists and who cared not a morsel for trendsetting. "We weren't that kind of band," said Mick Fleetwood in 2001. "We weren't looking to do anything other than play the music we loved. That wasn't even a thought. The reality is, that had no credence at all because we became very popular playing fundamentally straight-on blues music…Elmore James and early B. B. King-type shuffles. In fact, it was fairly extraordinary to see the first Fleetwood Mac album (eponymously entitled, it was the biggest-selling LP of 1968)—the greater portion of that album was Elmore James songs—up there with the Marmalade and bands like that. It's hilarious. We were doing what we wanted to do, and luckily having it be very successful."[2]

Fleetwood has long inclined toward the disingenuous. There was much more to the Mac's appeal and success, which was deeply subtle, than this simplistic "happy accident" explanation. The band released a string of unique singles that wandered through the genres before Green's departure in May 1970: "Black Magic Woman" (1968, written by Peter Green, Latin-flavored, later rendered even more famous by Santana's cover); "Albatross" (1968, instrumental, composed by Green, inspired by Samuel Taylor

Coleridge's 1798 poem *The Rime of the Ancient Mariner*, and the band's only number one on the UK singles chart); "Man of the World" (1969, Green again, the only Mac single on the Immediate Records label as the company imploded soon after its release, a British number two); "Oh Well" (1969, still Green, extraordinary, blues rock meets heavy metal, widely covered, UK number 2); and "The Green Manalishi (with the Two Prong Crown)" (1970, Green of course—but his final composition for Fleetwood Mac before he walked away from his own creation. A UK number ten and the band's last British Top 10 single until "Tusk" in 1979).

Band-quitting had become a trend by the time the sixties began to fade. David Crosby was shoved off his Byrds perch in 1967. Troubled Syd Barrett fell out of Pink Floyd the following year, ahead of the band's 1973 breakthrough, and was replaced by David Gilmour. John Lennon had declared his intention to leave the Beatles in September 1969, but it was Paul McCartney who made their dissolution official in April 1970. Peter Green eclipsed the lot of them, leaving not only the band of his own invention but checking out of his life.

"He came to stay with me and my second wife Angie in 1975," recalls David Ambrose. "It was only then that we realized how ill he was. The gossip and rumors about how he had become so are conflicting. My own understanding is that in 1970, the band had been in Munich among a bunch of jet-set Beautiful People, who lured them back to some aristo-type commune where it was all going on. It was there, so I'm told, that Peter ingested the hallucinatory drug Orange Sunshine: otherwise known as ALD-52, one of the most powerful mescalines in existence. It is comparable to LSD, and you have to be very careful indeed who you take it with. I took it myself, so I knew first-hand."

The rest of the band had left, leaving Peter at the mercy of said jet set. Knowing him, says Ambrose, he probably thought it would lead him to deep inspiration: "Being a true artist, he believed he had to experiment to reach the core of himself and harness his fundamental creativity. It has been said down the years that his drink was spiked, that he was unaware he had taken it, that someone else had been responsible. But I think he must have taken it deliberately. I'm sure, in fact, that he wanted to, convinced that it would help him to discover things. But as with all such substances, take it with the wrong people and the outcome can be disastrous. In Greenie's case, it led to a massive breakdown."

As Peter was by then homeless, David and Angie took him in. He refused to dress, and wandered around their home naked all day while David was at work. Which was somewhat disconcerting for the young wife. He refused all meals, consuming nothing but cake. It quickly became apparent that he was in dire need of medical support. Soon afterward, he was admitted to a psychiatric hospital.

"We didn't see him again for a long time," says Ambrose. Rumors did the rounds: he was living with gypsies in a cave in Granada, Spain. He had found his way back to England, had settled in Hastings, was married and had a child. He threatened accountant David Simmons with a shotgun because Simmons kept sending him large sums earned as royalties on his songs, and he disapproved of "ill-gotten gains": "As far as he was concerned," Ambrose adds, "music had to be pure, and for its own sake, untainted by filthy lucre. He wanted the whole band to give all their money away to a string of charities." Unsurprisingly, they were reluctant to agree.

His mental health improved a little. He started recording again, releasing a number of solo albums from 1979 onwards. He contributed to Fleetwood Mac's 1979 album *Tusk*, on the track "Brown Eyes," although he was not credited in the sleeve notes. He recorded with Mick Fleetwood on his solo projects, and started doing sessions. Ambrose last saw him in 2002, in the restaurant at rehearsal studio complex Nomis in Hammersmith.

"He started laying into me because I was no longer a musician, but had crossed over to 'the other side.' I started telling him about my latest project, *Dark Nebula*. He was delighted. His face lit up and his eyes glistened with tears. He was so glad to hear that I still had the music in me. He had heard it from the horse's mouth, and he was satisfied. He urged me to keep on playing. I promised him that I would. Because of him, I play to this day. We bid each other goodbye on a high that day. It was the last time I ever saw him.

"He was one of the greatest blues guitarists this country has ever produced," concludes Ambrose. "We are unlikely ever to see his like again."

CHAPTER 8

BIG MAC

Who hasn't considered the idea of clubbing together with a bunch of friends to buy a big house in the country, pooling resources, working together, playing together, eating, drinking and hanging together, and wallowing in a lifestyle if not exactly luxurious then at least community-minded and never lonely? Two former school friends and I have often discussed it. What sense it would make, later in life, to co-inhabit the kind of property none of us could afford alone. To share domestic staff, maybe even a driver and a vehicle if we were well-off enough, and to have room enough to put up our families and friends. It is a fantasy beyond the reach of most. Right-thinking adults in the real world don't do this kind of thing, do they? They do if they're Fleetwood Mac.

In 1969, even before Peter Green had formally walked away from his own band, there were rumblings among them about getting out of London and living and working together in perfect harmony, far from the evil distractions of the capital. The idea was probably inspired by the hippie communalism that was popular at the time, particularly in America. "The rural hippie communes were media attention-grabbers, full of photo opportunities, wild anecdotes, and the weirdest-looking people most Americans had even seen," says Timothy Miller, professor of Religious Studies at the University of Kansas at Lawrence and author of the paper *The Roots of the 1960s Communal Revival.* "Press coverage was massive from about 1969 through 1972, and a string of popular books soon emerged, most of them travelogues of the authors' visits to communes. A fair body of scholarship eventually developed as well."

Commentators seeking to explain the movement's revival often pointed to the disintegration of urban hipster life in hippie capital of the world San Francisco and its epicenter Haight-Ashbury, the late-sixties base of the Grateful Dead, Jefferson Airplane, and Big Brother and the Holding Company; also in New York's East Village, Chicago's Old Town and other, similar enclaves. "The hip urban centers, so the thesis ran, might have briefly been joyous centers of peace and love and expanded consciousness, but they soon devolved into cesspools of hard drugs, street crime and official repression of dissident lifestyles," offers Miller. "The hippies at that point fled for the friendly precincts of the countryside, where they built communes as new places for working out the hip vision."

We might assume that communalism would have appealed to Peter Green, given its roots in religious groups across America dating back to the Hutterites: the Christian Anabaptist group that arose out of the Protestant Reformation in Germany during the sixteenth century. Having migrated throughout Europe and settled in Russia, they crossed the ocean during the nineteenth century and founded many communities in America and Canada. To most involved with him during the late 1960s, Green had been gripped by religious fever. But he was a walking contradiction. He professed profound beliefs, insisting that he worshipped God and wished to do only whatever God had planned for him, but renounced his Jewish faith. He simply wanted, he tried to explain, to spend his time with like-minded others, and to be able to work with musicians other than those in Fleetwood Mac. The idea of living in a commune with his bandmates and their families brimmed him with dread. He opted instead to remain under his mum and dad's roof in Surrey.

It was the band's manager Clifford Davis who located and leased Kiln House for them, in the wilds of Hampshire, the county south-west of London and opposite the Isle of Wight. The converted oast house on Truncheaunts Lane, where hops and barley for beer were once kilned (dried), stood not far from Alton, the market town between Farnham and Winchester famous for its links with Jane Austen. The author spent the last eight years of her life in a cottage in nearby Chawton Village, where she wrote her six novels.[1] The gang moved in during March 1970, all pinching themselves. The large, rambling, perfect house stood in a remote spot a short drive from the New Forest. "We lived there for six wonderful months," recalled Mick. "I still look back on that time as some of the most creative and overall positive times of my life. It was summer in the country, and we eventually turned one of the wide kiln rooms into our recording studio. We brought lots of hash—great big blocks of it—that we had lying about for all to share if they chose to. Jenny and I got married there on 20 June 1970. I'd allowed the band's schedule to come first for far too long. It was time."[2]

While life looked harmonious on the domestic front, as far as the band were concerned it was anything but. The problem was that without Peter Green, their leader, composer and songwriter, these young, inexperienced musicians were headless chickens. Spencer and Kirwan did their best together to fill Peter's shoes, but it was heavy going. Danny had worked well with Peter, but was out of his depth with Jeremy. They lacked inspiration, and were incompatible as writing partners.

Jeremy, twenty-two, and his eighteen-year-old wife Fiona were devout Christians. They had been together since Fiona was fourteen, and had welcomed their first child when she was fifteen.

Where, we should ask, were her parents, her teachers, her GP and her priest, every one of whom failed to protect the gymslip mother? And how had Spencer managed to dodge the law for having corrupted a minor by engaging her in sexual activity? All those responsible for looking after this child had allegedly turned blind eyes.

"We finally moved out of our little apartment and bed-sitters, & terrible London life into this big house in the country along with other members of the band," said Fiona in her Testimony for Christian evangelical movement The Family International. "Dicon was two years old, Heidi was six months. It was nice to be out of the city, but there were other problems, feeling alone and feeling like I wasn't doing anything worthwhile. Through having children, going through the pregnancy & labor and being alone a lot, I was drawing closer to the Lord. I prayed & asked the Lord to help me do a work for Him, to do something with the children for Him. At that time, in that situation, it seemed a little far away, but I kept praying, asking, and believing that the Lord would work things out."[3]

The couple kept themselves to themselves in their room when the two guitarists were not struggling to work together. They spent their spare time, as if they had any with two tiny children to feed, water, exercise and occupy, studying the Bible.

Former insurance clerk Kirwan, now twenty—who according to Chicken Shack and Mac producer Mike Vernon played with "an almost scary intensity" and would weep as he did so—was in a fractious relationship with girlfriend Claire. Said Peter Green, "I feel badly, because I introduced him to this girl, an ex-girlfriend of mine…She was mad, used to hit him with his Les Paul!" Stress drove baby-faced Kirwan to drink. It made him volatile. He took out his frustrations on his fellow band members, creating an intolerable atmosphere. Danny, said Christine, was "really, really neurotic and difficult to work with…he was one of those people that would never look you in the eye…to be around him was a very nerve-wracking thing. So he and I never actually wrote together at all."[4]

John and Christine, still happily married, had moved out of their flat near London Zoo in London's Regent's Park to join the "commune." Christine's solo career was as good as over. The two consecutive *Melody Maker* gongs for female vocalist of the year and critical acclaim for her debut album had led to neither bookings nor billowing sales. Nor was she gainfully employed anywhere else. But this was all part of the plan. Being a "proper" housewife, washing, cooking, cleaning and taking care of her husband, she stressed, was all she wanted. Not that there could be any escape from music. Living with John in his band's crazy commune led inevitably to her being drawn into their rehearsals, for an upcoming U.S. trek to promote their first post-Peter album. The weaknesses in their sound created by his absence were deafening. Chris drifted into the gap, bringing her keyboard-playing skills and understated backing vocals to fill in the gaps. Some of which ended up on the record. Unfair though it seems, because she was neither an official member nor an official session musician, her contributions to the fourth Fleetwood Mac studio album went uncredited. She didn't care. The fine artist in her was chuffed when they allowed her to create the sweet, evocative artwork that graced the sleeve.

When asked during a 2022 interview for *Uncut* whether she expected to be invited to join the band full-time, she responded modestly. "I didn't presume," she said. "I was quite happy being a housewife, actually. I had given up my music to be with John, because otherwise we would never have seen each other. But without Peter, they were struggling, for sure. They wanted to carry on as a four-piece and not replace him. But they realized they needed another band member. Then one day Mick came out, followed by John and the other guys, and we all sat around a table. They said, 'I know it's short notice, but how would you feel about joining?' I said, 'You don't have to ask me twice.' Ten days after that I was in New Orleans with them. It happened that quickly. Gosh that was a moment, playing with my favorite band in New Orleans!"[5]

What made it work just like that, and how was she able to slot in so seamlessly? Because, she said in 2004, "John, Mick and myself were inherently blues-based musicians. I was part of the rhythm section. I was never Stevie Winwood. I am not a great keyboard player. I get by, but I nestled in with bass and drums."[6]

During her 2022 *Uncut* encounter, when her interrogator did not know that his subject was reaching the end of her life but Chris herself may well have done, she was quizzed about the mood in the band during that period. She came straight to the point. "I think they were worried, obviously, because they'd lost their main guy," she said. "Peter's style of writing, with things like 'The Green Manalishi,' had become quite dark. They were brilliant as well, but they were left without that element. We turned into a bit of a mishmash of everything. That darkness of Peter's was not there anymore, so Fleetwood Mac became a different object."

By the time *Kiln House* was released on 18 September 1970 —the day twenty-seven-year-old Jimi Hendrix was found dead in London's Samarkand Hotel from an apparent overdose of his on-off girlfriend's Vesparax sleeping pills—Mick had married "Jennifer Juniper" Boyd at the Kiln House, with roadie Dennis Keane as his best man.[7]

Before the Mac wended their way out of deepest Hampshire to board their flight and tour America, they had a big decision to make. By the time they returned, the lease on Kiln House would have expired. They could renew it pre-departure, and resume residence on their return, or they would have to vacate the property and relocate elsewhere before they left. Mick favored taking things further. He suggested that they actually buy another communal property in the vicinity. Amazingly, the others agreed. Off he went in search of a house. His lucky find was Benifold: a fine Victorian residence with twenty-two rooms, set in more than eight acres within dense woodland on the south side of the Headley Hill Road, East Hampshire. Manager Clifford Davis handled the purchase to the tune of £23,000. It would be the band's home, rehearsal and recording studio for the next four years. When they offloaded it four albums later toward the end of the decade, it went on the market for £65,000. Another forty-two years on and it was up for sale again—for £4 million. If only they'd had a crystal ball, they might have hung onto it.

Communal living was "for financial reasons, mainly," said Christine, casting her mind back in 2022. "If we wanted to have a big house with lots of garden area, we thought it was beneficial to share, because we weren't making much money at that point. So we bought the house between the band and split it up into three good-sized flats. That worked for a while. Everybody ended up in my kitchen because I cooked the best food." What was she serving up in those pre-fame-and-fortune days? "Very hippy vegetarian," she said. "Nut rissoles. That kind of stuff. 'Health Food.' I'll put that in quotes because we were probably drinking gallons of wine at the same time."

*

Following a mid-January warm-up tour of Scotland—during which Mick and Jenny's first child was delivered via an emergency Cesarean section that threatened to claim both mother and baby's lives—the band delivered their new American tour's opener in Vermont on 6 February 1971. Four days later they were in Vancouver for a pair of shows, following which they wended their way to San Francisco for four more at the Fillmore West. They would then point southwards to Los Angeles, where they were expected at the renowned Whisky a Go Go club on

Sunset Strip, West Hollywood, crucible of LA's live rock scene since its inception seven years earlier. There was no arguing with the Whisky. The Doors had been the house band there. Buffalo Springfield, the Byrds, Van Morrison's Them, Frank Zappa and his Mothers of Invention had all turned ears there. Now Fleetwood Mac were set to become part of its story. What could possibly go wrong? Nothing beyond a major earthquake and the departure of another key Mac member.

The 6.6-magnitude San Fernando Valley-Sylmar quake to churn the dead hit at 6 a.m. on 9 February 1971. One of the strongest ever recorded in Southern California, it killed 65, injured 2,000 and wrecked the region to the tune of $500 million. The first of significance since the Long Beach quake in 1933, this was the game-changer. It awoke the state into expanding seismic monitoring and upgrading both technology and public safety. News of which did little to soothe Jeremy Spencer. He was spooked. There was evil out there, the end of the world was nigh and the devil was coming to get him, was his take. This might have been prompted by the mescaline he had swallowed with Danny Kirwan in San Francisco. Telling the others he was just nipping out to find a bookstore, he never returned. The Mac's hugely anticipated gigs at the Whisky had to be cancelled. His desperately worried bandmates combed the city, searching in vain for their guitarist. They pleaded with the police, and crashed the HQs of cults. By the time they found him, four days later, he had made up his mind that he was not coming back. He had joined the Children of God in downtown LA. He was later flown to Texas, where his wife and their son Dicon joined him, leaving little Heidi behind in England to be brought up by Fiona's mother. Jeremy and Fiona became recruiters for the cult, and had four more children together. They separated in 1978.

Once again, Fleetwood Mac had been left in the lurch. To continue the tour and honor their commitments—there were still six weeks of dates left to go—they were going to have to replace Spencer. Had they opted to cancel the remainder of the run, they would lose a fortune and be forced to forfeit their new home. There was only one solution. Clifford Davis took it upon himself to call Peter Green and beg him to plug the gap. Davis couldn't have expected to get anywhere with the musical genius turned farm hand. He must have squirmed as he dialed the number. Against the odds, Green reappeared as their savior, only too happy to help his old friends out in a crisis. Unfamiliar with their newer numbers, he could at least get stuck in on the band's earlier hits. This in turn would set him off on ecstatic, extended blues jams, delighting both the audience and the band. Returning for a few nights to the Fillmore West, they forged on through California, New York, North Carolina, Florida, Maryland and Michigan. Back to Benifold they flopped, exhausted, in time for the release of a new single, Danny's "Dragonfly," with Mick, John and Danny's "The Purple Dancer" on the flip, and to set about finding themselves a new guitarist. Peter Green, more was the pity, wouldn't be sticking around for long. Back to the howling old owl in the woods for him.[8]

The word was out. Through friends they caught up with Bob Welch, a Californian based in Paris at the time, immersed in the jazz scene. He accepted their invitation to audition and crossed the channel to Benifold. He stayed for a fortnight, by the end of which, the others knew unanimously that they wanted him. He fitted perfectly, rubbed along well with each individual and with the band collectively, and his songwriting was strong. It worked well for a while until it didn't, as was to become the long-running theme of Fleetwood Mac.

"Bob brought vocal harmonies to the band, and he wrote with Chris, designing songs around their shared tunefulness," recalled Mick. "We'd done none of that in Fleetwood Mac before him, and it was his idea to integrate the male and female vocals in the band.

It became the blueprint for the sound that Fleetwood Mac is best known for, and the origins of it started with Bob Welch."[9]

They couldn't fail to be impressed by him. Not only on account of his technique, his musicianship and his obvious potential, but because he was a great guy to have around. Being in a band is not just about making room for different and sometimes clashing personalities, and everyone allowing each other to shine; it is also about chemistry: the collective personality that builds over time into a strong and unique identity. The sound and ethos of Fleetwood Mac depended wholly on chemistry. Relationships could fail, band members could leave and be replaced and any other band would collapse, its remaining personnel sent scuttling. But on Planet Mac, their bond and the music that arose from it would always see them through. What they had could not be defined. It was about family and co-dependency, yes, but it was much more than that. An understanding? It ran deeper. United they stood, divided they fell? Partly, but not only that. As Chris said, you had to be in it to get it. You could check out any time you liked, but you could never leave?[10] There would come a time when she would try everything in her power to do so.

"Bob's songwriting drove the next phase of our music, elevating us from what seemed like the gritty end into a new beginning," said Fleetwood. "He was a prophet of what was to come, because if we hadn't begun to experiment with the intermingling of male and female vocal harmonies, we might not have been capable of bringing Lindsey Buckingham and Stevie Nicks into our midst so quickly and easily once Bob had moved on."[11] The fact that Bob did not write with Danny Kirwan led to a sudden divergence of sound and feel.

Following their UK tour that summer, they checked in at London's Advision Studios to record the sixth Fleetwood Mac album, *Future Games*. This was the first Mac LP on which Christine was credited as an official member; and the first of theirs to showcase a line drawn under the blues. "We started being a bit more adventurous," Chris recalled. "Trying different things. [Bob Welch] had a West Coast, Wes Montgomery jazz sound that had a really great feel to it, and I just started harmonizing with him."[12] If the "classic Fleetwood Mac sound" was conceived during the recording of this album, it would dawn on them only in hindsight. But something crystallized. That surge in temperature, the prickle of recognition, affected them all.

"In the past no one did harmonies," Christine told Andrew Male for *Mojo* in 2017. "I remember saying to Danny Kirwan, 'Harmonies?' And he'd be, 'Ooh no, no! I don't want harmonies!' So it was only really with Bob that we started to develop a three-part harmony vibe."

"As the pop world embraced harmony with Doo Wop groups and white acts like Les Paul and Mary Ford [multi-tracking for the first time], the girl/boy-next-door groups, Fleetwood Mac and so on, this sound became synonymous with pure, almost bubblegum popular music," says platinum-selling songwriter and The Songwriting Academy co-founder Tim Fraser. "Even Neil Sedaka could harmonize with his own voice. Emerging from the exploding pop scene, there were 'purist' fans who wanted 'authentic' sounds like blues and even Dixieland jazz. The purists did not want their music to have anything to do with 'moronic' pop, as they saw it." With this hair shirt attitude, notes Fraser, the blues bands actively recoiled from vocal harmony. "Little wonder," he says, "why Danny Kirwan and all the others would sneer at vocal harmonies as a pollutant of their 'real' music. The same reverse snobbery would occur a little further down the line with punk, when harmony and musical competence were considered to be distinctly for hippies."

Christine sang the blues delightfully, Tim acknowledges. "But it was always in that stately, English, almost folksy style. It sounded beautiful, but it had nothing to do with gravelly blues shouters. The fans knew it—but they couldn't have cared less. The whole reason why Christine had such success early on was *because* of that very hybrid style of hers. I'm sure she loved the blues, but it wasn't a passion for life. Had she joined another type of band, she wouldn't have fought for purity. She just wanted to sing and be successful."

Harmony—when more than one note is sung or played on instruments at the same time—is a significant aspect of pop music. The way that chords sound together in a certain key can lighten or darken the mood of the song, raise or depress the sentiment, and generate a wide variety of emotions. Harmony brings personality to the melody—a series of notes played or sung in a specific order—and can make it more memorable. While the melody will provide the chorus and does not need harmony in order for it to be a tune, harmony will complement, embellish and enrich the sound to make the song much bigger. It supports the melody, adding depth and meaning. Think the Mamas & the Papas, Crosby, Stills and Nash, the Eagles. The way their voices sound together creates an instantly recognizable identity. If blues music is about simplicity and clarity, it is not difficult to understand resistance by some blues purists to the suggestion of the inclusion of harmony. Which is not to imply that blues harmonies do not exist. Get into a dissection of blues scales and pitches and they'll be there all night. But harmonies were the penny-drop moment in the evolution of Fleetwood Mac. Bob Welch liked them. Danny Kirwan didn't. The end. At least, it soon would be.

"Blues singing does not lend itself to harmonies," comments songwriter and composer David Mindel. "It is very much free form, allowing for a different rendition on each performance, adlibs and various phrasing repeats. There are plenty of examples of blues groups who had personnel changes that made them more pop and very successful, but hardly recognizable: not just Fleetwood Mac, but bands like the Moody Blues and the Doobie

Brothers." Purists such as Peter Green, he says, and to an extent Danny Kirwan and Jeremy Spencer, "would never have considered harmonies. Clifford Davis signing Fleetwood Mac to Reprise Records, and Bob Welch joining, seemed to change everything. Later on, Lindsay Buckingham's arrival, and him bringing in his girlfriend Stevie Nicks, would take it to another level; no longer blues, but making fortunes.

"I think it's fair to say," he adds, "that a great many music lovers couldn't tell you if a song has harmonies or not. Many know what they are, but not how they're achieved. And to some, my wife included—'How do they know what to sing?' she would say— they're a complete mystery."

"Harmonies? Acceptable incest," is Andrew Loog Oldham's provocative take. He suggests a quasi-sexual dimension to the sibling harmonies produced by the likes of the Andrews Sisters, the Everly Brothers, June Carter Cash and the Carter Family, the Beach Boys, the Osmonds et al. The fabled Stones manager never minces words. "A flash remark," he concedes, "but it's true. Keith [Richards] always protected himself by accepting the songs and the harmonies as a gift. The Everlys tour of 1963 was his university" —revealing that Richards learned the importance of harmony in songwriting at the knees of close-harmonizing, country-rocking sibling phenomenon Phil and Don. "Ever seen the Jonathan Demme, Neil Young Ryman show?" Oldham asks me, referring to director Demme's *Neil Young: Heart of Gold*, the acclaimed 2006 concert documentary filmed over two nights on 18 and 19 August 2005 at Nashville's Ryman Auditorium. "Instruments harmonizing in so many ways. And the looks between the musicians. I almost have a lump in my throat, saying this."[13] Demonstrating deftly that even the memory of perfect harmonies has the power to move us, years after the actual listening experience.

While there is no suggestion of incestuous misdemeanor between all singing siblings, it is a fascinating point that Oldham makes. Vocal harmonies created by members of the same family can sound almost indivisible. It's about biology. When siblings sing together, something spiritual happens. Physical clan characteristics—the same ears, the same noses, similar speaking voices—are all indicative of the likelihood that their singing voices will not only sound alike but will blend together seamlessly and exquisitely. The resonance of voice arises from sounds being enhanced in various chambers: the nasal cavity, the oral cavity, the pharynx ("throat"). Parts of the face and head act like the box of a violin or a guitar, to amplify and "color" tones. The size and shape of the mouth alter vocal quality. It stands to reason that members of the same family will produce the same "timbre" because their facial structure is the same or incredibly similar. Not only that, but "family personality" plays a part. People brought up together in the same household share history. They started out with shared values and attitudes. They can have similar temperaments and tastes. They can be put asunder: the Everly Brothers did not speak to each other for a decade following disputes over song ownership, while there were bad vibrations among Brian, Carl and Dennis, the three blood brothers in the Beach Boys (the other two being cousin Mike Love and school pal Al Jardine).

But perfect harmony is not restricted to singing brothers and sisters, as Simon and Garfunkel, the Beatles, the Hollies, Queen, ABBA, the Bangles, the Corrs, Fleet Foxes, Fleetwood Mac and the rest have proved.

The Greek philosopher Pythagoras "discovered harmony" in the sixth century B.C.E. He found that the beautiful musical relationship between notes was also a mathematical relationship when harmonious sounds were produced by vibrating strings with particular ratios of string length. His theorem had been known to the Babylonians a thousand years earlier, but he was the first, historians believe, to have proved it. Countless accounts have dissected the science of harmony, from J. P. Rameau's

1722 volume *Treatise on Harmony* to Frieder Stolzenburg's 2015 study *Journal of Mathematics and Music.*

Such theory, beyond the comprehension of the vast majority, must take a back seat to harmony's universal emotional effect. We require neither instrumental training nor notational ability to experience how we feel when we hear it. Quivers down the membranes, a tickle in the tonsils, something in the eye.[14] Music itself has the miraculous power to stir and move us; to elevate us to a higher plane or drag us to the depths; to lift us out of ourselves and transport us to extreme emotional realms via a mere earful of notes. While a variety of musical elements contrive to cause this effect, melody and harmony predominate. They shape the emotional impact. If melody is the heart of a piece of music, as well as the journey—its tempo setting tone and creating tension to the point that we become hooked on it and find ourselves humming or singing it at random moments—then harmony fashions and hones a song's emotional context.

But it's not just about what melody and harmony "do" to us. Our emotional responses to it depend on other factors, such as our cultural roots, our childhood, our relationship history and other personal experiences, and on the musical memories encoded in our brains. If a particular song reminds us of something similar from some other life, we are more likely to warm to it. However, one woman's chateaubriand is another chick's chuck. A sequence of notes that sparks a thrill that ripples through this listener will induce indifference, melancholy or even fury in that one. It depends almost entirely on past musical associations.

"Keyboard players in rock bands often raise the bar in terms of sophistication," comments James Graydon. The guitarist, songwriter, composer, producer, arranger and music educator has recorded and toured with a wide range of artists from Placido Domingo to Westlife, and has worked on numerous films including *Bohemian Rhapsody, Eurovision,* and Danny Boyle's

Pistol, the Disney Plus series about the Sex Pistols. "[Keyboardists] see harmony in a more visual sense than guitarists, and as such, can weave original and interesting textures," he explains. "It was Freddie Mercury's keyboard knowledge that took Queen into a completely different place, for example. I also believe it was George Martin's keyboard training that really defined the Beatles' productions from *Rubber Soul* onwards. With Christine, it was the vocal harmonies." Exemplary illustrations of which can be found on "Say You Love Me" from the album *Fleetwood Mac*, "Think About Me" on *Tusk* and "Temporary One" from *The Dance*. "Musically," adds Graydon, "she could be delicate and introspective, but could also rock out equally well. [U.S. conductor and composer] Leonard Bernstein always said he wanted to bridge the gap of critical and public acclaim. Give the people what they want, but at the same time, push the boundaries."

That's what Fleetwood Mac did in rock, Graydon says. "I think Richard Rodgers [American musical theater composer and legendary partner of lyricists Lorenz Hart and Oscar Hammerstein II] would have said, a song's ability to last mostly pins on the melody. Fleetwood Mac had great, great melodies. Lyrically, they deal with adult stuff. I can remember the music feeling a bit like rock for grown-ups when I was young! Funny thing is, you grow and you get some life experience, and some music you grow out of. Fleetwood Mac is a band you grow into—and that is why they are perennial. The music is always being rediscovered. It resonates with a new generation who are confronting the ups and downs of life and love."[15]

*

"Mick was very supportive," said Christine, "and it worked. Bob had this honey voice, and so did I. We sounded great together and worked well in the studio, me at the piano and him on guitar. Mick would make sure Bob stayed within the boundaries of a commercial song, because, given the chance, Bob could just take off into space." Three main songwriters had now emerged to dominate Fleetwood Mac. Bob and Christine blended well together. Danny was on an odyssey of his own.

*

Former *Melody Maker* news editor, U.S. editor and eventual Omnibus Press managing editor Chris Charlesworth visited the band at Benifold in July 1972. He arrived to find Christine and John in full domestic mode, painting the hall. "It's a kind of communal home where they can get away from each other if they want to: surely an ideal situation for a band," he wrote at the time and remembers today. Bob Welch, he reported, lived most of the time in Los Angeles, joining up with the other four when work demanded. It was "an odd situation, but one which seemed to work quite well." Christine opened up to him about life on the road during his visit, and about the different ways in which touring affected them on each side of the pond.

"In England, it means traveling by road and coming home each night in the very early hours," she told him. "But in America, you are staying in hotels. You don't feel it's such a tiring drag over there. If I am away, I like to be away, and that means completely away. We are doing positive stretches of work now, and then rest periods, rather than a few gigs and a few days off."

Mick Fleetwood confided to Charlesworth that living together in the same house had been a bonus. He confessed that, had it not been for the communal living arrangements, they would have broken up completely by then. "They have their own rehearsal room," reported Chris, "thus saving hire charges. And because they are so far out in the country, noise is no problem."

Soon, trailblazer Christine revealed, the group would be introducing a Mellotron synthesizer into their stage act, such as deployed by the Beatles on their "Strawberry Fields Forever" single recorded at the end of 1966, and also used on "Tomorrow Never Knows" (*Revolver*), "Flying" (instrumental, *Magical Mystery Tour*) and "The Continuing Story of Bungalow Bill" (*The Beatles*/"White Album"). The beauty of the Mellotron, an early synthesizer, was that the sounds of a range of instruments could be introduced without having to have those actual instruments, and musicians who could play them, in the room. Christine had already played one in the studio, and would be playing the band's own one on stage. "It's just a basic guitar sound, and we'll be using it as a background instrument," she said. "Bands seem to have a lot of trouble with them on the road, but we hope this doesn't happen. The one we've got (an M400, a simplified model) is specially designed for use on the road."

The Mellotron has been picked up on Mac tracks "Sunny Side of Heaven" and "The Ghost" (*Bare Trees*), and on "Bright Fire" (flute) and "Nightwatch" (possibly strings, *Penguin*). Chris would later use it to create the flute sounds on "Oh Daddy" (*Rumours*). She also commented that there was "a lot of Mellotron" on "Why" (*Mystery to Me*), but music critics have disagreed, insisting that those are "straight orchestral strings." Either way, it must have delighted her that the U.S.-conceived instrument was made in Birmingham.

*

Manager Clifford Davis, né Adams, was the toughest of taskmasters. Having worked for Beatles manager Brian Epstein, the East End Cockney go-getter was hired by promoters and agents the Gunnell brothers to run their agency, and was eventually appointed by Mick to manage Fleetwood Mac. Under Davis's rule, there would be no let-up. The band duly packed their bags. They spent the best part of 1972 on the road across the U.S. and Europe, opening for many high-profile artists including Deep Purple and Long John Baldry. They even swerved back into the studio to record their seventh studio album/second album in six months, *Bare Trees*: the one with the ghostly cover image shot by John McVie. This was the final offering to feature Danny Kirwan. He contributed five of the album's ten tracks, and he plays them for all he's worth. The tedium and exhaustion of the road are writ large in Christine's composition "Homeward Bound," a bouncy, upbeat number that belies its lyrics—"I don't wanna see another airplane seat/or another hotel room"—featuring superb drums and lead guitar. Chris's vocal stutters a little, and the faltering lyrics can seem clumsy. But the song is saved by the instrumental work, which is deliberate and moreish. The message is loud and clear: Christine is already sick of touring. She could not have known that there would be another twenty years of this tedium before she would make her first escape. She would revisit her hatred of touring in her 1990s songs "Temporary One" and "Hollywood (Some Other Kind of Town)."

Her other song on *Bare Trees*, "Spare Me a Little of Your Love" showcases poised songwriting that heralds the majesty to come. Her controlled, mellow vocal and neat phrasing put Christine up there alongside fellow songstresses Dusty Springfield and Sandy Denny. Its mid-song guitar solo oscillates beautifully. There is a lovely sped-up countryish coda to fade. Bob Welch's "Sentimental Lady" bought them a U.S. hit but was dismissed by British critics as trite. They ridiculed this and Welch's "The Ghost" while mourning the demise of their once beloved homegrown blues band. They didn't get it. All things must pass.

The Mac's popularity in America had surged ahead of their domestic profile. This album performed well, almost every show was a sell-out, and Van Morrison supported them at the Fillmore. But their schedule and routine were taking their toll. "I had to look no further than John and Chris to see the proof," rued Fleetwood. "Because the stress of it all was tearing their marriage apart. When his nerves were shot and he had reached the end of his rope, my emotionally reserved friend would explode. Since they were so close in every single way, Chris bore the brunt of it."

Kirwan succumbed to the booze. The demolition was ugly. Alcoholism rendered him condescending and pugnacious, particularly when he was around mild, amiable Bob Welch. As the band were touring the hard way at this stage, literally on the road in a pair of station wagons with their equipment bringing up the rear in a trailer, at least a couple of them had to ride with Danny. Nobody wanted to. Things came to a head that August, when a row over tuning erupted in the dressing room that culminated in Danny smashing his head into a bathroom wall. Blood all over the shop. He then destroyed the dressing room and bashed to bits his cherished Les Paul.

The show must go on. There was no choice. They fumbled through without their lead guitarist, unaware that he had gone out to the soundboard to join the crew and watch their limp-along performance from a distance. He was, he later indicated, delighted to see them squirm. After the show, he had the nerve to criticize them. Mick was enraged. "Danny had to go," he stated. "No one had ever been fired from Fleetwood Mac before. Danny was the first, but he wouldn't be the last." After he'd sacked him, Mick said, "I then went upstairs to John and Christine's room and was crying before I even got to the door."

CHAPTER 9

MYSTERY

Given the wealth of brilliant blues guitarists kicking around at that time, who else might have been hired to replace Danny Kirwan? By no stretch the shabbiest suggestion was young Mick Taylor, formerly of John Mayall's Bluesbreakers, who succeeded Rolling Stones founder Brian Jones after the latter's death in 1969. Taylor had hair-raising reasons to seek a new gig, a sexual liaison with Mick Jagger not the least of them. That and other experiences including drugs threatened his sanity, and were the reasons behind him quitting the Stones in 1974. Taylor had replaced Peter Green in the Bluesbreakers and would have been an obvious fit in Fleetwood Mac. He lost almost everything thanks to his sojourn with Mick'n'Keef and the boys. His career and life going-forward were largely a haze and a misery.[1]

Blues rocker Johnny Winter, a person with albinism, had been hailed by *Rolling Stone* in 1968 as the biggest thing to emerge from Texas since Janis Joplin. He bagged what was at the time the largest advance extended to a solo recording artist when he signed with CBS. His eponymous album for them released in 1969 won him a spot at the Woodstock Festival. With a new band and a big live album he was riding a crest. But he sank into chronic heroin addiction and disappeared until 1973, when he released a comeback LP, *Still Alive and Well*.[2]

String-bender Robin Trower, the former Procol Harum guitarist from south London, might have been an excellent bet. Quitting the band in frustration after their fifth album *Broken Barricades*, he pulled together a power group called Jude and released his debut solo LP *Twice Removed from Yesterday* in 1973. He followed it with the landmark offering *Bridge of Sighs*, prompting comparisons to Jimi Hendrix who had died four years earlier.[3]

Or they could have gone for gold and picked up the then twenty-three-year-old Bonnie Raitt, daughter of a pianist and a musical theater actor who had started playing guitar at the age of eight. The Californian with Scottish roots who had released her eponymous debut the year before peaked early then simmered steadily, earning the enduring respect of many acclaimed bluesmen and rockers.[4]

Instead, they got themselves two for the price of one. While Mick favored Plymouth-born blues and rock guitarist Bob Weston, one of Long John Baldry's men who had supported the Mac on their 1971 British tour, management had other ideas. The band, they decided, lacked the all-important frontman and singer. West Midlander Dave Walker, a singing rhythm guitarist with a percussive style, was heavily influenced by black American vocalists. As part of a band called the Redcaps he had opened for the Beatles, and was now fronting blues outfit Savoy Brown. He regarded himself as a jobbing musician. When asked in 2008 why he left Savoy Brown for the Mac, he said, "Fleetwood Mac paid!" Of the criticism he faced for having "pulled [them] in the direction of Savoy Brown," he retorted: "With my input into the band being so minimal, I don't see how I could be said to have been pulling anyone anywhere. Although in my opinion, it may have been a good idea at the time. Fleetwood Mac were always a good blues rock band. Why they quit playing it, I'll never understand."[5]

Weston and Walker duly trolled on down to Benifold to begin rehearsals ahead of a brief, successful tour of Scandinavia.

During the first days of January 1973, the band took delivery of the Rolling Stones' recording truck, referred to throughout the industry as "the mobile." They set about committing that year's offering to tape: the seventh Fleetwood Mac studio album, *Penguin*. The six-strong line-up of Mick, John, Christine, Bob Welch, Bob Weston and Dave Walker promised more than it delivered. The end result, released that March—why the rush? —begs the question: what were Walker and Weston even doing there? The contributions of both sound out of place.

While the rhythm of the whole feels disjointed, there is no denying that *Penguin* edges the band closer toward the fearlessly commercial outfit they would soon become. The most measured critics couldn't call it much more than "transitional." Neither one thing nor the other, it was at least a step in the right direction. The drummer surpasses himself. As for the songwriting, Welch and Christine do the heavy lifting. Her "Remember Me" is a vibe-y opener, boosted by Weston on slide. Almost choral in parts, its harmonies sound angelic. Chris's voice is as brilliantly controlled here as on "Did You Ever Love Me?" Co-written with Welch, it lilts along to an unexpected calypso steel drum beat, and is enhanced by a bewitching vocal. A Christine McVie hallmark is emerging here: that of a song that is baldly about heartbreak wrapped in brave smiles. "Hidden gem" runs through it like letters through a stick of rock. As for "Dissatisfied," you get pleading, plaintive, polished Chris to a deceptive rock-out tune. Listen: that Southern California sound creeping in. Hear it? Pre-echoes of *Rumours*. This, the highest-charting Mac album hitherto in the U.S., is infinitely better than the one the critics dismissed.

Their seventh studio album, released in March 1973, *Penguin* was the first to feature an image that would become indelibly linked with Fleetwood Mac, to the point that it would come to be regarded as their mascot. This was down to John McVie. When he and Chris had lived near Regent's Park, before they moved with the band to the Kiln House and then on to Benifold, he had got into the habit of sloping off to the zoo with his camera whenever time and itinerary allowed. Christine often accompanied him.

"Chris and I used to live round the corner from London Zoo," John said in a rare, undated interview. "On days off I'd go over and take pics of the animals. Usually ending up at the penguin exhibit. The display area is very interesting visually, and I found/find the penguins fascinating. When the band moved to a 'House in the Country,' we thought we could use a logo. Hence, the penguin."

John loved to photograph the seabirds, bizarrely, while they were copulating. He also got into reading up about the habits of the various species: eighteen in all, each one with its own unique characteristics. He loved their tapered bodies and streamlined shape, and was fascinated by their personalities. The spiritualists out there might claim that he identified with them. Penguins being social, caring, community-minded creatures who are protective of their mates and offspring. Although the Emperor penguin is not monogamous, many other species mate for life. A message to his Christine, that he couldn't quite articulate? No bonus for overthinking any of that.

John's curious obsession led to the artwork feature and to the adoption of the penguin image by the band. It was also behind the booze-fueled tattoo on his right forearm. "The tattoo came from a boring afternoon in the bar at the Riot House on Sunset Boulevard in [LA], recalled John, of the restaurant and bar at the Continental Hyatt House Hotel in West Hollywood that was a popular haunt of the hardest-partying rockers of the seventies, among them the Who, the Stones and Led Zeppelin.[6] "Right opposite is, or was, Lyle Tuttles' tattoo parlor. As the afternoon wore on, the idea of a tattoo became an increasingly 'GREAT IDEA!'...DUH!'[7]

The humble penguin would prompt an off-the-wall publicity stunt a few years later in 1977, when the Mac were the biggest band in the world. WMMS-FM, a Cleveland, Ohio radio station, got wind of John's obsession. The Mac were in town for two sold-out gigs at Richfield Coliseum that September. Contriving to steal a march on their competitors, WMMS-FM, whose logo was a buzzard, decided to get the band whose logo was the flightless bird to donate real-life penguins to the city's zoo. The band's record label, Warner Brothers, helped John to pick up a pair, worth $800 each, some $4,000 today. John and Christine, who were still legally married at the time but were in the process of divorcing, visited the zoo together. In the pictures, John is wearing the penguin ring Christine gave him as a parting gift before she left. They were photographed holding a Rockhopper penguin called Rocky, and presenting a check to the zoo's executives to purchase the seabirds, one of which would be named after Peter Green. The station milked the stunt for the next twelve months, until the Mac landed back in town for the following year's performances. Said the station's former program director John Gorman of Chris, "She was one of the most wonderful people I ever met in my life. I can't say enough good things about her. You would never know she was a rock star. I think Christine was probably like the den mother of Fleetwood Mac. She, as much as anybody, kept that band together."

*

Not another 1973 album? Oh, yes there was. Which first required the offloading of "front man" Dave Walker, who had pissed them off royally by propping up a bar at a local pub with John McVie throughout much of the recording of *Mystery to Me*. Fair criticism? Perhaps not, given that they hadn't exactly afforded him much else to do. But there was growing disgruntlement at his behavior on stage, where he was, they couldn't help but agree, something of a limelight-hogger. Wasn't that what they'd wanted, a stand-out front man, somebody to relieve the others of that pressure because none of them wanted the role? Maybe. Whatever, he had to go. That June, manager Clifford Davis was called upon to wield the stick. Walker was out.[8]

Frustrated and infuriated by her husband's relentless drinking, Christine "got tangled up with" ("as my mother would say!" she laughed) with Martin Birch, their married sound engineer, who at twenty-five was five years her junior. She convinced herself that she had fallen in love with him, and made her feelings known. Wishful thinking? Happens. John also played away, tit for tat, and drank even more. The atmosphere during recording sessions was unbearable. Although loyal servant Birch had engineered five albums for the band, Mick and John ruthlessly ejected him. What was that about? None of the males in this set-up was any angel. Against their own mounting misdemeanors, blind eyes were turned. When the woman in the group indulged in a clandestine liaison, however, they weren't having it, and she was having no say. Her affair was obliterated by the blokes, and she simply accepted it. Why didn't she object to this entitled, blatant sexism? Because she couldn't do anything about it. Faced with a similar dilemma today, she might have left the band and her husband, walked away from the toxic set-up and had another crack elsewhere. She was only thirty years old; beautiful, talented and in her prime. Why didn't she divorce John, cut her losses, and resume her solo career or join another band? Chicken Shack would have had her back in a beat.

Her hesitation was partly to do with a fear of "losing everything," she said. Not that there was much to lose at that point. "I wasn't brave enough frankly," she confided, years later, when we had the conversation entitled "Affairs." "There was still that stigma of being divorced in those days. "My pop [her father] would have been very, very disappointed in me," she said. "I didn't dare do that to him. In some ways, thank God my mother wasn't still alive to know about it. Martin was never going to leave his wife. I loved him, but I didn't want to be a mistress, horrible word, forever. It wasn't as if I could leave John and go straight into a new set-up with Mart. That was never an option, he made that clear. Neither of us had money, it was still only wages. And I was, you know, John's missis, not a person in my own right. There was no future in it."

Looking back on it, she said, "I could whine and gripe that I was used, but I don't want to bung all the blame on Mart. It was six of one, half a dozen of the other. There was something seedy about it that dented my self-respect. Maybe that was how the others made me feel. If they did, that would have been subliminal. Nobody actually said anything, which in some ways made it worse. I didn't like myself during that whole period. I sank very low. I loved John, too, of course I did, though part of me really loathed him."

Maybe another part of her thought it might work out with him eventually, and they would be OK again? "I don't know," she said. "I disliked my husband intensely for what he'd become, for what he was doing to me and to our marriage. We should have had kids by then. At least one, maybe. But in a way, thank God we didn't. I could understand completely how things had got so bad. We hated the sight of each other. The booze numbed the pain, as did the drugs. Yes, they were starting to kick in around then. Fleetwood Mac had become the mistress of us all. There was a sense by then that we could be on the verge of something, a breakthrough, dare I say it the big-time. The band had us by the short and curlies, she wasn't going to let us go." There was far worse to come.[9]

The Swinging Sixties had changed things, not least with more liberal social attitudes and the contraceptive pill. Britain's divorce rate had soared, with more than 50,000 filed in the UK in 1969 alone. The Divorce Reform Act that year was responsible, as it eliminated the requirement for one party to blame the other. In order to divorce, a couple simply needed to prove the irretrievable breakdown of their relationship. The 1973 Matrimonial Causes Act, the basis of modern divorce laws, established that a couple must be married for three years before attempting to apply for a divorce. By then, John and Christine had been spliced for five. Although their marriage was broken, neither was ready to abandon it.

*

The release of *Mystery to Me* in October 1973, its title coined by Jenny Fleetwood in reference to her growing attraction to a man who was not her husband, remains exactly that: a mystery, given everything else that was going down. Again, why the rush? That can only have been down to management, and contractual obligations. With Dave Walker out of the picture, Bob Welch had got down to it and had written six of the songs by himself, plus a seventh with Christine. She contributed four more. The twelfth track, which appeared as the penultimate offering on the B-side, was a cover of the Graham Gouldman composition "For Your Love," a hit in 1965 for the Yardbirds. Chris's BVs on track one, side one are sound. But her songs "Believe Me" and "Just Crazy Love" are weak by her standards. Lending her voice to Welch's "Keep on Going," she redeems herself, and then runs with it. Back on the B-side, her courageous confessional "The Way I Feel" with its quaintly Elizabethan texture is a blatant romanza to Martin Birch. Its vocal and instrumental control are superb. The album's parting shot, Christine's "Why," signs off from that ill-fated relationship with sad philosophy. Easing in with a stunning blues solo on slide guitar played by Bob Weston, its dark, doom-laden drums are offset by the deliberate lightness of Christine's piano. This is by far, to date, her strongest writing and singing. The track heaves with all the Fleetwood Mac brilliance to come. "My heart will rise up with the morning sun," she sings, "and the hurt I feel will simply melt away." Was she willing herself to rise not up, but above—despite the unmissable credit on this album to her erstwhile lover on acoustic guitar? There is wondrous vibrance in the song's majestic strings. Did that surge of harmonies relieve her? If only. It was the best she'd ever done, yet the best was as yet unwritten. The future of Fleetwood Mac begins here.

*

"It's the voice," affirms multi-platinum-selling songwriter and SongCentre founder Tim Fraser.[10] "Christine's vocal style was unique and completely natural. She seemed to have a soprano voice almost in the English Folk tradition, but chose to bring her range down to an alto. This was a fantastic instrument, and so accurate that on harmonies and double-tracking the whole effect was an almost sparkling sound. Her tone and style were thoroughly English and unusually dignified, no matter what musical noise was going on behind her. She never punctuated her singing with yells or whoops. In fact, her dynamics remained steady throughout a song. There were no exaggerated Americanisms or accents, unlike her contemporaries Elton John, Rod Stewart et al."

Christine's cool approach, explains Fraser, was never "cold." It directed the listener to the song and the lyrics without distraction. And within those lyrics, he points out, there was always a story that stayed with the listener for the long run. "Incredibly, in the 1960s," he reflects, "when female singers were storming the airwaves—Dusty Springfield, Lulu, Sandie Shaw, Petula Clark, Cilla Black—it was quietly spoken Christine Perfect who won the *Melody Maker*'s award for the best UK female singer in 1969 and 1970." But it is also, he reminds us, about the songs. "And it is a challenge to grade them. She knew how to write hits, and Fleetwood Mac became the juggernaut that steamrollered those records into the public's collective brain. She knew how to exploit the up-tempo powerhouse of Mick Fleetwood and John McVie and their storming shuffle, and decorate it with a serene performance that filled the airwaves, coffee houses and 'fern bars'[11] of California, and then conquered the world."

The point being that Fleetwood Mac had found their sound, their writing rhythm and their raison d'etre well ahead of the arrival of "the Americans." Though Lindsey Buckingham and Stevie Nicks have so often been credited for having revived a "flagging" band, and hailed as the musicians who guided them into the stratosphere, the Mac were already getting there of their own accord. By then firm favorites on U.S. "underground" FM radio, their music did not belong on the crammed-with-Top-40-bop-alongs AM frequency. But a change was gonna come on that front too, and soon.[12] "I am sure," agrees Fraser, "that as soon as Christine harmonized with Bob Welch, the die was cast. Fleetwood Mac was already set before Buckingham and Nicks arrived."

*

If any other Mac member was aware of the frustration and loneliness that drove Jenny Fleetwood to drink and into the arms of another behind Mick's back, they kept schtum. The band were back on the stateside road, touring *Mystery to Me*. A fortnight in, Jenny—who unusually was along for the ride with the kids instead of remaining home alone with their children—confessed to her husband her infatuation with another man. No random man, either, but one of Mick's chosen ones. So blinkered had he been to his neglect of his wife and their family, he had not even noticed anything was amiss. He seemed paralyzed and emotionless when Jenny and the girls withdrew from the tour and went to Los Angeles, where Nancy, the girlfriend of Bob Welch, took them in while Jenny made arrangements to get them home. But not to

Benifold. Faces and future Stones guitarist Ronnie Wood and his first wife Krissy offered them a berth, where Jenny assessed her future and her men.

Retreading her own footsteps in her compelling 2020 memoir *Jennifer Juniper*,[13] she paints a chilling picture of the collapse of the Fleetwood marriage. Their daughters were only three years and seven months old at the time. It raised the stakes. Mick exerted his usual band authority, did the inevitable and fired Bob Weston. Then he did a runner, cancelling the rest of the tour and disappearing off to Zambia. Bob Weston flew to London and made his way down to Benifold to be with Jenny, which she hadn't wanted or expected him to do. Under the influence, she succumbed. Only when he uttered telling words under the covers one night did she snap to her senses. "Mick might have had the power to kick me out of the band," said Bob, "but I have his wife in my bed." Her nagging sense of unease had been on the money. Jenny twigged that she was being used. Her loyalty to her husband surged through her like a billion-volt shock, and she knew the affair was over. "I was married to Mick and he was the one I wanted to feel connected to," she wrote. "Even so, the feelings of guilt, shame and betrayal were almost unbearable, knowing I would never be able to turn back the clock."

"It didn't take long for her to figure out that she didn't love Bob, she loved the part of herself that he allowed her to get in touch with," said Mick in his own memoir.[14] "The child-like part she could no longer access with me. She felt that I'd abandoned her for the band, so she had done the same."

Christine later referred to the episode and to 1974 generally as "a total fuck-up."

"Eurgh!" she sighed when interrogated about the period for *Mojo* in 2017. "Nobody knew what was going on. I just drifted with the strongest wind. My marriage to John was kaput by then. We were living together but no…because of…" She didn't have to say the word "bottle." "There was also that tawdry affair where Bob Weston slept with Mick's wife. That was very acrimonious, and obviously Bob had to be sacked…I can't quite remember how it all happened. That was the point where we all decided to move to America. We were only planning to go there for three months, get a record deal, get on the road and make some money. Then Bob Welch decided he couldn't see any future in Fleetwood Mac, so he left to go solo." Leaving Mick, John and Christine bereft of guitarists. What now?

*

Although the significance of what happened next has evaporated, the fall-out at the time was cataclysmic. With Mick off gazelle-gazing in the Zambian wilds, the other Mackers followed suit and shot off on holiday too. Following which, they would regroup at Benifold. They could not have known that their chancer of a manager would seize the day, claim their name and assemble an alternative line-up to finish the abandoned U.S. tour. Some of this "new," fake Fleetwood Mac line-up were members of another band managed by Davis called Curved Air. Retaining funds advanced to him for use by the genuine Mac on the rest of the tour Mick had just cancelled, Davis set Mac Mark II on the road. "If there was ever a time to call it quits," recounted Mick, "this was it. There we were in England, far from what had become our core audience, thousands of miles from our record company and with our band in tatters, as our trusted manager of seven years tried to move on without us. It was heartbreak heaped on heartache."[15]

But Fleetwood wasn't about to concede defeat. The McVies, drowning in their own sorrows, were not much help. The thought of having to endure the process of finding yet another guitarist, of having to sack their manager and then engage in extortionate legal proceedings simply to retain what was already theirs, eclipsed everything they had survived hitherto. How to handle it? They strolled in the woods, built huge bonfires and sat around staring into the flames, as if the clues were to be found there. They gathered around the kitchen tables of their apartments, weighing up the options as they tried to find a solution. It was soon agreed that they would dispense with management. Mick would manage the band himself, with support from Bob Welch. They would sue Clifford Davis in the U.S., where he was touring what was no more than a tribute band—"Fleetwood Mock"?—to retrieve ownership of their name, reassure their fanbase and restore their reputation. Fearing that the legal battle could drag on for many months, and that constant returns to the U.S. for court appearances and lawyers' meetings could cripple them financially, they agreed to relocate to LA. This meant that they must surrender their beloved Benifold.

Did they relocate for nothing? Their lawsuit kicked off in London's High Court, as reported by *Billboard* on 27 July 1974. "Fleetwood Mac Win a Round in Name Tiff," ran the headline. The sizable news item proceeded to outline the issue: that the band were trying to stop a management company and three musicians from using the same name. Fleetwood Mac Promotions and members of the band were duly granted an injunction against Clifford Davis as Clifford George Adams and his company, Clifford Davis Management Ltd. His defense was that the band had split up. The band countered that the split was only temporary. The order restraining three members of the new group from passing themselves off as Fleetwood Mac was made by Mr. Justice Goff. "The original group had a reputation through the name Fleetwood Mac that Davis thought was worth using," said the judge. Davis claimed the right, in a letter, to "take charge of the situation." He had said he was going to form a group to go to America, and certain members of the group could go with him if they wished. But if not, they would not stop *him* going. But they did get to pull the plug.

"John McVie had had enough of all the Clifford Davis stuff, and cleared off for a while," recalls their first bassist and close friend David Ambrose. "Mick asked me to start jamming with him, just in case. It was all very messy and they were terribly upset. But I was quite out of it by then. I'd met two hippies in Morocco, who I took round to see Mick. They were great to me, and I was in love with them. Jenny Fleetwood took one look at them and said, 'Get them out of the house, *now!*' She protested that they were smelly, and had germs. But they wrote some truly lovely songs, and set me free from my horrible life for a while. I thought they could be good for Fleetwood Mac, especially given the way things were changing all the time, with so many comings and goings and now an international lawsuit."

He and Mick really were like brothers, sighed Ambrose. "I thought we were going to do it all over again. I really thought John was going to quit the band and I could sneak back in. But Jenny threw the boys out, I had to leave with them, and that was that. Once again I was left high and dry, thinking about what might have been."

While at Benifold, Ambrose and Christine "started talking about how terrible things were, and how awful it was that there was another Fleetwood Mac strutting around America. Mick, Christine and John did save the name eventually. But it took some doing. There's an old saying in the music business: 'It depends on who's doing the business.' The three of them had to fight their corner with Warners, their record company. It took years. They went to America. Mick hadn't found a guitarist. Then he went to check out a studio, heard this amazing guitarist having a go, and that was Lindsey Buckingham. Mick offered him the gig in Fleetwood Mac, and Lindsey said, 'Stevie comes too.' They reached an agreement with Clifford Davis to keep their name. Then, after a couple of warm-ups, they went and did this fuck-off incredible album. Which was retribution in a way. Two fingers to Davis. Up *yours*."

Bass players always know the story, Ambrose tells me. "Because we're watching. The bassist is the rock. He invents melodies. Invents lines. Bassists are also randy bastards. The girls always love them. Why? Because we feel the beat. I mean, look at Bill Wyman."

So they say?

"So *he* says."

*

Cut to November 2023. Via a global sale instigated by Clifford Davis as Clifford Adams, hundreds of items of Fleetwood Mac memorabilia documenting the band's rise to fame changed hands for the disappointing sum of £20,050. Somebody needed the money. There were "bids from all over the world, from Australia to the U.S.," enthused Robin Fletcher, manager of Hansons Auctioneers Kent in Tunbridge Wells. Among the collection was a fifty-year-old personal letter to Davis from Fleetwood Mac's founder Peter Green, explaining why he left the band. It changed hands for £2,000. Gold and platinum discs were also available. Claiming to have been Fleetwood Mac's "co-songwriter and agent" as well as manager, Davis stated that his memorabilia offered fans the opportunity to "gain an insight into what life was like for the band in the early days, and why Peter Green chose to walk away." He also parted with Green's personal driving license, for £460. He and Green, he insisted, had always been "really good friends."

"He trusted me," he said.

*

LA's fine, the sun shines most the time.[16] Swinging London was swung-out. The heyday of New York's Brill Building, the biggest generator of popular songs in the post-war Western world, was over. The West Coast was happening, in particular Laurel Canyon, which had become the epicenter of America's music scene during the early 1970s. This was the leafy cathedral of the decade's new music, folk-rock-country fusion. Songwriters had wagon-trained it across country from Manhattan's concrete jungle to settle in the eucalyptus-scented serenity of the Hollywood Hills. There, north of Sunset Boulevard, was where the golden age of California Dreamin' had begun. Out of the dregs of hippie idealism came the mecca of rock'n'roll. For the susceptible, as members of the Mac surely were, there was everything to entice them. This narco-fueled, hedonistic realm was where the acid freaks hung, where cocaine cowboys rubbed shoulders with cultists, groupies and dudes, where whatever you fancied was a fistful away. It was also where Christine McVie truly, absolutely did not want to live. Until she got there.

"It was to save the band," she remarked in 2017, "and once there, I didn't mind it much. We were living in relative pauperville in Laurel Canyon, in John Mayall's house for two months. Then we found an apartment down the hill and gradually started to make a bit of money, and then moved to Malibu where we started recording 'The White Album' (1975's *Fleetwood Mac*), driving to the valley every day from the beach. We were in a real bubble then. I was so overawed by these guys as writers that I stepped my game up. I wanted to impress them."

"These guys" were songwriting guitarist Lindsey Buckingham and singer-songwriter Stevie Nicks, a Californian duo in need of a break. "[Mick] went to the Valley, the studio where he heard Lindsey, and thought, 'Fuck, who is this brilliant guitar player?'" Chris recalled. "The engineer said, 'Oh, it's this couple who've just finished this duet album.' So Mick got the number of Lindsey and said, 'How would you feel about maybe joining Fleetwood Mac?' and Lindsey says, 'We come as a couple.' So, somehow, we meet up in this Mexican restaurant and…it was that chemistry, and it started round that table."

Mick arranged a New Year's dinner for the final three Mackers plus Lindsey and Stevie at El Carmen, a Mexican restaurant in LA. The deal was that, while the tequila and tacos flowed, Christine would size up Stevie and get the measure of her at her own pace. If she didn't feel they could rub along together in the same band, the right to refuse would be hers. While this was a cool, gentlemanly move on Mick's part, how come it had never been applied to potential new *male* members? The girls got along famously. Just as well. Said Stevie down the line, "We went for Mexican food with them, and we laughed and laughed, because you English people have a very strange sense of humor. Even Lindsey had fun—he didn't want to, but he couldn't help it."[17]

"Then we had another meeting at Mick's house," said Chris, "and then we went into rehearsals. I started playing them 'Say You Love Me' on the piano, and we got to the chorus and the two of them just chirped into the perfect three-part harmony. I just remember thinking, 'This is it!' Then Lindsey picked up his guitar, Mick his drumsticks, John his bass and it happened like *that*…" A snap of the fingers and a brand-new day. It's LA.

*

How many years to overnight success? Neither Stevie nor Lindsey would care to count them. A lot of blood has been let since then. What happened next was less about timing, more about chemistry. The thing about chemistry in bands is that it depends as much on differences as on similarities. "The Brits"—a lofty thumper in a troubled marriage and a dysfunctional, wed-by-a-thread bassist and keyboard player—were alluring to the Americans as twee strangers in a foreign land. More popular there than back home among their own, they were an eccentric, mismatched trio with a long and fascinating history. "The Yanks" were to some extent familiar. They were also exotic, because American culture was king. The U.S. music scene was a rich, heaving smorgasbord and an escape from the buffet back home, where the Beatles as solo artists, the Stones, Elton, Cat Stevens and their brothers dominated. Cult followings in metal had boosted Deep Purple, Black Sabbath and Led Zeppelin. The navel-gazing prog rockers —Pink Floyd, Genesis, Emerson Lake & Palmer, Yes—were taking themselves very seriously. Bowie and Bolan, Roxy Music and Queen glammed a good dance for which America wasn't yet ready; while Slade, Sweet and their ilk went mental, but peaked mid-decade and would be gobbled by punk. You wait. Synthpop, anybody?

In the U.S., post-Beatles and the British Invasion, post-counterculture, hippie soul-searching and Vietnam, the parallel rise of white American rock and black soul and R&B and the emerging dominance of funk, Philly and the disco craze that hustled in during 1974—George McCrae, Anita Ward, a reborn Earth, Wind and Fire—not only swirled a heady cocktail but reflected the mood of their time. Hundreds of American singer-songwriters flocked west and tried to launch careers during the early 1970s, many of them via a trio of record labels that were part of the vast Kinney Leisure corporation. Warner Brothers, Elektra and Atlantic releases were marketed collectively under the WEA name. It evolved into the massive musical success story of the seventies. The artists they signed were strongly identified with the new "rock jet set" based in—where else—Laurel Canyon.

It was there, right there in the songs. The press descended. Joni Mitchell bleeding her guts about her affairs with James Taylor and Graham Nash set the precedent. Open your heart, kids, and splash it all over your sleeve: that's the way to explosive record sales. Suddenly anyone who displayed even a streak of promise was heralded as "the new Bob Dylan," "the new Joan Baez," "the new Simon and Garfunkel." Superstar artists guested on each other's albums—Crosby, Stills, Nash & Young on Joni's, James Taylor on future spouse Carly Simon's, she on his—thus establishing the elitist canyon as an incestuous, mystical domain. You don't do this stuff, you're not one of us? The door's behind you. The studied American-ness of much of the music, the honoring of rock's country and blues roots, the Disneyfication of swamps, river boats, the frontier, the trail of the lonesome guitarist that had surged back in the sixties, championed by the Band, Creedence Clearwater Revival, the Allman Brothers Band and more had, by the mid-seventies, become sanitized and repackaged by the Eagles, the Doobie Brothers and the British-American trio called America. Their country-infused harmonies and gentle, agreeable odes sat nicely on FM radio. But FM, too, was changing. AOR, adult-oriented rock—in those days, "adult" indicated that you were over twenty-five—was now recognized as the "true" music of the 1970s. Linda Ronstadt, Andrew Gold, Bonnie Raitt and friends heeded the whistle.

You see where this is going—and how Fleetwood Mac evolved into who they became. The accidental rather than calculated move could not have been more timely. Such things are only obvious in hindsight. They were immersed to the roots and were blinking on stars. The canyon consumed them.

*

Yet again, to know Chris, we must unpeel the incomers. Because their absorption into the line-up didn't just enlarge and refine the sound. It also unlocked and volumized the creativity and personality of the existing members. Specifically, Christine. The Mick'n'John rhythm section remained the solid, reliable backbone. Chris, the Mac's muse, songwriter and voice, would now flourish in the company of the new kids. But who were they, and where had they come from?

Stephanie Lynn Nicks hailed from Phoenix, Arizona, where she was born post-war on 26 May 1948. Her first exposure to music had been at the knee of her grandmother "Crazy Alice," who sang her old lullabies and read her fairy stories. Her paternal grandfather AJ, Aaron Jess Nicks, a bit of a hillbilly who played fiddle, guitar and harmonica, started Stevie singing when she was no more than five. The first harmonies she learned were to the nineteenth-century Western folk ballad "Oh, My Darling Clementine." The pair were soon performing in local saloons, Stevie dressed in a cute cowgirl rig-out stitched by her mother. AJ began to picture the realization of a lifelong dream: that of making it to the Grand Ole Opry, Nashville's home of country music. Stevie's parents put their foot down, and a rift ensued. Stevie could have been Shirley Temple in teeny tiny cowboy boots. Where would she be now?

The family relocated frequently, as her father, Aaron Jess Jr., pursued corporate success. She would later recall that she was "always the new girl." At a Catholic school in Texas, the nuns tried to make left-handed Stevie write with her right hand. It is interesting that this happened to Stevie in 1950s America but not to left-handed Christine (who wrote and later smoked "southpaw") in England.[18] In 1962, when Stevie was fourteen, the clan moved again, to moneyed Arcadia in the San Gabriel valley around thirteen miles north-east of downtown LA. She joined the a capella choir and teamed with beautiful Robin Snyder, a fellow pupil who became the sister she'd never had. She got into music, especially the Beach Boys, and pleaded for guitar lessons for her fifteenth birthday. She was gifted her first instrument, joined a school group, and wrote her first love song, "I've Loved and I've Lost," about the boyfriend who dumped her on her sweet sixteenth. And she was bitten. "I *knew*," she later said, "from that second on, that I was not going to sing a lot of other people's songs. I was going to write my own."

Two years later, during the summer of '64, a few months after the Beatles had turned 73 million heads on 9 February with their performance on *The Ed Sullivan Show*, the Nickses upped sticks again. They moved further north, to San Mateo on the San Francisco peninsula, the region known today as Silicon Valley. Stevie enrolled at Menlo-Atherton High School in Atherton, twelve or so miles down the coast. It was at an evening church session for budding musicians the following year that seventeen-year-old Stevie met sixteen-year-old Lindsey Buckingham. He was playing "California Dreamin'" on the church piano. Stevie ambled over and started harmonizing with him. It led to nothing. Three years passed. She had landed and lost her first recording contract and had started at junior college by the time they saw each other again.

Lindsey Adams Buckingham started life on 3 October 1949 in Palo Alto, and was raised in Atherton. He was the youngest of three sons in a typical Californian family. All three swam competitively. Elder brother Greg, who swam for Stanford University, was the most successful, taking silver in Mexico at the 1968 Olympic Games. Lindsey fell early for strumming cowboy Gene Autry, and received his first instrument, a plastic Mickey Mouse guitar, when he was six. He was soon imitating Elvis, and getting into local groups. He learned guitar and banjo in high school, and followed Elvis, the Everlys, the Beach Boys and Hank Williams. In 1966, aged seventeen, he co-founded Fritz, his first band. His Rickenbacker was borrowed, their first gig a school assembly. He graduated from school that summer, and started at San Jose State public university in the autumn. Keen to keep Fritz going, he was dismayed by the departure of a couple of members including the band's female singer. Then he remembered Stevie...who happened to be studying speech therapy at the same university. In 1968, the year she left her teens, Stevie found herself quivering on Lindsey's Atherton doorstep, awaiting an audition. She got the gig. When her parents left for Chicago, she did not move with them but stayed behind. She was now in Lindsey's band, but she was not yet his girlfriend. He already had one. Stevie bided her time. She wrote poems and lyrics in journals. She had always known that she was going to be a star.

Fritz got gigs all over the peninsula, at high school dances and colleges. Their reputation grew. One by one, the serious bookings started coming in, at important venues such as the Winterland and the Fillmore West. They found themselves opening for named artists: Creedence Clearwater Revival, Chicago, Leon Russell, the Santana Blues Band. They attracted attention from local radio and television. They played the Monterey/Carmel Pop Festival, the one that heralded Woodstock. While things didn't always go their way—they were turned down as opening act for Led Zeppelin in San Francisco, and were never invited to support Fleetwood Mac—but they did get to open for Janis Joplin's new backing group the Kozmic Blues Band. The year 1970 was the turning-point. They supported Janis again, this time fronting her Fill Tilt Boogie Band; and got up ahead of Jimi Hendrix's Band of Gypsies for an estimated 75,000 fans. But by the end of the year, both Janis and Jimi, both twenty-seven, would meet their Maker. Fritz disbanded amid much squabbling. Their manager announced he was moving to LA, and wanted to take them with him—for greater exposure and a better chance at getting signed. Stevie didn't fancy fake Tinseltown. She was not alone. But she and her bandmate were overruled. Plans were made to head south in order to look for a decent producer.

Downbeat Sound City recording studios' chief engineer Keith Olsen got to hear about them, and to listen to their tapes. Impressed by their harmonies and by the chemistry between Stevie and Lindsey, he arranged some free off-schedule studio time for them. But in the studio, the band sounded lackluster. Olsen took Stevie and Lindsey to one side, told them they'd never get anywhere with this band, and proposed that they record as a duo. They "ummed," "ahhed," quit Fritz, left their respective partners, and were suddenly an item. Stevie was twenty-three, Lindsey a year younger. "I loved him before he was famous," she would declare years hence in a television interview. "I loved him before he was a millionaire. We were two kids out of Menlo-Atherton High School. I loved him for all the right reasons." Little did they know that this tumultuous, euphoric, all-consuming love would soon erupt volcanically, generating songs that remain beloved half a century on.

Lindsey succumbed to glandular fever. Their move south was delayed by several months. They trod water by writing. Stevie's new songs were already an outlet for her arrogant, repressive and at times maddening boyfriend, who forced his musical education and songwriting technique down her throat. Blinded by stars, she took it, but the cracks were there from day two. Love finds a way. Lindsey was also a pothead, and grumpy because he was missing his fix. His physician had banned the indulgence until his health improved.

*

When they moved to LA, Stevie and Lindsey dossed at Keith Olsen's place and Stevie worked as his cleaner. She also took a job as an assistant at a local dental surgery, but was out by the end of the first day. She signed up as a waitress and as a hostess, and stashed her tips away. On her earnings, Stevie did her best to support the two of them. "We were broke and starving," she told *Rolling Stone* years later. "I was cleaning the house of our producer for $50 a week. I come home with my [cleaning equipment and products] and Lindsey has managed to have some idiot send him 11 ounces of opiated hash. He and all his friends are in a circle on the floor. They'd been smoking hash for a month, and I don't smoke because of my voice…" What she resented was that it was hash *she* had paid for. Not only that, but she'd get in every day and find herself not only tip-toeing over bodies but having to clean up around them. At the time, she put up with it, relieving her frustrations by writing about it in her journals alongside her lyrics.

She and Lindsey recorded demos, did auditions and even had an audience with Lou Adler, the label owner who had signed the Mamas & the Papas. That went nowhere. Olsen gave them an old upright piano, and Stevie tinkered. She also started reading fantasy novels about her distant Welsh heritage. A year on, they were performing Eagles covers in bars and steakhouses. Keith Olsen bagged them an industry showcase, but only two people turned up. At the point at which all seemed lost, Buckingham Nicks landed a recording contract with Anthem Records. That one fell through, but another opportunity came good, for Anthem to have a distribution deal with Polydor, and suddenly they were in possession of a recording budget. Olsen lined up a bunch of respected session musicians to work with them, and they were on their way. But when it came to shooting the cover art, Stevie found herself being bullied by Lindsey to appear semi-nude. Under pressure, she did it, but never forgot how it made her feel. Not that very many people saw the picture, at that stage.

The album, released in September 1973, was in every way other than musically a shabby product. It took an instant dive. Despite which, Lindsey pulled a band together so that Buckingham Nicks could at least play some gigs in support of their debut album while dishing up the inevitable covers. After they supported John Prine at the Troubadour, things looked up. They traveled east for further gigs including the Metro club in Manhattan, and were reviewed by *Billboard*. Not entirely favorably. Some gigs down south went better than most. They seemed to have a following there. So they were surprised when, after only three months, Polydor let them go. Stevie put her waitress's pinny back on. Lindsey insisted they were in it for the long haul, and forced her to carry on. Both started writing fervently for the next album: Lindsey throughout the day, lazing about, surrounded by stoner sycophants; Stevie through the night when she got in from work. Their relationship was already hitting the rocks, which drove Stevie to write the rudiments of gems: "Rhiannon" and "Landslide." That December, into Olsen's ambled Mick, looking for studio time.

*

The first album the Mac recorded in LA—for the only time as a quartet—was *Heroes are Hard to Find*. It would be Bob Welch's swansong with the band, which was ironic given that he knocked out seven solid songs for it. Christine brought up the rear with four, and outclassed him, particularly with the heart-melting, hugely underrated "Prove Your Love." She also yielded the orchestral, country-infused "Come a Little Bit Closer" and the funky, horn-driven title track. But although this record slotted seamlessly into the AOR groove and made the U.S. Top 40, it didn't even chart back home. It was perhaps unsurprising, with its diverse range of numbers, styles and influences that steered them ever further from the blues.

Just as they were hitting the road to promote it, Bob Welch quit. Mounting drama, relationship fallout, financial disarray and inter-band animosity had proved too much for him. He went silent for a while before re-emerging in November 1977 with his acclaimed solo album *The Kiss*. Eight more studio albums followed, which were less successful, but he kept on recording regardless. His undoing, during the mid-1980s, was a wild friendship with the members of Guns N' Roses that got him hooked on heroin and cocaine. By 2012 he was ailing. Acute back pain forced him to submit to spinal surgery. The operation failed to relieve his agony. During the early morning of 7 June, Welch shot himself dead in his Nashville home, leaving a suicide note and a love letter for his wife Wendy, who found him. He was sixty-six. Four years later, Wendy's own life was claimed by heart disease and COPD. The couple are buried side by side in Memphis.

Back at the Olsen ranch, Keith played Mick a Buckingham Nicks track to showcase the sound quality his facility was capable of producing. The track was "Frozen Love." A fortnight later, making contact through the producer, Mick offered the guitarist a gig. Olsen explained that Lindsey and Stevie came as a pair.

History rewrites. Mythology would have us believe that Christine was as impressed as the others by the Buckingham Nicks album that Mick carried back for them to listen to; but that she balked at the suggestion that the band should absorb another woman, with all the potential to upstage her and steal her thunder. It wasn't like that.

"It was critical that I got on with [Stevie]," said Christine, recalling the moment, "because I'd never played with another girl. But I liked her instantly. She was funny and nice, but also there was no competition. We were completely different on the stage to each other," she remarked much later, "and we wrote differently too."[19]

When Christine joined, she became one of the boys. She had no choice. Their unsavory habits, bloke-ish behavior and toilet humor on the road in the back of a clapped-out van desensitized her and thickened her English-rose skin. Hanging with them gave her, she admitted, a filthy mouth. She didn't seem regretful. Her attitude was, so what? Mick's wife Jenny became a lovely, loyal ally and supporter in those early days. Their friendship would last for the rest of Christine's life. Four years into her tenure and they found themselves dealing with the Buckingham Nicks onslaught.

So much was made, at the time and ever since, of the fact that Fleetwood Mac now had *two females in the line-up*. What fresh hell? Wouldn't they bitch each other to oblivion, murder each other with their mic stands, scratch each other's eyes out with razored nails? No good could come of it? Men, oh men. Get down. It's the seventies. Hadn't they got used to the idea a decade earlier, via groovy folk-rock quartet the Mamas and the Papas—they of "This is Dedicated to the One I Love,""Monday, Monday" and "California Dreamin'," who boasted voluptuous Cass Elliot and waif Michelle Phillips alongside the latter's lascivious husband, band leader John, and pudding-bowl-coiffed Denny Doherty? How come three men in the same group was never a problem, while two women always would be? Hey, crusty critics of yore. The world didn't care. It was too busy getting off on Fairport Convention, Jefferson Airplane, Velvet Underground with Nico, the Carpenters, Gladys Knight and the Pips. All with girls. Get over it. And there were ABBA, Blondie, the Human League, Joan Jett & the Blackhearts, Thompson Twins, Middle of the Road, No Doubt, Heart, Peaches & Herb, The Talking Heads, The B-52's et al to come. None of these females was there for decorative purposes.

Christine and Stevie "felt like, together, we were a force of nature," said Stevie. "And we made a pact, probably in our first rehearsal, that we would never accept being treated as second-class citizens in the music business. That when we walked into a room we would be so fantastic and so strong and so smart that none of the uber-rockstar group of men would look through us. And they never did."

"When I met Chris—this sounds like a movie, right?" Stevie also commented, to the 1975's Matty Healy for *The Face* magazine in May 2020. "...when I met Christine McVie...she's five years older than me, so we were like 28 and 33. And Christine is a full-on, you know, trained concert pianist person and an amazing artist, painter. So there was so much more to Christine than just music, and when I met her that night at the Mexican food dinner, I was just like, I was awestruck with her."

All things being equal. Two women, one group? They had no idea. It was to prove the least of Fleetwood Mac's worries.

The morning after the dinner came the call. Stevie and Lindsey were in. Let's do this.

CHAPTER 10

RUMOURS

Fleetwood Mac's eponymous tenth studio album and second nominative offering was recorded at Sound City in LA, together with their new recruits. They would refer to their July 1975 release as "the White Album" to distinguish it from the band's 1968 debut of the same name. The alternative title was ironic. In nicknaming it to avoid confusion with the earlier offering by the Mac's original incarnation, they established something that would instead be confused with an altogether different album also labeled "the White Album," released by the Beatles in 1968 —during the same year as the Mac's debut LP. With me? That sparkling gem, the one featuring McCartney's "Back in the USSR" and "Blackbird," George's "While My Guitar Gently Weeps" and John's "Julia," and encased in a stark white, wordless sleeve (apart from a tiny, embossed band reference) was actually entitled *The Beatles*. You could forgive the Macs-to-Macca tongue-in-cheek. But it backfired. Although a smash in America, it didn't even chart in the UK, which was a travesty. Because this is the album that showcases two of Stevie Nicks's evergreens, "Landslide" and "Rhiannon"; Christine's and Lindsey's frantic debut collaboration, "World Turning"; and Chris's "Over My Head" and "Say You Love

Me"—on which all five musicians distinguish themselves brilliantly and on which Christine, Stevie and Lindsey's harmonies crystallize perfectly. "Falling, falling, falling," lilts the dream-sequence coda, and *Rumours*-era Mac are out of the blocks. "Rhiannon," "Say You Love Me" and "Over My Head" scored them American Top 20 singles. The album whisked them all the way. Having achieved so much at their first attempt, would there be no stopping this souped-up line-up? Would jealousy between their two obviously contrasting females thwart them? Because from the off, ethereal, angelic Stevie was already into her center-stage, attention-demanding, twirling-in-chiffon thing. Even when there wasn't a stage. "Sure, I got jealous," admitted Chris, candidly. "It didn't last long. You soon realize where your role is…I could no sooner do twirls in chiffon than Stevie could play the piano."

"She would never have let me know that," was Stevie's response. "She would have known that would have freaked me out…she never reined me in." Also, "She always would say to me, 'I don't want to be out in front. I like being over here playing my piano, being one of the men.'"

*

"It wasn't cool to like Fleetwood Mac in 1977," reflects Richard Hughes. The clinical psychotherapist, who was still at school at the time of the *Rumours* release, remembers that to admit liking the band would have been "playground suicide." "First of all, we thought of them as an *American* band," he recalls. "Secondly, they just seemed so obvious. At least ABBA, who were more or less their contemporaries, had something mysterious about them. What we would call nowadays a 'Scandi-noir' interest to them."

BBC television's *Top of the Pops* was crammed with clashing acts that year, from Bowie, Bob Marley, Leo Sayer and David Soul to Hot Chocolate, the Jacksons and Rod Stewart. There were moments for the Sex Pistols, the Stranglers, Elvis Costello and the

Jam. Queen rode the crest, as did queen of disco Donna Summer. Elvis Presley expired in Memphis on 16 August and leapt high up the charts. Marc Bolan died in a car crash in Barnes, west London on 16 September, and would be deified as the dominant glamster.

But before all that, on 4 February that year, out crept an album destined to become not only the musical phenomenon of the decade but this curious band's magnum opus. It would change the lives of those who created it, both musicians and technicians. It would move millions of people all over the world for nearly the next half-century—and possibly in perpetuity. It would cost almost a million dollars and the best part of a year to create; score ten hit singles from eleven tracks; and bag them the 1977 Grammy Award for Best Album. Pause to consider the musical climate into which it sailed. The number-one single in the UK that week was David Soul's "Don't Give Up On Us, Baby," and the number-one album was Slim Whitman's *Red River Valley*. Stateside, Mary MacGregor was celebrating her chart-thrasher "Torn Between Two Lovers," and at the top of the LP tree perched the Eagles with *Hotel California*, having toppled Stevie Wonder's wondrous *Songs in the Key of Life*.

*

Although they were fizzing from what they'd achieved together on "the White Album," it had not yet earned them any hits. All that was to come. They had exhausted themselves throughout the summer and autumn of 1975 touring America relentlessly, showcasing the new album and converting their fans to their revitalized line-up. Hot, tight and galvanized, thoughts turned to what they would record next. Preoccupied though the five of them were when they convened, toward the end of January 1976, at Record Plant studio in Sausalito—over the Golden Gate Strait from San Francisco—to begin work on their follow-up, it was not by chart positions.

Another Fleetwood Mac misconception is that *Rumours* was constructed as a chronicle of the breakdowns between the band's three couples: Mick and his wife Jenny, Christine and John, and Stevie and Lindsey. Although that's what the songs were mostly about, there was no pre-planned structure. But so disruptive was the disintegration that discolored their chemistry and threatened the band's future that the drama bled inevitably into their songwriting. Without confiding in each other about their personal tragedies, dashed ideals and wrecked romances, Fleetwood Mac's trio of writers opened their hearts and allowed raw emotion to drive the narrative. Drugs, booze, illicit sex and imprudent affairs played their part. The result, sometimes referred to as a "journey" or even a "concept album," was anything but. It just happened that Christine, Stevie and Lindsey came to the table with cathartic pieces laying bare their own pain, suffering, anger, despair and even a little hope that matters would improve. Extreme feelings splashed about by one band member were absorbed by the others. Emotion shook down into songs that would resonate universally. It was as though they had taken the advice of "father of American literature" Mark Twain, whose Golden Rule of Writing was, "Write what you know."

Here was songwriting that avoided the vague and the abstract to go straight for the jugular, cutting directly to real-time experience. The heartbreak and the fall-out were ongoing. These songs gelled so perfectly because they shared fundamental truths about human love and loss. Didn't they? They have stood the test of time, and remain relatable. Haven't they? We have all been there. We identify with these people. We suffer with and are drawn to them, because they understand our own pain...

*

The engineers who co-produced *Rumours* with the band members were Richard Dashut, who routinely oversaw their live work, and Ken Caillat. "What's ironic is that throughout the *Rumours* journey," commented Caillat in his highly personal, subjective memoir *Making Rumours*, "Fleetwood Mac went from one end of the fame spectrum to the other. That day in Sausalito, when we walked into the studio to start recording, they were an established band, but you could hardly say they were rock stars. Before we even released *Rumours*, that had changed dramatically."

Young and relatively inexperienced though he was at the time of this recording, Caillat could read the room. He quickly had the measure of those five distinct personalities, their habits and foibles, their insecurities, their relationships with one another and the hierarchy within the band. He was soon aware that he was dealing with five headstrong, eccentric, unpredictable obsessives who would clash frequently.

Band leader Mick was the control freak, beating the others on relentlessly. He would go all night if he could, and sod the home life. John, his trusty collaborator, was, or at least seemed, out of it half the time. But he was in the habit of flooring them every now and then, usually when they least expected it, with a brilliant new bassline. Stevie was "the new girl" with the most downtime on her hands. She tied her tambourine with long black ribbons, did her twirl, and was infuriatingly precious about "her words." Woe betide he or she who suggested a cut here, an alteration there. She wasn't having it. Stevie was the band's new poet, for whom every last obscure syllable mattered. The tone and meter of her lines were exquisitely crafted. She wasn't going to stand for them being shredded by anyone just because they failed to understand them. As for the "extraordinarily talented, extraordinarily opinionated and extraordinarily annoying" Lindsey, the guitarist's outbursts could be terrifying. When he gave in to violent rage and became confrontational, the others, knowing what to expect, just ignored him.

As for Christine, her obsession was her piano. She was almost impossible to please. "Lord, how we suffered for her piano," remembers Caillat. Being blessed with perfect pitch, Chris insisted that her Steinway grand was always in tune. This exasperated Ken, who found her "picky." Even the shirt on his back would annoy her if she wasn't in the mood. "Christine and I always got along very well," he reports, "but she never withheld an opinion." He would go so far as to say that the outsider may well have concluded that Chris and Lindsey were the most antagonizing, abrasive and demanding members of the band. But no. That honor went unequivocally to Mick Fleetwood.[1]

Of the relationships within the band, the McVies were the most fascinating. It seemed obvious to anyone who was half-paying attention that John McVie still "loved" his wife. Although he had a funny way of showing it, he would have jumped at the chance to repair their marriage. But John was maintaining the most dangerous kind of mistress. A heartless sort who had the most sinister hold on him. She lived inside the bottle, and was impossible to relinquish. Having made her decision and called time on the marriage, Christine appeared resigned. She was able to rise above her feelings to put the band first. She was more than willing to work with John provided he controlled himself and behaved like a mature adult. Which he could rise to when he was sober—so not that often—but lamented her when in his cups. He must have known as well as she did that they were beyond reconciliation. Was his jealousy fueled by the knowledge that she was savoring a tasty morsel on the side? Because Christine was by then involved with yet another Fleetwood Mac hand: this time their suave, sexy lighting director, Curry Grant. As for her songwriting, she outlined her businesslike approach to the task to writer Cameron Crowe. "I don't struggle over my songs," she said. "I write them quickly, and I've never written a lot. I write what is required of me. For me, people like Joni Mitchell are making too much of a statement. I don't really write about myself, which puts me in a safe little cocoon…I'm a pretty basic love song writer."[2]

Ken observed that Chris and John would usually begin a fresh session in a relatively good mood, addressing each other politely. The vagaries of the previous day, however extreme, would usually have been forgiven and forgotten. But as the new day progressed and as more and more alcohol was imbibed, their dialogue grew terse and light friendliness evaporated. The slightest thing would set them off. In a beat, they would be arguing, until Christine could take no more. She would then cut her estranged husband dead with, "John, you're being ridiculous, you've had too much to drink," before walking away. If he continued, she would retort that he should tell it to his bass. "I had to do it for my sanity," Chris told Cameron Crowe in 1977. "It was either that or me ending up in a lunatic asylum. I still worry for him more than I would ever dare tell him. I still have a lot of love for John. Let's face it, as far as I'm concerned, it was *him* that stopped me loving him. He constantly tested what limits of endurance I would go to. He just went one step too far. If he knew that I cared and worried so much about him, I think he'd play on it. There's no doubt about the fact that he hasn't really been a happy man since I left him," she admitted. "I know that. Sure, I could make him happy tomorrow and say, yeah John, I'll come back to you. Then I would be miserable. I'm not that unselfish."

Ken hadn't clocked that Stevie and Lindsey were also in meltdown. He had assumed them to be in an open relationship, which says it all. As for Mick and Jenny, they had divorced during the autumn of 1976, but had turned around and remarried four months later. Their relationship was troubled again almost immediately. Caillat describes Mick as "a womanizer and an alcoholic, so his relationship with his wife was doomed because he couldn't change his ways."

The engineer couldn't imagine how all this turmoil and negativity could possibly lead to a credible album that stood a chance at chart success. After it was finished, he found it miraculous that they had managed to keep it together for long enough to get through it. He would later describe the process as "brilliant group therapy in which we all—wittingly or unwittingly—participated." And he acknowledged the not inconsiderable roles that sex, booze and substances—pot, cocaine—had played. Beyond that, he didn't get involved. "Successful musicians are not normal," he concluded. "Your average person doesn't have the kind of single-minded, relentless determination it takes to spend three hundred days a year on the road playing dive bars and half-empty clubs in pursuit of some elusive, vaguely defined dream of stardom."

*

While the boys shacked up together for the duration, Christine and Stevie were accommodated separately, first at a plush local hotel and later in a pair of neighboring harborside condos. Each was accompanied by a tiny dog that would be carted to the studio each day to be fussed over. Christine's pooch was Dusty, while Stevie had her poodle, called Ginny. Though he appreciated Stevie for both her visual appeal and her sweet nature, Caillat found Christine, then thirty-three, the most "intriguing" member of the group. "She had a very sharp tongue," he noted. "One time I was walking through the studio, whistling something to myself. 'I *hate* your mindless whistling, Ken,' she said. 'I hate when people do that!'

"Christine drank like one of the guys," he revealed, "and she swore like one too. The only woman I ever met who could do it better was Grace Slick [formerly of Jefferson Airplane and Jefferson Starship]. Christine smoked up a storm, but she played killer keys and sang great hooks. Christine [is] quite possibly the queen of English blues."

*

Rumours was released on 4 February 1977 in the U.S., and a week later in the UK. It sold ten million copies that first month. Its singles—Lindsey's "Go Your Own Way," Stevie's "Dreams," and Christine's "Don't Stop" and "You Make Loving Fun"—all went Top 10 in the U.S., though only "Dreams" scored them a No. 1. Voted Album of the Year at the 1978 Grammy Awards, it went Diamond around the world. By February 2023, it had sold more than 40 million copies. In the UK, the Official Charts Company places it at thirteenth in the list of best-selling albums of the 1970s.

Every track on the album is as familiar to those of a certain age as the gems on *Sgt. Pepper's Lonely Hearts Club Band* remain to the original Fab Four generation. The songs are worth revisiting one by one for the stories behind them, for how they reflected the writer, and how they impacted on the group as a whole.

"Second Hand News" is the upbeat if bitter little opener, prompted by a brief affair that Lindsey, its writer, had with a New England chick. The theme is rebound sex, and the arrow is aimed at Stevie. The message is that they are through and no way will he miss her, he has too many other girls to do. Lindsey and Stevie's tight harmonies here are haunting. They sound so together, but could not have been more apart. The quick-fire, wordless syllables of the chorus could be said to give the impression that there are simply no further words. Lindsey cracks this song like a whip, setting us up for anguish to come.

It is followed by "Dreams," a melodic number of shuddering sadness, carried by Stevie, Christine and Lindsey's harmonies, punctuated by spiteful wails from Buckingham's guitar and throbbed along by the Mick'n'John rhythm section. There is such dignity in Stevie's lyrics, which spilled out of her in one go, and in her brave, melancholic delivery, that it is almost too gut-wrenching to listen to. Spotify says otherwise: more than 1.1 billion streams to date, and counting. It has become an anthem of both rejection and survival. It seems to imply that he who had it all but gave it away will be the ultimate loser. "Even though 'Go Your Own Way' was a little angry, it was also honest," commented Stevie in the 2013 *Rumours* reissue sleeve notes. "So then I wrote 'Dreams,' and because I'm the chiffony chick who believes in fairies and angels, and Lindsey is a hardcore guy, it comes out differently. Lindsey is saying, go ahead and date other men and go live your crappy life, and [I'm] singing about the rain washing you clean. We're coming at it from opposite angles, but we were really saying the same exact thing."

The plaintive "Never Going Back Again," another Lindsey number, was, he said, written toward the conclusion of the album's recording; when he and Stevie had the benefit of hindsight, and when he was ready to leave her behind, go forward and devote himself to someone new. The finger-picking track is a blatant dig at Stevie. He has to force her to see that he is doing well without her in order to feel OK about not having her anymore.

"Don't Stop" is classic, upbeat Christine with a little help from her friend Lindsey. Delivering welcome respite, it's his voice that opens the song and hers that carries it into the second verse. Some listeners find the two indistinguishable. There is rock-out guitar, a note of hope in Stevie's harmonies, and an optimistic pay-off: "O-o-hh, don't you look back."

"Go Your Own Way," the album's lead single, is Lindsey's hit-back at Stevie for "Dreams." McVie, J. and Fleetwood excel, as though thrashing the two warring ex-lovers apart. A nutcase drum pattern, killer guitar solo and throat-shredding lead vocal from Lindsey ram it home: that even though he no longer wants her, he hates her, he resents her, he despises her, he is in absolute agony. Lindsey just can't let his ex-girlfriend go.

As for "Songbird," the side one closer and the all-time favorite of millions of Mac fans, has there ever been a piano ballad more sublime? How are we supposed to listen to it now that she's gone? She had no idea where it came from, she said. For Chris, this was a spiritual visitation. "That was a strange little baby, that one," she mused. "I woke up on the middle of the night and the song just came into my head. I got out of bed, played it on the little piano I have in my room, and sang it with no tape recorder. I sang it from beginning to end: everything. I can't tell you quite how I felt; it was as if I'd been visited. It was a very spiritual thing. I was frightened to play it again in case I'd forgotten it. I called a producer first thing the next day and said, 'I've got to put this song down right now.' I played it nervously, but I remembered it. Everyone just sat there and stared at me. I think they were all smoking opium or something in the control room. I've never had that happen to me since. Just the one visitation. It's weird."

Ken Caillat recalled the day they recorded it. Sensing that the song was in need of a different vibe from what they could achieve in the studio, he booked the Zellerbach Auditorium on the campus of the University of California, Berkeley, for 3 March 1976. Her Steinway grand piano was positioned on the stage, and he had arranged eight tube microphones around the auditorium to capture the "lovely nuances" of the piano. Christine's singing and playing would be recorded by the Record Plant's mobile studio truck, from which cable after cable were snaked into the hall. There was also, beautiful touch, a bouquet of roses resting on the piano, which were lit from above by colored spotlights. "I really wanted to set the mood!" said Ken. Before Chris entered the hall, he had the house lights dimmed so that her eye would be drawn directly to the flowers glowing in the spotlight. It worked. She almost broke down in front of them.

Tears of frustration fell almost as fast. Anticipating issues with tempo, Ken requested that Christine play along to a click track in her headphones, just as Mick Fleetwood did. Ever the professional she was willing to give it a go, but was soon tearing the 'phones from her skull. "Ken," she cried, "I can't play my lovely song with this bloody fucking clicking blasting my ears!" He understood. Various solutions were suggested, including Lindsey playing along to the song on his acoustic guitar, across the hall, so that the sound wouldn't be picked up. There was also the issue that she couldn't be allowed to sing while she was actually playing the piano, because her voice would "leak." In all, it made for an extremely long session. Still at it beyond midnight, they did achieve two clean, separate recordings of voice and instrument so that Caillat could blend them together. He got what he wanted in the end, he said, "this perfect recording for the world." More than what's here, the sentiment of the song is impossible to describe. A great excuse to listen to it.

*

There is only one song on *Rumours* that is credited to all five members. Given that Mick and John didn't write, this made it highly unusual. "The Chain" originated as a song of Chris's entitled "Keep Me There." It features superlative performances from every musician, is a patchwork stitched from bits and pieces of discarded songs, and boasts an energy and dynamism unlike any other track on the record. Widely used on film soundtracks, it has become indelibly linked with Formula 1 as the theme of the motor sport's television coverage. Its famous bridge is one of music's most iconic, coming as it does at a lull in proceedings, rumbling steadily into earshot before detonating into a cataclysm of instrumental and vocal sounds. "Chains… keep us together," chant the singers, bleeding to fade. The metaphor is crystal. Fleetwood Mac are bound together against the odds. Breaking the chain would spell the end for the band.

Follow that? So they do, with Christine's "You Make Loving Fun." This is an aural, choral flirtation with her new lover, Curry Grant, and the meaning is obvious. She's getting lighthearted, no-strings passion from this gorgeous guy, and it's as much as she wants. To avoid recrimination and blood-letting, she told her outgoing spouse that she had penned it about her dog. Sweet, wonderful you.

Chris and Curry cohabited for about a year in her home above Sunset Strip, West Hollywood. "I haven't been without a man in my life for…God, it must be twelve years," she confessed to Cameron Crowe the following year. "I can't imagine what it's like not to have an old man…but I have no intention of getting married. I don't think I'm in love…I don't really know what the hell love is."

But she was proud, she insisted, to have been McVie's wife. She continued to wear the ring he had given her, just on a different finger. "Maybe we don't feel the same about each other anymore," she said, "but I wouldn't like to wipe that off-board. John can't handle Curry too well, even though he's much more at ease with other women around me than I am with men in front of him. He's making an effort. But if I was the kind of girl who wandered in with a new boyfriend every week, enjoying my newfound freedom, I don't know how he could handle that."

Had she felt inclined to throw caution to the wind and put herself about a bit? "It would be a new experience! Sure, you know." She mimed making a telephone call. "Kenny Loggins, call me up! I'd love to have a load of dates. I haven't done that since I was at college. But it's really out of the question. I mean, I hardly meet anybody. I'm so involved in the band…" But: "Seven more years until I'm forty. Then I'll start all over again!" She was already thinking about a life beyond Fleetwood Mac, though that would take longer than she anticipated.

Back to the album. Up pops Stevie again, with the exuberant, cathartic "I Don't Want to Know." She spars with Lindsey and she makes her point. He responds with defiant licks and a perfect vocal to match hers. She was spitting blood because her masterpiece, "Silver Springs," the royalties from which she had promised to her mother, had been left off the track listing of *Rumours* because it "didn't fit." This number's inclusion is her compensation. Stevie would have the last laugh eventually, as "Silver Springs" would make its bonus-track way onto future reissues of the album.

If there's a weak link on *Rumours*, fans have tended to single out "Oh, Daddy." Widely assumed to be about her lover Curry Grant, Chris has indicated that she wrote it about Mick and his wife Jenny. They had somehow managed to rescue their marriage... Or had they?

Six foot six tall, Mick's nickname within the group was "Big Daddy." It may not be the album's most popular number, but it's a decent track carried by Christine's organ playing. The production values are superlative. "'Oh, Daddy' is a lesson in less is more," Mick told Ken Caillat. "It's one of my favorite songs that Christine has ever recorded. I think it's a fantastic song."

Bringing us to "Gold Dust Woman," which plays the album out. Stevie's cryptic closer is dark and dangerous. Its subject matter is the seamier side of LA, as well as her own spiraling cocaine addiction. Dependency, helplessness and a threatened loss of control loom like a storm as Stevie warbles a stark warning: "Rock on, gold dust woman/ Take your silver spoon, dig your grave." On the day of recording, she stood at the microphone shrouded in a black veil, in the manner of a woman delivering her own eulogy. Those who witnessed it later described their discomfort, and recalled Stevie as having seemed possessed. Her quivering voice, the frontier twang of metal on steel strings, a chill up the vertebral column at the eruption of a drum beat that gives warning of awakening the dead: it felt sinister. The most haunting sound of all was achieved by Mick smashing glass plates with a hammer in a mic'd up side room. Stevie's cold-sweat howls as the song plays out more than "shatter the illusions of love."

Rumour has it, just like every song she has ever written, Stevie is singing about herself. But the piece is also inspired by "lost girls in the streets and groupie-type women who would stand around and give Christine and me dirty looks. But as soon as one of the guys came in the room, they were overcome with smiles."[3]

CHAPTER 11
HONKY CHÂTEAU

The band hit the road again in breath-taking style during February 1977. Gone were the tired station wagons, the grim food, cheap liquor, iffy drugs and flea-bitten budget hotels. From then on, everywhere they stayed, every mode of transport that conveyed them, every item and commodity they used and consumed would be deluxe. "Our rider was extensive, detailed and exhaustive," recalled Mick Fleetwood. "We had fourteen black limos at our beck and call, for a time Stevie wanted her room to be pink with a white piano (we'd often have to hire a crane to lift the piano in through the window), and the list went on. We were pleasantly out of control."[1]

Now international superstars, their wildly anticipated Rumours Tour paced them through fourteen dates around America over the first month. Seven more saw them through England and into Scotland, commencing at the Birmingham Odeon on 2 April: a poignant homecoming for Chris, who dragged along her proud "Pop," her stepmother and other family members to witness her success. In London, they sold out three nights at the fabled Rainbow Theatre, Finsbury Park.[2] That temple to entertainment is riddled with rock'n'roll ghosts. This was where "Britain's Elvis"

Tommy Steele had got picked up; where the great jazz band leader and composer Duke Ellington had swung them in the aisles; where the Beatles had fabbed a Christmas season into January 1964; where Jimi Hendrix had first incinerated a Fender Stratocaster in a stunt dreamed up by Keith Altham, then a writer on the *NME*, and wound up in hospital; where the Osmonds gave their first UK performance, and where David Bowie, Yes, Eric Clapton, James Brown, Stevie Wonder, Marc Bolan and T. Rex, Bob Marley and the Wailers and seemingly endless more performed unforgettable shows. It was also where bassist turned A&R man David Ambrose experienced an unsettling reunion with his erstwhile bandmate Mick Fleetwood.

"1977 was their year," Ambrose told me. "They had been transformed by *Rumours* into global superstars. This excruciating, compelling, addictive multi-platinum soap opera was Music to Get Divorced By if ever there was. *Rumours* was the landmark, the moment of truth. Every track was a knife to the heart. Nothing for this band would ever be the same again. When they unpacked in London on their triumphant world tour, I trolled sheepishly along to the Rainbow and caught up with Mick backstage. So did Peter Green, though we managed to miss each other. How did that happen? What a reunion it would have been. I remember Mick's eyes glistening with mischief as he stood staring at me in his florist's shop that doubled as a dressing room. '*Dave!*' he said expansively, throwing his leg-length arms as wide as the Thames. 'All this could have been *yours!*' 'You know me, Mick,' I smiled, 'the one who got away.'"

He would be lying if he said he didn't care, Ambrose admits. "Fleetwood Mac were the biggest group in the world at that point. The quintessential rock superstars. They were buying mansions the way the rest of us buy books. I pictured them bathing in champagne, wafting about on clouds of coke, having mind-blowing sex with whoever took their fancy in Learjets and on the back seats of limousines. Their tangled love lives made A-list movie stars look like losers. They were more, *much* more than mere rock stars. They were gods and goddesses, living the dream."

This was all so far removed from the quaint little plans Mick and Dave had once sat around making as teenagers, projecting themselves into a rock'n'roll stratosphere they doubted could really exist, that Ambrose burst out laughing. "I nearly choked, I couldn't help myself," he recalls.

"Did I regret walking away from Fleetwood Mac? Not especially. I knew myself too well by then. The stark truth was that I would never have survived what they had become. I would have gone for it, hell for leather, no holds barred. I would have drunk too much, drugged too much, fucked too much, died too much. I would have been the ultimate rock'n'roll suicide."

Because, as David Ambrose well knew, it looks easy from the outside. As an insider, he knew too well that it was anything but. "In their shoes, I would have gasped my last on my way to the nearest body bag." He rolls his eyes as if to say, what can you do? "Some are born to live their life in the limelight. To put up with the spleen-splitting drag of touring and performing, having to create to order from scratch in the studio when you've been sick to the stomach all night, being deprived of any semblance of private life, getting mobbed wherever you go, needing security just to go for a piss. Of that sinking feeling that everyone wants a piece of you, never knowing for certain whether you've got a friend or whether they love you for the money and the glory, and would no longer want to know you when your luck changed. Because it *always* changes, however long it takes. The crest of the wave must always come in to land."

David reminded himself, that night at the Rainbow, that *he* was the lucky one. "I may be a has-been—a never-was, more like. I may be living from wage packet to wage packet on an income that would never cover the outgoings. But I had my beautiful wife and child, my friends were genuine, and I knew where I belonged. There were tears in my eyes as I hugged Mick goodbye. I wondered, as I walked the long way home, whether I'd ever see him again."

*

The band of the moment marched triumphantly into Europe, where they performed to great acclaim in Paris, Amsterdam, Munich and Frankfurt. They returned, briefly, to Amsterdam, then soldiered on to Düsseldorf. Two Swedish dates, in Stockholm and Lund, saw off April. Five days later, they were opening at Folsom Field, Boulder, Colorado, at the hem of the Rocky Mountains, and preparing to advance across the USA and Canada for the next five and a bit months. Highlights? Get this: *two* performances at New York's Madison Square Garden—make it there, you'll make it anywhere; two more at the Chicago Stadium, and three at the Forum in Inglewood, LA. They wrapped up the U.S. leg on 4 October, and a month later were stepping out on stage at the Western Springs Stadium, Auckland, New Zealand…by which time, Mick and "Steamy Knicks" (as Stevie was dubbed by fork-tongued members of Her Britannic Majesty's press corps, well aware that she was putting it about) were involved in a passionate affair behind Jenny Fleetwood's back. Couldn't they see it coming.

"It was bound to happen, I suppose," admitted Mick, "because the two of us are cut from the same cloth, but we're more brother and sister—soulmates, not romantic partners—which is why it didn't last. We are so much the same that we fell into each other's arms, albeit at the worst possible time." He fell in love with her, declared Fleetwood, acknowledging that he really shouldn't have acted on feelings that "everybody" had for Stevie. "It was chaotic, it was on the road and it was a crazy love affair that went on longer than any of us really remember—probably several years by the end of it."[3]

The worst of it is the thought of poor, unsuspecting Jenny going about her day, her marriage apparently happily reestablished, her children thriving, her mood optimistic. She had not an inkling that her husband was playing away. Mick and Stevie met "in secret," explained Fleetwood casually, because "I was with Jenny and Stevie had a boyfriend"…who happened to be Don Henley, founder, drummer and co-lead vocalist of the Eagles. Stevie would later write and record her underrated masterpiece "Sara." Henley stated, during a 1991 interview with *GQ*, that the song was about the child they had conceived together, but which Stevie quickly aborted. "Sara" would have been their daughter's name.[4]

Stevie corroborated the claim during one of several interviews we did together, this one in June 1994 in Los Angeles. She told me for a piece published in the *Daily Express* that Mick Fleetwood had "made her" have *four* abortions—she conceived by four different partners[5]—because he couldn't stand the thought of a billowy, pregnant frontwoman, her sequinned chiffon get-up straining at the seams. The suggestion was that pregnancy contradicted the image of the band. "I bitterly regret that," she whispered to me in her tiny, candlelit library, her "favorite room" in her mock-Tudor Encino home. She remarked, indicating that she still inhabited a fantasy Hansel and Gretel realm, that echoes of all the songs from her new album, *Street Angel* featuring Bob Dylan, were "hanging in the air like silk shrouds." You had to wonder sometimes what planet she was on.

"How I wish now that I'd had one or two of those babies [how about all of them?]," rued the then forty-five-year-old. "You have no idea how much that hurts, but you do what you have to do at the time. For me to have stopped in the middle of Fleetwood Mac to have a baby would have set the town on fire. I do wonder what it would be like to have several children now."

She had spoken previously to me, I reminded her, about adopting a child on her own. "I did, didn't I," she smiled sadly.

"Thing is, I never really worked on it that hard. I was so busy. I felt if it was going to happen, it would happen. If I'd got the baby, I would have made the time, but all the stuff you have to do to get one, it's not that simple. I didn't have the time…having a child means cutting off a whole bunch of other people in your life and stopping a lot of things that you like to do. It's just not fair to take on that responsibility if you are not going to live up to it." So she felt that having those abortions, I couldn't help blurting, were somehow *more* responsible? "Please don't judge me," she replied, "and I will not judge you."

While she was poking about in her sadness, she said she couldn't help wondering whether she was destined never to find true love or real happiness. After all, she insisted, most people don't. Many continue the search after marriage. Take Mick Fleetwood. "I am coming to terms with that," she said. "In case this is it. But I haven't given up hope. There's time. Age is only numbers." That interview was published thirty years ago.

*

Off went the circus again, trekking to Queensland's Gold Coast. It rumbled on down to Sydney, Melbourne and Brisbane, circled back to Sydney, then voyaged on to Perth and Adelaide. Deep breaths, back on the plane, where to next, what day is it? If it was the first of December, they must be in Japan. They opened at the Nagoya Civic Assembly Hall, played the Osaka Festival Hall two days later, and on 5 December appeared at Tokyo's hallowed Nippon Budokan. They didn't know whether they were coming or going when they landed in Honolulu, where they started to wind down the tour on 7 December and finished in Lahaina two nights later.

"It's a far cry from the turmoil Fleetwood Mac knew only a year ago," reported journalist Dave Marsh in January 1978.[6] "For now, the rumors of disintegration have virtually disappeared.

John McVie is at his home in Hawaii. Christine McVie and Stevie Nicks are off somewhere, presumably packing for the group's tour of the Orient and South Pacific, but definitely incommunicado. Lindsey Buckingham is rushing to finish the production of American rocker Walter Egan's second album. (Buckingham and Nicks had co-produced Egan's first.) And Mick Fleetwood, the band's co-founder, drummer and manager, is sitting in a wheelchair (that he did not need, but was having fun zapping himself around in), auditioning keyboard players for a group led by Bob Welch, the guitarist who left Fleetwood Mac more than three years ago, creating an opening for Buckingham and Nicks, the very situation that made Fleetwood Mac millionaires."

*

The Five reconvened after a brief Christmas and New Year break, to work up songs for their next album and to plan yet another tour. Managing themselves, as they now did under the banners Seedy Management and their tour company Penguin Promotions, there was less room for error and they could do more or less as they pleased—within the confines of the expectations of Warners, their record company.

Come July 1978 they were off again, on their Penguin Summer Safari, performing another seventeen dates across the States including the Cotton Bowl Dallas and Philadelphia's John F. Kennedy Stadium—where a stressed, burned-out Lindsey collapsed in his hotel-room shower and was found unconscious by Carol Ann Harris, his girlfriend. Conveyed rapidly to hospital, he would later be diagnosed with epilepsy and would require medication for life. He was soon back up and running, and stayed with them all the way to the conclusion of the tour on 30 August at the Tiger Stadium in Louisiana's Baton Rouge.

*

As for Christine, she had gone and fallen in love. Completely and all-consumingly, with a toxic partner so utterly wrong for her that she simply couldn't let him go.

Most of the rumors then doing the rounds about Beach Boy Dennis Wilson were true. The notorious, hell-raising womanizer boasted of having yielded his virginity at the age of twelve. His nickname was "The Wood"—"always hard and ready for action" —and he had been expelled from school at sixteen for hurling a screwdriver at another pupil. Christine met him around the time, post-Rumours world tour, when the band were preparing to begin work on *Tusk*, its follow-up. While she could have run into Wilson anywhere on the LA circuit, at any venue or among any group of friends or musicbiz folk, they actually came face to face in the recording studio.

A year and a half her junior, Dennis had experienced monumental fame and adulation as a teenager during the early 1960s, pre-Beatles, with his brothers Brian and Carl, cousin Mike Love and close friend Al Jardine. Influenced by R&B and fifties rock'n'rollers such as Chuck Berry, the Beach Boys perfected the art of vocal harmony, crafted multi-layering elements inspired by producer Phil Spector and others into a distinctive "new" sound, extolled the virtues of California's beach-centric lifestyle of surfing, hot-rodding and girls and became America's biggest band. In fact, Dennis was the group's only surfer. He was also, as the black sheep of the clan, self-doubting and insecure. While everybody loved him, he didn't, couldn't, love himself. Although hits such as "Surfin' USA," "California Girls," "Fun Fun Fun" and "I Get Around" have endured and are played to this day, the band were knocked sideways by the impact of the boys from Merseyside. Brian Wilson, their innovator, quit the road (the rest continued to tour), peered inwards, ingested more drugs, got God and raised his game—hitting back, in 1966, with a deliriously brilliant album, *Pet Sounds*, featuring singles "Sloop

John B" and "Wouldn't It Be Nice/God Only Knows." This is the album that, according to Paul McCartney, was a major influence on *Sgt. Pepper's Lonely Hearts Club Band*. Brian followed it with the game-changing 45, "Good Vibrations," widely revered as the greatest pop single ever made. These releases are valued today as among music's most groundbreaking and influential creations ever. Dennis, incidentally, sang but did not play drums on *Pet Sounds*. That honor went to session man Hal Blaine.[7]

But the Beach Boys, eclipsed by the Beatles, had peaked and were on the wane. Not until the mid-seventies would they enjoy a resurgence, eventually becoming a parody of their former selves, as virtually all rock artists and groups do, if they stick around for long enough. By the time Christine and Dennis met, she was a superstar and he was hot again.

Dennis, born 4 December 1944 in Hawthorne, Los Angeles County, was thirty-five. Chris was seventeen months older. Both had been married: she just the once, to John; Dennis four times —to Carole Freedman, with whom he had a daughter and an adopted son; to Barbara Charren, who gave him two sons; and twice to the actress and model Karen Lamm, former spouse of Chicago's keyboard player Robert Lamm, in 1976 and again in 1978. The latter was the year that almost relieved him of his freedom. After a Beach Boys gig in Arizona, Dennis was caught in a hotel room with a sixteen-year-old girl, plying her with booze and drugs. Protesting that he had been set up, the father of four was arrested. That incident cost him $100,000 in legal fees.[8]

Four marriages, as many kids and a creepy encounter with a minor were not enough to put Christine off this self-destructive thrill-seeker. But it does seem surprising that gossip about his most scandalous association didn't send Christine running for the Santa Monica Mountains. We're talking his association with serial killer Charles Manson.

One day in April 1968, when Wilson was cruising in his car around Malibu, he happened upon a pair of female hitchhikers. He had no way of knowing that Ella Jo Bailey and Patricia Krenwinkel, known as "Katie," were members of Manson's sinister circle. He would soon find out. He bumped into the same girls a couple of days later, probably not by chance. He told them about the Beach Boys' experiences of the Maharishi Mahesh Yogi, the spiritual guru who had lured the Beatles to Rishikesh, India, earlier that year. Dennis had been the first Beach Boy to discover the Maharishi, and introduced the others to the guru and his ways. But he soon grew bored with the rituals of transcendental meditation. Mike Love was the one who pledged himself to the regime, and joined the Beatles in Rishikesh.

That May, the Beach Boys undertook a U.S. concert tour with the grinning guru. They played, and the Maharishi lectured. The girls informed Wilson that they too had a guru: a man they referred to as "Charlie," who was enjoying his new-found freedom after a dozen years inside. Had Ella and "Katie" been dispatched on a mission to find their leader a rich, influential and unsuspecting associate? Dennis took the girls back to his place to have sex with them. Soon afterward, he returned from a recording session to find Manson, an insignificant-looking figure only 5 ft 6 in tall, waiting for him on the drive of his rented home, an old Sunset Boulevard hunting lodge that had once belonged to the vaudeville and silent movie star Will Rogers. Even more sinister was the presence of a dozen naked, mostly female members of Manson's "Family" in and around the Wilson residence, partying wildly, helping themselves to his booze and food, having sex with each other and on standby to service his every need. Wilson appeared to be thrilled by all this, welcoming the invasion as in the spirit of the modern age. He and Manson became close friends. Dennis called his interloper "the Wizard." In an interview with *Record Mirror* entitled "I live with 17 girls," he divulged: "When I met [Charlie] I found he had great musical ideas. We're writing together now. He's dumb, in some ways, but I accept his approach and have [learned] from him." Manson and Wilson started recording together. When the Beach Boys recorded their 1969 album track "All I Want to Do," released as the B-side of the single "I Can Hear Music," it featured fleeting, ecstatic "sex sounds" said to have been provided by Dennis engaged in carnal activity with a female member of Manson's Family.

The counterculture had its dark side. The gullible Beach Boy was sucked in. Dennis found himself providing financial support for a murderous clan to the tune of around half of everything he owned. Of the Family's hundred or so members, some twenty-five, the majority of them attractive young women from respectable homes, lived in Dennis's house at his expense for most of 1968. Dennis coughed up for their doctors' appointments and gonorrhea treatment. When they "borrowed" and totaled his car, he was the one who paid for its replacement. He also picked up the tab for Manson's recording studio time, and introduced him to influential musicbiz friends.

He wised up eventually. At around the time when he was fretting because he had failed to secure Manson a record deal and was afraid of what he might do—especially since Manson had once or twice pulled a knife on him—the lease on his home expired. Dennis moved out, thus drawing to a conclusion his notorious "Sunset Boulevard" period. The landlord evicted the Family, who were forced to go and leech off some other poor, unsuspecting victim. Hooked on LSD and other hallucinogens, Manson's followers were brainwashed into believing that their guru was a manifestation of Jesus Christ. They fell for his prophecies and did his bidding, committing crimes and even murder in his name. The regime came to a devastating end in August 1969, with the Tate–LaBianca murders: of actress Sharon Tate, the eight-and-a-half-months pregnant wife of film director Roman Polanski, and four other victims. The killers were convicted of nine counts of first-degree murder. They were suspected of having slaughtered at least a dozen others, but these lacked evidence. Manson claimed to be both God and the devil, and blamed the Beatles' "Helter Skelter" for his corruption. In 1971, he and the four murderers were sentenced to death. When capital punishment was abolished by the State of California the following year, their sentences were commuted to life imprisonment. Though they did eventually become eligible for parole, their applications were always denied.

*

By 1978, Dennis had the look of a Californian beach bum. He scuffed along boardwalks in jeans, shredded T-shirts or a light, unbuttoned cotton shirt that exposed his tanned, muscular chest, and a battered jean jacket on cooler days. His floppy, sun-bleached locks were lank with brine, and his handsome, bearded face was cracked by the sun. More often than not, he went barefoot. He wore a brooding expression, smiling infrequently. When he did, his ocean-blue eyes dazzled. There was invariably a cigarette between his teeth or pinched between his fingers, and he was rarely more than a yard from a bottle of booze. Of the Beach Boys, Dennis—Denny to friends and family—was the one who got the girls. A sixties sex symbol, he had them all, from Ronald Reagan's daughter Patti to the Strip's lowliest hookers. His prowess was fabled. But it wasn't just sex. There was something else about Dennis that reeled them in; knowing that he would betray them, resigned to the realization that they would forgive him, and all too aware that he would do it again and again.

Barbara Charren, his second wife, put his restlessness and his wandering eye down to an emptiness that he could not fill, no matter how hard he tried. Poorly educated and inarticulate but sensitive and demonstrative, he had grown up with a pronounced stutter that he fought hard to disguise. It was more than likely provoked by the extreme beatings, burnings and hurlings against walls that he and his two brothers, Brian and Carl, had sustained as children. His relationship with his abusive father Murry never truly recovered. Which made life difficult during the years when Murry Wilson was managing the band. Dennis would refer to him as "the asshole," and in 1964, colluded in his sacking.

As a Beach Boy, Dennis was the least musical but the most intensely popular, particularly with women. This gave rise to jealousy and resentment among the others. Intoxicated by his own youth and beauty, his downfall occurred with the dawning that such qualities are ephemeral, and that he would have to grow up, come to terms with their fading, and find a way of moving on. He was ill-equipped to do so. The child in Dennis remained his driving force throughout his life. There is no doubt, said Steve Kalinich—his lifelong friend and collaborator who wrote songs with all three Wilson brothers, including Dennis's "Little Bird" and "Be Still"—that Dennis's boyishness and apparent helplessness were the main reasons women fell for him. "They all wanted to mother him," he told me, "and no one wanted to mother him more than Chrissie. She honestly believed she could be the one to fix him, and bring him to a point where they could enjoy an equal partnership. I never had the heart to tell her that it would never work, that he would never be totally there for her. He wasn't even totally there for himself. You see, there were very dark depths to Dennis. He had a tortured soul. He was plagued by obsessions that got him into deep, deep trouble. But the incredible music he made remains testament to the good in him. He was a man of extremes. To me, he was magnificent. It wasn't hard to see how a woman as amazing as Chrissie could fall for him."

Dennis was in love when Christine met him…with his third boat, a 50-foot (or was it 62-foot? Both are quoted) yacht he had named *Harmony*. He purchased her in 1974, spent the next two years restoring her, and moved on board in 1976. Although she was moored at Marina del Rey, he would regularly sail her out to sea. "Whenever the mood us upon me, I can capture the feeling," he said. "My greatest passion, after my music, is the sea. I love its mystery, its high adventure, and its peacefulness. It's the only place I can truly relax."[9]

By 1976, riding a tsunami of nostalgia, the Beach Boys had become huge again. CBS came for Dennis as a solo artist, to record on their Caribou label, for which he achieved a six-figure advance. At last, Dennis came into his own musically. His superlative album, *Pacific Ocean Blue*, was released on 16 September 1977. It was so good, the industry buzzed with excitement that a new solo superstar had been born. For a while, it seemed that Dennis Wilson would never need his fellow Beach Boys again. He had apparently broken the spell, found his way and unleashed his dormant genius.

"Everything that I am or will ever be is the music," he stated. "If you want to know me, just listen." His subject matter is an unlikely blend of love, ecology and the dangers of fame and where it can lead you. The title track is the most arresting: "We live on the edge of a body of water/warmed by the blood of cold-hearted slaughter." I mean. The album was received most favorably by the critics. *Rolling Stone* went so far as to compare Dennis with John Lennon—don't laugh, listen—rating the offering a minor masterpiece. Which helped to shift 250,000 copies. Not millions, but not bad. He was booked on a short live tour to take it higher, but his label couldn't or declined to meet his extravagant touring demands. He cancelled. He also quit the Beach Boys—*not again*—with a declaration in *Rolling Stone* that he had walked away. The relative success of his solo album had got the green-eyed monster rearing. Tensions within the band had become unbearable. He could take it no more.

He left them wallowing in their jealousy and went his own way. By that time, Dennis was imbibing enough to sink ships. He was using heroin. He divorced his latest wife Karen in 1977, went on tour with the band he had just left, as good as overdosed on heroin and almost wrecked the entire excursion. He was at his lowest ebb when a golden-haired heroine unwittingly rode to the rescue: the songbird of the world's most popular band.

*

Did Chris and Dennis meet by chance, or did Dennis contrive to make it happen? He had a reputation for pitching up wherever rich, successful, limelight folk were hanging, and for turning new contacts to his advantage. He befriended Mick Fleetwood and John McVie, and made a point of fixing himself in their frame. They would of course have been flattered by intense attention from the rock'n'roll legend.

He turned up one day toward the end of 1978 at LA's Village Recorders studios (known commonly as "the Village") on Butler Avenue, a place teeming with ghosts. The former Masonic temple had been used by the Maharishi to teach transcendental meditation. Dennis had lately been working on tracks for what was intended to be his follow-up solo album, but had lost his way. When he heard that Fleetwood Mac were going to be in that day, he dropped everything. He made his way there, and he met Christine. She experienced a *coup de foudre* that she described as "absolute love at first sight. It had never happened to me before, and I just knew it was real." Just like every other female who had fallen for Dennis before her, she was smitten and she didn't care who knew it. "Dennis has thrown me into the deep end," she declared, "literally and figuratively."

"Dennis walked into the studio one night and whisked me off my feet," she would later tell *Rolling Stone*. "It was probably the experience of a lifetime. Dennis was such a character. Half of him was like a little boy, and the other half was insane. A really split personality." Hadn't Mick Fleetwood said the same thing?

The curious thing was, she was not his type. Dennis's taste in women was predictable: young, giraffe-legged, pneumatic, blonde, babe-like. Christine, clearly flaxen-haired and with striking good looks, was not what you could call glamorous or overtly sexy. It was Stevie Nicks who ticked those boxes. Chris was a sweetheart. Easy to hang with. She exuded a quintessentially English charm that some Americans find intensely alluring. She was a brilliant musician, singer and songwriter, and she had banked a fortune. The rub? Remember, he was drinking more heavily than ever, and was also using heroin. Both weakened his resistance to cocaine. She introduced him to her own drug of choice—not the other way around—which in turn made him drink more. Dennis was soon addicted, he said. To Christine, or to the endless supply of Peruvian? Because Fleetwood Mac were making the *Tusk* album in what has been described as "a cocaine blizzard." In a beat, the pair had become rock's ultimate power couple, the industry's greatest love affair. He unlucky in life, she unlucky in love; doomed to be together; destroyed, ultimately, by rock'n'roll and all that it demands. Except that it was nowhere near as poetic as that.

Dennis moved into the guest suite of Chris's majestic property in the Crest Streets north of Sunset Boulevard. The exclusive enclave between Coldwater Canyon and Trousdale Estates is almost encircled by Beverly Hills, which gives it a rarefied air. Christine's estate had belonged previously to Anthony Newley and his wife Joan Collins, and to Elton John. The exterior featured landscaped gardens, which included a rose garden, pools and breathtaking views of both mountains and the sea, while the interior of the main house boasted lavish entertaining spaces, walk-in fireplaces, wood floors and the ultimate in showcase kitchens. Chris had installed a small English-style pub there, as well as a sculpture studio. Dennis's room was furnished in a cutesy style that you might say clashed with his personality. Tiffany lamps, a dinky piano and silk and lace upholstery suggested a boudoir bespoken for someone like Stevie Nicks, not a rugged, seafaring male.

Regardless, Dennis kicked off his sneakers, made himself at home, and mused a little more about his important second solo album, working title *Bamboo*. He was also considering a collection of duets with Christine, and what that might do for his bank balance. The couple crept off regularly for romantic trysts aboard the *Harmony*. Bathed in moonlight and lulled by the waves, they would lounge below deck planning their beautiful future. "I'm in love with Dennis and I will marry him the minute he's free to ask me," Christine announced. LA folk would see them out and about together, and would wonder. What on earth did the Mary-Poppins-neat English singer see in that disheveled old tramp? It must, they concluded, be an attraction of opposites. Call it love.

Dennis was so immersed in Fleetwood Mac during the recording of their *Rumours* follow-up, *Tusk*, that his face is all over that album's inside sleeve. In John McVie he had landed himself a new drinking partner. He also forged a firm friendship with Lindsey Buckingham, who would pay tribute to Dennis after his death with "D. W. Suite" on his 1984 solo album *Go Insane*.

All too soon, the Mac were on the decadent, hedonistic march again. They embarked on their mammoth *Tusk* world tour on 26 October 1979, performing thirty-two dates across America, ten in Japan in February 1980, seventeen around Australia and New Zealand straddling February into March, and pitching up in Honolulu at the end. Christine naturally wanted her man by her side, every step. Dennis couldn't handle such saturation. He was non-committal, pitching up without warning when he felt like it. He would devote himself to his beloved while he was with her, but would soon be gone again: back to his boozing, snorting, puffing partners in crime, and to his leggy, pneumatic blonde babes.

Hawaii, however, marked a turning point. Dennis had a big surprise in store for Chris. In front of the whole band and their entire entourage one night, he got down on one knee and proposed. Christine had not seen it coming but was over the moon. Though when, given their current punishing schedules, were they going to have time to get married? What about children? Surely he would want a proper family with her. "My lifestyle is fairly settled in terms of accommodating myself to children," she said at the time. But she couldn't quite make up her mind. She did, however, she revealed to me later, look into the possibility of tubal ligation reversal, having had her fallopian tubes tied at around the time of her divorce from John. Hey, the girl just wanted to have fun. Plus, she had witnessed first-hand what Stevie had gone through during a string of enforced abortions.

Christine discussed her childlessness with Kirsty Young on BBC Radio 4's *Desert Island Discs* in 2017, insisting that she had never wanted to be a mother. "And she says it with a slight bitterness, a throwaway certainty," says clinical psychotherapist Richard Hughes. "Her tone of voice is slightly different. A little defiant. Defensive. It comes across as the lady doth protest too much. You feel yourself jolted by it. Getting her tubes tied was quite a controversial procedure to undergo at that time. It does suggest that she was keeping her options open."

*

Back to the U.S. and Canada the tour thundered, the curtain finally dropping at the Joe Louis Arena, Detroit, on 24 May. Eight days later, on Sunday, 1 June, they were opening at the Reitstadion Munich. Through Germany, Switzerland, Belgium, the Netherlands and France they progressed, at last landing in England on 15 June. They gave two performances at Bingley Hall in Stafford near Birmingham. Dennis was with Christine to meet the family.

"Fleetwood Mac singing star Christine McVie was back home in Smethwick today—to introduce Beach Boys star Dennis Wilson to his future mum-in-law," trumpeted the *Birmingham Evening Mail* on Monday, 16 June 1980. "Christine and Dennis are to be married on her 38th birthday next month [12 July], when both groups are back in the USA. And, as Fleetwood Mac are playing the first of two nights at Stafford's Bingley Hall, tonight, while the Beach Boys top the bill at the Knebworth Festival on Saturday, it was an ideal chance to meet up with Christine's father, Mr. Cyril Perfect, for the first time in two years. The former music teacher said at his home in Lightwoods Hill, Smethwick, this morning: "I met Dennis for the first time in Los Angeles two years ago, when I went on a visit. But he has never met Christine's stepmother —my wife Lesley—before."

Chris was on tenterhooks. Dennis had the foulest mouth, and she knew he wouldn't hold back in the company of her father and stepmother. Nor did he. Her father didn't seem offended. "It was all 'Motherfuckin' this' and 'Motherfuckin' that.' Pop just got used to it in the end, and turned a blind eye," she said.

The Beach Boys' major tour that would reestablish them as a big live concert act would continue for several years. It was mounted to promote *Keepin' the Summer Alive*, an album in which Dennis had barely been involved. Commencing mid-January 1980 with the Cambodian Relief Benefit concert alongside Santana, Jefferson Starship, the Grateful Dead and Joan Baez, they gigged across the homeland for the next four months, played Toronto on 27 April, then zapped to Norway, Sweden and Denmark. In London they gave two historic concerts at Wembley Arena, supported by Chris Rea, crossed to Paris, then the Netherlands, and on 21 June, supported by Santana, Elkie Brooks, the Blues Band, Mike Oldfield and Lindisfarne, headlined at Knebworth Park, Hertfordshire. It marked the last time that all six members—Brian, Carl and Dennis Wilson, Mike Love, Al Jardine and Bruce Johnston—would perform together live on a British stage. It would turn out to be Dennis's last visit the UK. Back at their hotel, Al, Bruce, Dennis and Christine gathered round the piano in the lounge to sing Beach Boys songs—"Barbara Ann," "Lady Lynda" and "Please Let Me Wonder"—while Christine treated them and a number of taken-aback hotel guests to some good old English pub ditties.

The Mac tour blasted on. Six consecutive triumphant nights at Wembley Arena preceded their return to the U.S., where they started in Lakeland, Florida, on 5 August and finished on 1 September at the Hollywood Bowl. The Beach Boys' tour would continue relentlessly across America. They played the parting shot of that exhausting outing at the Forum in Inglewood, LA, on New Year's Eve. For the past six months, Dennis and Christine had spent barely any time together. They'd had a few snatched days together here and there at the most. Dennis was taking full advantage of the benefits of the road. Worse, the Beach Boys' tour resumed on 16 January 1981 in San Diego, and kept them away until the end of February. They took April off but then resumed again, conquering America state by state all the way to December. They spent Christmas and New Year performing, controversially, at Sun City, Bophuthatswana, South Africa, supported by sixties pop singer Lulu. Their appearance there was a violation of the boycott against apartheid, in place since June 1959. From January to December 1982, they were back on the march across America.

Dennis's drugged, drunken enthusiasm for marrying Christine waned in direct proportion to his infatuation with a sixteen-year-old blonde by the name of Shawn Marie Love, whom he had met toward the end of 1981. Chris cut her losses and broke off their engagement. She didn't want to listen to the gossip: that Shawn Marie and a girlfriend had gone to Dennis's house in Venice Beach next to Marina del Rey, and had both wound up in bed with him. Shawn Marie informed Dennis that she was the illegitimate daughter of Mike Love, his cousin, bandmate and lifelong nemesis, and that her mother was Love's former secretary Shannon Harris.[10] He warned her to shut up about it. A close friend later revealed that Dennis had only started a relationship with her to antagonize Love, and to get back at him for all the years of grief. He and Mike had hated each other since the earliest Beach Boys days. This must have felt like retribution.

Dennis and Shawn Marie had a son together in 1982. When they married on 28 July 1983, she was nineteen to Dennis's thirty-nine. The twenty-year age gap defeated them. He carried on drugging and boozing, and often hit on his wife's young friends right in front of her. The couple fought viciously. On one occasion, an infuriated Shawn Marie crashed their car into the front door of their house. On another, Dennis smashed all the windows of the same vehicle with a baseball bat.

The last live show featuring all five original Beach Boys (and Bruce) took place on 3 August 1983 in Costa Mesa, California. A drunken, disorderly Dennis hugged his brother Brian, who in turn was moved to pay tribute to him. "This my brother Dennis, you remember Dennis!" he exclaimed to the audience. The kid croaked a response. "You know, folks," said Dennis, "if you knew what it was like to be singing, and playing…thank you so very much. You are so beautiful to me." Six weeks later, on 26 September, Brian did not appear during their Pomona gig. He was not there to witness Dennis stumbling and rasping through his final rendition of "You Are So Beautiful," the song he co-wrote (though he goes uncredited) with Billy Preston and Bruce Fisher, and made famous by Joe Cocker. The proof was in the pudding: Dennis had often performed it with the Beach Boys, usually barely accompanied, as an encore. It clearly meant the world to him. It did that night.

But the man was a wreck. He was bringing the band into disrepute. His brothers and bandmates issued an ultimatum: get sober or get off the tour. There would be nothing further from them. No more road, no more money, no more sibling support. Wilson blood was like any other family's: only so thick. The warning was enough to shock him into rehab. Did the treatment fail, or did he fail at the treatment? Either way, shortly after he left the facility, he was back on the drugs and booze. He and Shawn Marie separated, and she initiated divorce proceedings.

He was virtually homeless when, on Wednesday, 28 December 1983, a few weeks after his thirty-ninth birthday, he got into a fight and emerged badly battered. He retreated to Marina del Rey to lick his wounds, though not to the *Harmony*, which had been sold at a knock-down price at auction to cover debts. He'd wept hard over that one. He spent the afternoon hanging out on his friend Bill Oster's boat, the *Emerald*, where he demolished a bottle of vodka. There were plenty of people around. So how come no one stopped him when he went into the freezing water to retrieve belongings thrown over the side of the *Harmony* in about the same spot, years earlier? Why did no one talk him out of it when he insisted that he could find them, diving back and back into the bitter depths until he apparently crashed his head against the underside of the boat, and failed to resurface?

"Dennis drowned before he ever hit the water," said Steve Kalinich. "I think if he'd had more outlets and encouragement with his creative expression, he might have taken a less destructive path…he was like a person without a country."

"My secretary called me up and said, 'Dennis has drowned,' Christine recalled to Mark Ellen for *The Word* in July 2004. "And I said, 'Ooh, God, is he all right?' Shock, I suppose."

Back in Smethwick the following day, it was Christine's stepmother Lesley who was forced to face journalists on the doorstep. "I'm shocked by this news," she told the chap from the *Birmingham Mail*. "Dennis was a very, very nice man. He was always considerate, and very homely. He enjoyed home cooking, and always wanted to give little presents. Christine will be very upset over this."

*

"Why do people stay with people?" Christine reflected in 2004. "Cos they love them, I guess. And I loved him for a while. He was very charismatic, great looking, very charming, very cute—if you can call a guy with a beard and a voice like Satan 'cute.' He used to draw people into his life, strangers off planes and off the streets, and they'd become his best friends."

Although his brothers Brian and Carl insisted that Dennis be laid to rest in the Wilson family plot within Inglewood Cemetery, his widow objected. In accordance with his wishes, and with special Presidential dispensation from Ronald Reagan, he was cremated and committed to the Pacific by the U.S. Coast Guard on 4 January 1984. During his memorial service, a recording of his raspy, haunting voice singing "Farewell My Friend" from *Pacific Ocean Blue* was played.

Shawn Marie remained in Los Angeles with their son. Also a drug user, she developed stomach cancer and liver problems. When informed that she needed a transplant, she appealed to Beach Boy Mike Love, her alleged father, for help. He declined. She died in September 2003, at the age of thirty-nine…the same age as Dennis at his own demise.

*

Christine and Dennis did record together: for his song "Love Surrounds Me," written for his intended second solo album *Bamboo*. When he handed this song over to augment the Beach Boys' 1979 album *LA* (*Light Album*), it became clear that there was never going to be a second solo album. Christine contributes cooing, angelic vocals over Dennis's gnarly snarls. The Beauty-and-Beast dynamic imparts a mere lick of the kind of brilliance they might have achieved together, had Dennis been able to drag himself back from the brink and make a go of their relationship. As it was, he fell into a hell of his own making, losing his fiancée, friends and the colleagues who had helped him to record those very special songs for *Bamboo*.[11]

As for Chris, she wrote endlessly about him, as though trying to eradicate him from her soul. "Only Over You," composed during their ailing affair and released on Fleetwood Mac's 1982 album *Mirage*, is her self-crushing admission that love couldn't save them. This was her "last declaration of love" to Dennis, affirmed Jon Stebbins, musician, friend and collaborator. The record sleeve even extends him a credit: "With thanks to Dennis Wilson for inspiration." But no song of hers sums him up better than "Ask Anybody" on her 1984 solo album *Christine McVie*, the lyrics for which she had written while they were still together. "He's a devil and an angel...he's a saint and he's a sinner... I guess he's still a child..."

*

In years to come, Christine would naturally blame herself for the failure of their relationship. She also blamed the Mac. She blamed anyone but Dennis, defending him to the last. "As a band, we personified dysfunction," she explained to me. "We seemed to destroy all who came into our sphere or who had more than passing contact with us. A lot of people believed that Dennis was the one who destroyed me, with his boozing and womanizing. I wonder now whether it wasn't I who destroyed him.

"*All* lovers are a crutch," she went on. "Someone to lean on, someone via whom to deflect and defer the pain. *The Pain*, capital letters, is what makes you become a musician in the first place. But you can't get rid of the bloody fucking pain. You lug it along with you, everywhere you go. You have no choice. The lovers are your mind's, your subconscious's way of kidding yourself—that all you need is a fine, stable relationship to be able to deal with everything that life throws at you. Only there is no such thing as a stable relationship in rock'n'roll. What happened to us was every bit as much my fault as it was his."

Dennis took the piss, squandered her fortune and shagged around. She loved him. She couldn't help herself. She believed that they were pre-destined, but she had to sack him to save her sanity. She never stopped loving him, she said. His drowning affected her deeply. There were times when she refused to accept her former fiancé's death; when her grief contrived to convince her that he would somehow return. "Madness, I know," she said. "Complete and utter madness. It's what heartbreak does. They call it 'magical thinking' in America, what we call 'wishful thinking.' I was in denial."

She returned to her senses only when it was brought to her attention that Dennis and Stevie had slept together. "Unable to resist the obvious temptation, Dennis made love to Stevie Nicks just when he was supposed to be settling down with Christine," said friend Jon Stebbins. "He also returned to [former wife] Karen on a fairly regular basis. He just couldn't seem to give her up. To make matters even more insane, he began cutting a passionate swathe through the entire Fleetwood Mac extended family, leaving no female untouched."[12]

"Dennis had sex with every woman that was in any way remotely involved with Fleetwood Mac," revealed another close friend. "Singing members, wives, girlfriends, secretaries—every one. It was unbelievable."

"Dennis would even call Karen when he was with Chris," admitted Stephen Kalinich. "He's with the girl he's going to marry and he's calling his ex-wife. That's intense, isn't it? And Chrissie put up with that. She loved him that much. But he always knew when he'd done wrong. He was always regretful. After he slept with Stevie Nicks, he said to me, 'You know, I did something terrible. I went with her best friend.' We discussed it. He *did* stuff like that. I couldn't fathom it. I couldn't have done it. But *he* did. With Chrissie, he abused the relationship, but he really didn't want to. His addictions got him in trouble. His body would let him down. The flesh was weak. Very weak.

"Chrissie was a really good person. Although there was still a certain dependence on Karen, who also mothered him, Chrissie was the love of his life. She was more of a normal person. Because of that, she liked his grand gestures. Like her birthday party, for example. Dennis performed the song he helped to write, 'You Are So Beautiful,' at that, in front of a full orchestra. And he dug her a heart-shaped garden, which she loved. They were two special artists who bonded through music and loved writing together. When you really think about that, it could never have worked."

He didn't know "Chrissie" that well, Kalinich admits. "He wasn't with her that long. Could he have changed for her, had he really wanted to? You're asking me. I'll be honest, I don't think so. Though Dennis definitely had that other side. The good side. How else could he have a totally straight, un-druggy, non-drinking best friend like me? He was one of the most talented people I ever worked with. He had a lot of love, and he was in reverence of creativity. He'd have a classical piano player come to the studio in Santa Monica to play us some Beethoven and get us in the mood to write and record. He did things like that. Then we'd go for a walk, down on the beach, to the dam, to the ocean. We'd go eating. And wherever we went, there were girls. They never left him alone. And that was it. He just couldn't resist them."

But he loved him, Kalinich says. "Like a brother. He was one of the great persons in my life. He influenced music. He was a non-commercial musician. He wrote from his feelings and from his gut. Very few musicians do that. Very few *can* do that. The point is, for me, that Dennis and Chrissie had a love without all the complications. What they had was real. It was pure. She was his first real adult love. He was a mix. He wanted to be happy and to be joyous, but he never felt he was appreciated enough. Which is probably why he went to other women. I wish he hadn't. The love Chrissie brought him was pure, wholesome and real. I know they saw something in each other that the other one didn't have. That's what makes a real attraction of the soul. It's such a shame it didn't last. But I'm so thrilled he was able to have what he had with her. She was special."

"In the end," Christine said, "you are falling in love with figments of your imagination. And so are they, by the way. You want him to be or become this or that. When he fails to live up to the *that* that you have projected onto him without his permission, it becomes his fault, not yours. Even though he was never that in the first place. There is comfort in this, I suppose."

CHAPTER 12

RETREAT

The musical departure that was 1979's *Tusk* album precipitated sweeping change, both for the group and for the individual members. Realizing that they hadn't a hope of topping or even matching the brilliance and impact of *Rumours*, as the record company expected and required, they agreed to go along with Lindsey's newfound passion for punk and new wave. That then dominant hybrid genre was the one toward which he was leaning for inspiration, if only because it represented dramatic departure. A volte-face seemed the only viable option. Buckingham's plan was wildly ambitious; some felt too much so. He proposed that they create a double album featuring twenty diverse tracks that would showcase their collective and solo talents, by which both fans and newcomers to their music would be refreshed. Though by no means the first to try unorthodox methods of making and recording sound, they went out on a limb to prove their versatility. Why use a conventional drumkit when a tissue box would do? Why stand upright to sing into a microphone when you could lie on the floor and do it without holding on?

This is the album that opens with Christine's "Over and Over," so sorrowful and pain-soaked that it is almost unbearable to hear. Her heavy-hearted lead beats over layers of ghostly backing vocals that swell and recede like tides. "Did you ever need me…and would you know how?" she asks rhetorically, all too aware of the answer. It's obvious who this is about. It prompts suspicion that the end of her love affair with Dennis was a self-fulfilling prophecy. The Golem effect was at work.[1] She comes in again at track three with "Think About Me," a number more upbeat and sparky, with divine harmonies that fail to disguise her inherent sadness. Her next shot is the third track on side three: the shimmering, choral "Brown Eyes." It is followed by her "Never Make Me Cry." Such melancholy. She drains the blues from her voice to the point that it sounds almost folky. She then imparts a defiant message of hope: "Go and do what you want, I know that you have a need…You'll never make me cry." And yes, that's Peter Green on guitar on the fade. On side four she steps up with both the opener, "Honey Hi"—bongo beat, nice riff, acoustic guitar, piano, beautiful BVs—and the closer, "Never Forget." Stevie Nicks triumphs with "Sara," "Storms" and "Sisters of the Moon."

The rest does feel like manic Lindsey making a point and going off on one. It was reported that he snipped off all his hair with a pair of nail scissors during the recording. What was that about? Did anyone think to question it? Because cutting off one's hair, we recognize today, is symbolic: of tradition or crisis, of letting go of the past, of getting something or someone damaging "out of one's hair," of drawing a line under things, and of lightening one's load as one advances into a fresh future. But whenever there is a letting go, there is grief for what has gone.

"Recording *Tusk* was quite absurd," Christine commented in hindsight. "The studio contract rider for refreshments was like a telephone directory. Exotic food delivered to the studio, crates of champagne. And it had to be the best, with no thought of what it cost. Stupid. Really stupid. Somebody once said that with the money we spent on champagne on one night, they could have made an entire album. And it's probably true."[2]

Warners were devastated. Watching their Christmas bonuses disappearing down the pan, they denounced the album as a "failure" soon after its October release. This despite the fact that it would shift around five million. John McVie later remarked that the album sounded like the work of three solo artists; implying that there was no discernible coherence, no recognizable Mac sound. But look, it did earn them No. 1 status in the UK. Six single releases including the title track, with an ambitious marching-band backing, secured them two American Top 10s. "Failure," in this instance, simply meant "not as successful as one of the most successful albums in rock history."

The *Fleetwood Mac Tusk Tour* documentary, accessible online, offers compelling insight into the dynamics of the band during this crossroads in their evolution. To witness Mick sucking piped oxygen through a mask before dragging himself back onstage to resume berserk behavior behind the kit on "Sisters of the Moon"; Lindsey lost in music, in his manic riffs; Stevie delirious under the gauze shawl draped over her head and the crowd going wilder and wilder, yelling themselves inside out as she yields her soul to the groan. And Chris? She's out of sight, behind the keyboard off to one side, pounding and cooing her vital part, yet never limelight-hogging.

"In the context of the whole, *Rumours* took longer to make than *Tusk*," declared the heavily criticized but defiant Lindsey. "One of the reasons why [it] cost so much is that we happened to be at a studio that was charging a fuck of a lot of money. During the making of *Tusk*, we were in the studio for about ten months and we got twenty songs out of it. *Rumours* took the same amount of time. It didn't cost so much because we were in a cheaper studio. There's no denying what it cost, but I think it's been taken out of context."

*

The Tusk tour concluded in September 1980 and was, reflected Mick, "the very height of our touring at the top of excess. We had a team of karate experts as our security guards, a full-time Japanese masseuse, our catering was supplied by top-notch California chefs, and it usually went uneaten. We had our own airliner and we booked the best hotel suites around the world. We had rooms in those hotels repainted in advance of our arrival, specifically for Stevie and Christine. We had a huge cocaine budget and the usual fleet of limos waiting for us at every port of call." It was, he admitted, "fabulously expensive, wonderful, and sometimes depraved. But in the end, it wasn't a good time because more than ever, our musical family was as distant from each other offstage as our music was intimate onstage. To be frank, that tour nearly killed the band."[3]

When it ached to a close at the Hollywood Bowl on 1 September 1980, the band were wrung out both physically and emotionally. They could hardly stand to be in the same room together. "I used to go onstage and drink a bottle of Dom Perignon, and drink one offstage afterward," Christine confessed. "It's not the kind of party I'd like to go to now. There was a lot of booze being drunk, and there was blood floating around in the alcohol, which doesn't make for a stable environment."[4]

Excess all areas took its toll. Both Stevie and Lindsey withdrew from Mick and pledged their careers and earnings potential to new managers. Profits from the album and tour had been predicted to soar off the scale, but actual earnings fell shockingly short. The band's accounts were audited. Mick, who until that juncture had acted as both manager and leader, was accused of having allowed excessive spending to drain the coffers. He protested that he had been the one attempting to rein in some of the more outrageous spending, but that he'd been shouted down by the others. Where had the money gone? Up their noses, mostly, though nobody was inclined to admit that. Mick was "released" as manager, and he could not have been more hurt. Their tour manager John Courage was also "let go." After which, The Five retreated into their own self-obsessed worlds.

"By the end of it," said Mick, "Stevie's voice was a ruin and Lindsey had pulled his back out so badly that he needed a spinal tap. During the last shows of that tour, Lindsey told our audiences that it would be a long time before we toured again. Boy, was he right."[5] It was indeed the end of an era. They needed an extended rest period. They needed time away from each other. Some of them craved, and demanded, the freedom to get on with other projects and to develop planned solo pursuits. Mick was fearful that this would prove the beginning of the end. For some, it was exactly that.

*

Personal problems were only ever a page away. When a lifestyle is that extreme, that complicated, the relationships within it are bound to suffer. Mick, while still hopelessly entangled with Stevie, started seeing someone else behind her back. This was doorstep defecation on a ludicrous scale. Not only was the other woman married—to Jim Recor, manager of pop duo Kenny Loggins and Jim Messina—but his newly beloved, Sara Recor, was one of Stevie's closest friends. She was also the second inspiration for the ethereal lead track on the *Tusk* album (the "great dark wing" in the lyrics is a blatant reference to Fleetwood and his black Ferrari). Mick knew he was dicing with death. "I didn't care," he said. He treated Stevie ruthlessly, not even telling her to her face that he was dumping her for Sara, but penning her a "Dear Jane" letter instead. He excused himself on the grounds that Stevie had carried on seeing other men all the time they were together, so what difference could it make? Unbeknown to him, he claimed,

Stevie turned out to have been far more emotionally invested in their relationship than he had thought. "It surprised me that she was so hurt," he said. "But then again, she wasn't expecting me to take up with her best friend…She couldn't help but ask, 'Really? It had to be her?' Stevie wasn't wrong, but love is not a rational thing…Stevie wouldn't talk to me, and my other bandmates expressed their disapproval. Sara's friends completely cut her off, so she was stuck with my circle, one of whom was the best friend she had betrayed. I'm not sure there could be a worse start to a relationship."[6]

Mick escaped to Africa, recorded a solo LP, *The Visitor*, in Ghana, and later reunited, yet again, with his ex-ex-wife Jenny.

*

Stevie's solo debut, *Bella Donna*, appeared in July 1981, one month after Mick's. The album was an instant sensation, selling ten million copies, falling just short of the Top 10 in the UK and scoring a No. 1 in America. This was Nicks' broadside to the band; her acknowledgment that they needed her more than she needed them. Lindsey brought up the rear that October with *Law and Order*, for which he wrote and composed every track and on which he played almost every instrument, with the exception of Chris's keys and Mick's drums. Which made it, but for the absence of John and Stevie, an almost-Fleetwood Mac album. Standing in for Stevie was Carol Ann Harris, who by then had been Lindsey's romantic partner for more than three years. Where was Christine's follow-up solo effort? Give it time.

*

The Mac sabbatical was shorter than some had anticipated. Before those three solo LPs were even released, they returned to the studio to begin work on the next Mac album. For the first time in eight years, however, they did not record in the U.S.

This time they returned to Europe, specifically to France, where they had booked themselves into the Château d'Hérouville.

It was an early Elton John album that lent the eighteenth-century château its sobriquet "Honky Château." Tucked away in the charming village of Auvers-sur-Oise—where Vincent van Gogh committed suicide in 1890 at the age of thirty-seven, and where he and his brother Theodorus are buried—the small castle was formerly the residence of the Polish composer and pianist Frederic Chopin, as well as the location of his secret affair with Amantine Dupin, otherwise known as George Sand, the novelist. A long, sweeping drive led up to the château from the main road in those days—parts of the estate have since been sold off—where it was guarded by huge cast-iron gates. Its formidable walls stood six feet thick in places, making the château an impenetrable fortress; not to mention the ideal kind of venue in which to house paranoid, security-conscious superstars during the precarious process of recording an album. French composer Michel Magne had converted the château into a residential recording studio during the mid-1960s. A decade later, its Strawberry Studios had gained a reputation as a premier facility with what was at that time state-of-the-art sixteen-track recording equipment. Both instruments and vocals could be recorded in the studio or outside in the open air. Untroubled by flight paths and by the hustle and bustle of neighboring settlements (there are plenty of those today), the quiet of its rambling grounds was punctuated only by wild birds and animals, the wind and the rain.

Picture The Five with the run of this thirty-bedroomed, dual-winged residence, its solid walls heaving with ghosts, and with enough history, tragedy and intrigue to fire their collective imagination. They could relax in its pool, hang in its outhouses, challenge their courage in its haunted chamber, partake of the château's own wine (with its frankly pornographic bottle label) and feast on home-cooked fare served by comely jeunes filles at refectory tables laid out in front of roaring log fires. Every temptation was up for grabs. Little wonder that the cream of the rock fraternity including Pink Floyd, Cat Stevens, the Bee Gees, Iggy Pop, Elton John and Marc Bolan had all availed themselves hitherto. Bolan had recommended the château to David Bowie, who recorded *Pin Ups* there in 1973, and *Low* four years later.[7]

Stevie and Lindsey detested the place, according to Ken Caillat, their co-producer on *Mirage*. "We got there and Lindsey and Stevie became the biggest babies I've ever seen," he divulged during an interview with *Tape Op* magazine. "It was like, "I don't have any TV. I don't have anything to do. I'm bored." He recalled that they were ready to quit and return home before they had even unpacked. "So we stayed as long as we could, and we finally flew home," he said. "Stevie was so miserable."

"I just sat there and watched as these paned doors, two stories high, flew open," Stevie would later recount to *Rolling Stone*. "The glass doors opened on a wrought-iron balcony overlooking a wishing well. It was quite dramatic, and the desk went over like *whamp*! I went into the kitchen, and the people who worked there said it was the ghost of the château."

Christine, not given to complaining, tended to look on the brighter side. She was well aware that their use of this facility was all part of a mammoth cost-cutting exercise, which would be to her own advantage in the end. The unlimited luxury and indulgence to which the band had grown accustomed were off the menu for now, while management and money men steered them back to black. So she was determined to make the most of it. She made no mention of paranormal activity. While conceding that the past-its-best establishment was "rather beaten-up," she pointed out that they had at least been able to use the wine cellars as echo chambers. It probably helped that she was within driving distance of her original home, less than 400 miles southeast.

France, the French, their cuisine and culture were more familiar to Chris, Mick and John than to the Americans.

At least relations in the studio were harmonious. A civilized attitude prevailed. Lindsey curbed his tendencies to bully the others and throw his weight around, twelve tracks were laid down quite swiftly, and the band and their reduced entourage returned to Los Angeles after only two months to spend the next seven mixing, overdubbing and perfecting at Larrabee Sound Studios and at the Record Plant.

The problem with *Mirage* is by no means the songwriting, which is as sharp, observant and honest as ever. It suffers simply from the fact that it was recorded during the eighties. During that era, there prevailed a tendency to interfere, over-egg, mix metaphors and put too much slap on; to add embellishment where it could do without. But more was more during the decade that gave us Michael Jackson's *Thriller*, Prince's *Purple Rain*, Kate Bush's *Hounds of Love* and Bruce Springsteen's *The River*, Cyndi Lauper's *She's So Unusual*, the Police's *Synchronicity*, Bowie's *Let's Dance* and George Michael's *Faith*. We had U2, we had Culture Club, we had New Order and Joy Division. We also had the Specials and Def Leppard. Such was the diversity and energy of young artists and bands during those years that those pushing forty and upward had no choice but to raise their game to stay part of the bigger picture. We hadn't yet hit the era of dinosaur rock, celebrating the continuation or resurgence of artists *because* they had broken the age barrier. When Tina Turner launched her solo career in 1984 at the age of forty-four, she also established the concept of the rock comeback. Her timing, miniskirts and stupendous legs had MTV-era scrawled all over them. Follow the rabbit down the hole and here we are, worshipping at the altar of seventy-eight-year-old "goddess of pop" Cher, eighty-two-year-old Paul McCartney and octogenarian Stones Mick'n'Keef. Rock stars who once hoped they'd die before they got old would now do anything, if not for love, then to live forever.

Did Fleetwood Mac try too hard with *Mirage*? Undeniably. The result is an underwhelming collection redeemed by Stevie's iconic "Gypsy," its subject the poet's beloved childhood friend Robin Snyder, who had taught Stevie "how to sing, how to use my voice." The track was, commented Mick, "A perfect portrait of the people we were at the dawn of the 1980s." And, "It has a wise, world-weary melancholy that's as poignant as anything off *Rumours*."[8]

There were also Lindsey's "Book of Love" and 1950s parody "Oh Diane," a UK Top 10 hit, and Christine's odes to Dennis, "Only Over You" and "Hold Me," the latter, like "Gypsy," a huge hit single. Delivered to market in June 1982, the album topped the U.S. chart and climbed in Britain to a respectable fifth place. Results that would have thrilled the average outfit disappointed the Mac. "We had decided that we'd go in and do something that was expected from us, and it failed," Christine told the press. "From our points of view, I think I can say that we were all disappointed. It reeks of insincerity to me." Why, exactly? Because it lacked passion. "*Rumours* had been born out of strife and tensions," she explained. "During the recording of *Mirage*, the band members were boringly friendly again. We were no longer the musical soap opera we used to be!" Rarely a truer word.

The promotional tour for this album was brief, just two months long. In marked contrast to their previous global rampages, this one remained stateside and encompassed only thirty-three dates. Mick Fleetwood contradicts the facts in his autobiography, remembering "eighteen dates" and a tour that lasted "about a month." The primary reason for the condensed outing was that Stevie's solo career had taken over. Other contractual commitments over an extended period prevented her from committing to a longer run. This was hugely frustrating for Mick, who felt that they could have kept *Mirage* top of the shop for longer than five weeks had it been afforded the tour it deserved. Commencing on 1 September in Greensboro, North Carolina, this trek sidestepped New York but did give LA's Inglewood Forum two nights. It terminated on Hallowe'en in Austin, Texas. Until *The Dance* excursion in 1997, fifteen years hence, this would be Lindsey's last tour with them. Stevie, too, stepped aside, informing the others that she no longer wished to tour as part of Fleetwood Mac. It was time for her to concentrate on her enormously successful solo career.

But her decision was not entirely work-related. Stevie had been dealt another huge emotional blow. Her childhood best friend Robin, who worked for Nicks' company Modern Records, had been diagnosed out of the blue with leukemia. Robin and her boyfriend Kim Anderson married in haste, and she gave birth to their son Matthew in October 1982. A couple of days later, Robin died. Grief-stricken Stevie and Kim, both wanting to do whatever was best for the child, turned around and married each other, with the intention of sharing responsibility for raising the baby boy. This well-meaning but deranged move proved catastrophic. Horrified friends and loved ones struggled to process it. Christine refused to buy them a wedding present, implying that they were making a mockery of marriage. In time, the couple awoke to the enormity of what they had done. Within eight months, they were divorced.

*

John McVie was now remarried, to second wife Julie Ann, and was living on the Hawaiian island of Maui. He led a low-key existence and minded his own business when not recording or touring. Until 23 December 1980, that is, when their home was raided by police after a cocaine delivery was traced to their address. When they searched the house, officers also uncovered a stash of unlawfully retained firearms. Thirty-five-year-old John and Julie

Ann, six years his junior, were arrested. John was charged with the felony possession of cocaine, as reported by the *New York Times* on 8 January 1981. The couple were released on bail. As a British subject, John could have been deported, and also prevented from re-entering the United States in perpetuity. Which may well have spelled the end for the band. Although the outcome was never fully explained, they somehow got away with it.

Mick moved back to Malibu and bought the big house he'd had his eye on. Now that the others were putting their solo projects first, his only option was to join in. He opened the doors of his new home to any and every musician of a mind to work with him, and the place soon became a doss house. The musical collaboration acquired the name "Mick Fleetwood's Zoo." They would tour their music on and off, on a low-key level, for the next several years. Mick stayed out on the road as much as possible for three reasons: he had crippling money problems, he was failing as a father, and his world-famous band—his focus, and the meaning of his life—was in hiatus, perhaps never to return. The road let him live in denial…until 1984, when he was once again forced to file for bankruptcy. He lost his home, cars and possessions. He also lost Sara. Had he been able to pull the band back together for a new album and tour, he could have lifted himself from the mire. Alas, the rest of the band were busy elsewhere.

*

Christine had faced her demons. She had also recorded a song, "Got a Hold on Me," that earned her an unexpected hit. Its placings— No. 10 on the Billboard Hot 100 and No. 1 on the Billboard Adult Contemporary and Rock Tracks charts—were just the boost that she needed to wheel herself back into the studio to begin work on a possible follow-up solo album, thirteen years after her 1970 debut. To boost her confidence during this brave undertaking, she decided, she needed the support of dependable old friends.

So she brought back "The Colonel," "The Gatekeeper," Fleetwood Mac's long-serving tour manager, MC, butler, psychotherapist and nanny, rolled into one.

So indispensable had John Courage been, many regarded him as the band's sixth member. Few in the outside world could comprehend why he had been dismissed. Widely believed to have been the inspiration for the road manager character Ian Faith played by actor Tony Hendra in Rob Reiner's 1984 rockumentary *This is Spinal Tap*, this stern, Belfast-born, steely-eyed descendant of the famous Courage Brewing Company ran a tour like a drill sergeant. He was known to the band and their entourage as "JC." His voice was recognizable to millions of Mac fans the world over during their *Rumours* and *Tusk* era, thanks to his nightly introduction, "Ladies and Gentlemen, would you please give a warm welcome to…Fleetwood Mac!" In this new role, he would not only caretake Christine's solo career but also help her make the album she refused to record in America. Removing herself from the fray, she had JC book her in at Mountain Studios in Montreux on Switzerland's Vaud Riviera, and reserve her the most superior lakeside suite he could secure at the best rock hangout in the world, the Montreux Palace hotel.

The well-heeled, retro town of Montreux nestles on the edge of Lac Leman in the shadow of the Chablais Alps. Anyone of a certain vintage who has worked in the music and press industries knows it well, thanks to its long jazz heritage and the world-famous music festivals staged there annually for decades. During the 1980s and '90s, I attended most of them. Local businessman Claude Nobs held his inaugural jazz festival at the Montreux Casino in 1967. It attracted legends: Ella Fitzgerald, Aretha Franklin, Miles Davis, Nina Simone. On 4 December 1971, the old casino burned to the ground after a fan fired a flare during a Frank Zappa and the Mothers of Invention gig. The members of Deep Purple, in town to record their album *Machine Head* at the casino, observed the incineration from a hotel window. Ritchie Blackmore was prompted to coin one of the most recognizable riffs in rock history, for "Smoke on the Water."

By 1975, the casino had been rebuilt. A state-of-the-art recording studio was installed. Dubbed "Mountain Studios," this facility was the first in the world to feature a pair of 24-track recorders that could be synchronized for 48-track recording. Mountain subsequently recorded every artist who performed at the Montreux Jazz Festival, from the Stones, David Bowie and Michael Jackson to Led Zeppelin, Sting and Phil Collins. In July 1979, Queen purchased the studios for their own personal use. They installed their own engineer, David Richards, and went on to record seven albums there. They would later sell the studios to Richards after Freddie Mercury's death.[9]

*

Before she left LA for Montreux, Christine spent three months preparing songs for the album. "I had wanted to do a solo record for a long time, but I was nervous about it," she said. "After all, I'd been so used to being a fifth of a band, and suddenly it had reached a point where this record was expected of me. The only things I was sure about were that I didn't want the responsibility of producing it myself, and I didn't want to write all the songs on my own."

Her primary collaborator was young Cleveland-born guitarist and songwriter Todd Sharp, whom she had known since 1978 when he joined former Mac member Bob Welch's band. Daryl Hall and John Oates hired him to play lead guitar for them in 1975, when Todd was only nineteen. He played and performed with them for the next three years. He would go on to work with a host of greats, including Rod Stewart, Mick Fleetwood—on *The Visitor* in Ghana—Bonnie Raitt, Al Stewart and many more, as well as to record solo albums and to market his own range of amps.

"We literally went into my music room at my house and played with ideas and riffs that we both had and wrote the music and words together," Chris said. "I enjoy writing that way now because when you can inject somebody else's personality as well as your own, the songs come out stronger."[10]

"I worked with another FM family artist—Danny Douma, and that is when I first really got to know Christine McVie," recalled Todd Sharp in 2022. "We spent a few nights together with Danny and his producer Nick Van Marth, at Village Recorders overdubbing on Danny's *Night Eyes* record. Fleetwood Mac was recording *Tusk* in the next room.

"Christine was, from my perspective, a very comfortable rock star," he said. "She was fun, easy to know and she would often ring [his wife] Angela and I to come over and have dinner and hang out. We became good friends. Even best friends for a while. I spent the next few years bouncing around LA trying to get a band going, writing songs, recording demos and doing any sessions I could get. One night, I played Chris a demo I had just recorded. She loved the song and volunteered to come to the studio and sing background vocals on it."

Before long, Chris approached Todd to ask him whether he fancied helping her pull a band together, and to write some songs with her for a new solo album she was planning. "In about 1983 she picked me up, dusted me off and said, 'Come on, we're going to write a batch of songs and put a band together and record an album in Europe with producer Russ Titelman.' And don't you know, I have nearly every record Russ Titelman and Lenny Waronker have produced in my collection."[11]

The next few months were spent writing at Chris's home. Having secured the services of bassist George Hawkins Jr., and Average White Band, George Benson and Jeffrey Osborne drummer Steve Ferrone, they decamped to Montreux to record. "Lindsey Buckingham popped in and added his brilliance to a few of the tracks," recalled Todd. "[Guitarist] Stephen Bruton joined us…for the follow-up tour, and [guitarist, singer and songwriter) Billy Burnette lent a hand as well. These people have been my lifelong friends. I introduced Chris to her [future] husband [musician and songwriter] Eddy Quintela, who I had become friends with at Montreux. She took me to England with her, where we worked with Steve Winwood, Eric Clapton and Ray Cooper, at the legendary Olympic Studios in London. James Taylor stopped in for an afternoon and we just hung out…"

"We were so well-prepared that the album only took three months to make," said Chris. "Montreux is a really beautiful place, and I loved it there. I treated being away from home as an adventure. I mean, if you're going to make a record, you might as well make it as much fun for yourself as possible." She found, she remarked ahead of the album's release, that collaborating with other songwriters took her own writing in new directions. "It also seems to lift me out of my own insecurity as a songwriter when there are a few more ideas floating around from someone else."

"It's a very up, rock'n'roll record," she concluded. "More gutsy than people would expect from me. The lyrics and songs are very happy and positive. They're not the love-lost, miserable-type songs that I'm accused of writing all the time. I'm proud of this record because I know I've done my very best on it."[12]

Christine McVie, released 27 January 1984, produced the Hot 100 Top 10 hit "Got a Hold on Me" and Top 40 "Love Will Show Us How." "We wrote both songs together," said a proud Todd Sharp.[13]

"The Smile I Live For" is the only track on that album written solely by Christine. Of her extensive work with Todd, their collaboration "The Challenge," named in honor of her former husband John's boat and featuring Eric Clapton on guitar, encapsulates her best at this stage in her career. A blues undercurrent overlaid with honed pop production techniques is a winning formula. Stevie Winwood's keys and vocals reassure that the blues are never very far away.

Nor were they in her personal life. Eddy Quintela, the Portuguese keyboard player, composer and songwriter who contributed to this album in Montreux, appeared to personify respite. He got under her skin, paradoxically, in a way that may not have occurred had she not still been pining for Dennis. The rebound relationship can prove difficult to resist because it represents the easy answer. It's there on a plate. The news of Dennis's drowning in December 1983 shocked Chris so deeply that she virtually reeled into Eddy's arms. She had turned forty the previous July. While its impact is largely diminished today, "the big four-oh" was still a blow for women like Christine who had come of age during the early to mid-1960s. It was perceived as the age of midriff bulge, elasticated waists, bubble perms and stout shoes. It delivered decline in libido and fertility, heralded menopause, and caused irreversible loss of youthful attractiveness. Ultimately, for a woman, it spelled invisibility. Acutely conscious of her motherless status but hopeful that she might still be in with a chance—*just*, if she got her skates on—she admitted that the last-ditch possibility influenced her decision to get involved with the dark-eyed, olive-skinned Iberian musician lurking in her rented studio. "We just kind of drifted into being together," she remarked to me later. She didn't want to elaborate, she said.

Come the day of their wedding, 18 October 1986, Chris was forty-three. The thought that she and Eddy might still start a family together had begun to recede. Conspicuous by their absence at the ceremony and reception were Christine's band-mates, whom Quintela, allegedly, neither liked nor trusted. He was keen for his bride to quit the band, and concentrate instead on writing and recording with him. He was adamant that she should refrain from going on the road with them again. Chris found flattering to begin with the urges of her new man to control her.

The novelty wore off. Her insistence on making her own decisions and doing as she pleased was the source of mounting conflict between the two.

Why did she marry Eduardo Quintela de Mendonça from Estoril? "I convinced myself that I loved him, because I was lonely," she admitted. "I hated going to bed by myself every night, and waking up alone every morning. By then, I had talked myself down from the idea that true love was really a thing. I'd decided that the secret was simply to look for someone you could rub along with and get on OK with most of the time. We were happy for a while, I think. He was by no means perfect, but I kept telling myself that neither was I. Beggars can't be choosers. I had to quit holding out for Mr. Right and settle for Mr. Good Enough. Because life is neither a fantasy nor a fairy tale. We kid ourselves, and I was frustrated by it. It was time I bloody grew up. What mattered to me at that stage in my life was having someone who would be there for me, who I could rely on, who would have my back. I also wanted someone to grow old with. The idea of facing all that by myself filled me with dread."

But her efforts served only to toss her out of the frying pan into the fire. "What I ended up with was another bloke I was going to have to try and fix," she continued. "Another guy who spent half the time hopping in and out of bed with other women [including her own personal assistant: another double betrayal] who had a penchant for spending my money. I knew within a short time that it was not going to go the distance, but I didn't want to admit to myself that I'd made another mistake. The only consolation was that it didn't hurt so much as the last time. What I went through with Dennis must have immunized me."

She couldn't say more. Because of lengthy "legal shenanigans." While he was said to have come from wealth, there was still a jugular to go for. Although she and Eddy collaborated on a number of songs together—including "Little Lies" and "Isn't it Midnight" on

Fleetwood Mac's 1987 *Tango in the Night* album, "Save Me" on their 1990 *Behind the Mask* album, and "Temporary One," which made its debut on the live 1997 album *The Dance*—the concepts were likely all hers, and her husband's input may have been inferior to hers. She appears to have shared songwriting credits to help boost his career and reputation. They would separate for good in 1998 when she left the band and Los Angeles and returned to England. She and Eddy had been married for twelve years.

Quintela left the States in 2000, and returned to Estoril. He sought solace in the local music scene, collaborating with a variety of Portuguese musicians. He had been working for some time on a rock opera based on the life of assassinated U.S. president John F. Kennedy when he died on 16 October 2020. So low-key and private had been his existence that not even the date of his birth nor the cause of his death were public knowledge. He is believed to have been about seventy-six at the time of his death. On her Facebook page, his then seventeen-year-old daughter Sara Mendonça mourned him, and thanked Mac fans for their condolences. At the age of almost sixty, Eddy had become a father following his return to his homeland. If word of the existence of a post-marital "step-daughter" ever reached Christine, she never referred to it in interviews. Another chapter in her complicated life was firmly closed.

CHAPTER 13

SENHORA

In 1985, Chris was invited to record a cover of the Elvis Presley hit "Can't Help Falling in Love" for the soundtrack of American comedy feature film *A Fine Mess*. Written and directed by Blake Edwards, it starred Ted Danson and would be released the following year. What a song! Why Christine? She would have been the first to ask. It had been covered by almost anyone you could think of before her. By Doris Day, Perry Como, Alma Cogan, the Stylistics, Shirley Bassey and Engelbert Humperdinck, to name some. That safe, enduring classic would be covered ad infinitum. Still, she wouldn't stare the nag in the gob. She asked Fleetwood Mac's touring producer Richard Dashut to produce her, and he suggested they should get Elvis enthusiast Lindsey to play guitar and sing BVs. Buckingham leapt. Richard then beckoned Mick and John on board, and presto: but for the absence of Stevie, a Mac reunion that would lead to other things.

The promo pictures are interesting. They feature a bronzed Chris in a *very* (for her) low-cut, tight black top that reveals tan lines left by a strappy bikini bra. The skinny black ribbon knotted at her throat may or may not be symbolic. Why is it there? It's not attached to anything. It's not holding together a collar, nor does

227

a charm or trinket dangle from it. Whatever, there is something endearing about the image. As though someone had said to her in passing, "You wanna sex yourself up a bit," and she had taken them at their word. The fragility of the forty-something is evident.

There were other, more personal obligations that year. In June, Christine dropped everything and dashed home to Smethwick. Having promised both her father and herself that she would spend his eightieth birthday with him, regardless of whatever else she was committed to at the time, she kept the promise and turned up to sing for him. Not only to sing, in fact, but to host a full musical tribute in his honor. The evening was by invitation only.

"When dad, Cyril Perfect, from Lightwoods Hill, Warley, walked into a city hotel room," reported Paul Cole, the *Birmingham Mail*'s pop writer (later that newspaper's Executive Editor) on Saturday, 22 June 1985, "he was stunned to find his very own concert party. Around 60 musicians and friends gathered at the Plough and Harrow in Edgbaston last night to spring the surprise show on Cyril—and left him speechless. During the party, a string quartet and band played, and Christine got up to duet with brother John in tribute to their veteran violinist dad." Cyril, the journalist explained, was one of the best-known musicians in the Midlands, and still gave recitals and made occasional appearances with the City of Birmingham Symphony Orchestra.

"I live in Los Angeles, but I wanted Dad's eightieth birthday to be really special," Chris said. "So I set about getting the show together. It took countless calls across the Atlantic. Dad is very special to me. He's a marvelous musician, and he's the youngest eighty-year-old man I have ever met."

"Next month," concluded Cole's report, "Christine will be back in the studios helping to record a new Fleetwood Mac album, and there could be a tour in the New Year."

Five years later, on 16 July 1990, the same newspaper reported Cyril's death. "One of the region's most respected classical musicians and former viola player for the City of Birmingham Symphony Orchestra died peacefully at home in Smethwick." Aware that he was ailing, Chris had flown in the previous week to be with him, pulling out of several dates on the band's Behind the Mask U.S. tour. Her father's funeral took place promptly, on Thursday, 19 July 1990, a week after his daughter's forty-seventh birthday. He was buried at Quinton Cemetery, Halesowen in Dudley, the West Midlands. Christine attended, but couldn't hang about. She was soon back on the plane to rejoin her bandmates, so that the tour could resume.

Something clicked, then, for Christine. Something changed. There was the usual sense of loss, as well as an overwhelming realization that important things were removing themselves from her life. Things that she could not get back, that she would never have again. She found herself reliving the loss of her mother twenty-two years earlier, in 1968. She had managed to sweep her grief under the carpet at the time of Beatrice's death, because she was young, in love, impatient, and there was new married life to be getting on with. She hadn't yet known better. Her father's passing rekindled that long-buried, unprocessed agony. Christine realized to her shame that she had never dealt with it.

"Losing Pop made me begin to look at my life differently," she said. "I could suddenly see that so much of it was pointless. Devoid of worth. A lot of it was going through the motions, and I was deferring actual living. For what? To satisfy the insatiable, ever-increasing demands of a record company? To keep the band going? To help keep the rest of them, the profligates, afloat? To make sure the fans carried on buying our records and seeing our shows, which in turn fed the record company? And there was that moment when I saw myself as a hamster in a wheel. I was rich beyond anything fifteen-year-old me could ever have imagined, 'just' from making music. But no amount of money, I knew, could buy me love or peace of mind. I woke up. I just didn't want to live that lifestyle anymore."

"Dad dies and she finally gets to mourn her mother," nods clinical psychotherapist Richard Hughes. "This is so common. When our final parent dies, we are at last able to mourn the loss of family, the loss of being parented, and also the deficits that are still deeply needed. Hers was clearly a very close and supportive family, but there were frustrations. She spoke about her father always living beyond his means, continuing to perform in concerts as if he felt he had to maintain that air of 'being someone,' his largesse in the bar afterward, his drinking, wearing his hair shoulder-length at a time when men of his standing didn't." Perhaps this also explained Cyril's ultimate act of self-reinvention: his remarriage to a much younger woman soon after his beloved's funeral. His second bride was a woman young enough to be his daughter, and similar in age to Christine. She arrived at his doorstep with a little girl. She would all too soon make him a father again, well into his sixties, when she delivered him another son.

And at that point, perceives Hughes, Christine begins to understand her mother. "Finally," he says, "she gets her. I was prompted to revisit her signature, 'Songbird.' Christine spoke to Kirsty Young during her *Desert Island Discs* interview about her psychic mother having a spirit guide called 'Silver Shadow.' I thought about the most common songbird, the sparrow, which has a silvery breast and beigy brown wings. It is, in a sense, a little shadow. And I am convinced that *that* is who Christine was writing about in the song: her own mum. About that deep, spiritual part of her mother to which she was deeply drawn, but of which she was also terrified."

Was Christine rewriting history during that interview, or was her mind and/or memory playing tricks? Because the "spiritual controller" of whom Beatrice spoke in her own press interviews was a "Red Indian" called "White Eagle." "I sit down and ask for White Eagle," Chris's mother said, "and I feel a cold band pressing across my forehead."

Christine would not be the first rock superstar to reconfigure her own story. I have encountered the phenomenon many times. Perhaps it's simply a case of them needing to adapt old tales to fit a new narrative that they feel suits their legacy better. Mick Fleetwood, after all, wrote two memoirs, the second of which often contradicts the first.

"Or could it be," asks Richard Hughes, "that Christine created her own spirit guide, subconsciously, which of course relates to her own story?" Either that, or did Beatrice have more than one spirit guide, and spoke publicly about only one of them? We'll never know.

We should consider, the clinician says, the piece of music Christine chose as her favorite for her *Desert Island Discs* episode: Ralph Vaughan Williams's "The Lark Ascending," inspired by George Meredith's eponymous poem. "The piece is a violin solo," Hughes points out. "It is likely that she witnessed her father performing it. It would have reminded her of him, but it would also have evoked her mother. This time, the lark is the songbird. When she talked about the spiritual experience that inspired her own 'Songbird'—about having no idea what had inspired it, insisting that it simply 'came' to her—I got the feeling that the song also haunted her. There is a very strong sense that she felt it came from her mother. That she believed the song was no random thing, but was delivered to her."

*

Lindsey, Mick and Stevie all produced further solo albums. Stevie was about a year behind with hers, because she was also dealing with the collapse of yet another love affair. This latest had been with record producer Jimmy Iovine (John Lennon, Tom Petty,

Bruce Springsteen) who had been steering her new offering, *Rock a Little*, before their relationship disintegrated. The baton was passed, full circle, to her and Lindsey's old friend and early supporter Keith Olsen. To think that Stevie had started out as his cleaner, mopping his studio floors. Now here she was, the global superstar, with the man who had given her a welcome break on *her* payroll. Which may not have occurred to her at the time. She was so smacked out on coke and booze that she would make it to the stage but be barely in the room. Her promotional tour flashed by in a haze. Six months on the road in 1986 concluded in her admission to the Betty Ford treatment center, Rancho Mirage, in California's Coachella valley.

When I interviewed her at home in LA three years later, during the campaign for her fourth solo album, *The Other Side of the Mirror* (produced by her latest lover, Rupert Hine, Alice-in-Wonderland-themed, part-recorded in Buckinghamshire and the one with the hit "Rooms on Fire"), she needed no encouragement to relive in acute, excruciating detail the experience that had saved her: $6,000 and twenty-eight days of her life, she declared, had been well spent. "I knew if I didn't go soon, I would be dead," she confided. "I was existing on false hopes and fake substances… I could, and have, stopped drinking. Many times. But the cocaine got the better of me. I needed that energy to keep up the pace. I'd get up in the morning and panic. 'How can I possibly make it to a photo session and three rehearsals?' And I'd be reaching for the coke. I was obsessive, addicted. And one day I just woke up and knew I didn't want to die."

Betty Ford, the clinic founded by U.S. First Lady and wife of President Gerald Ford who had herself become addicted to prescription medication, had brought Liza Minnelli, Liz Taylor and many other distinguished figures back from the brink. "It was worth a try," said Stevie. "Funny thing is, there is no cure as such, no stringent rehabilitation program that they put you on.

Your cure comes through talking, facing up to your problem and looking your 'drug of choice' in the eye.

"What did it for me was seeing so many people in much worse shape than me. I had three men friends in their late sixties, all rich, all from Texas, who sat down and told me the stories of their lives. How they'd had it all and lost it all, betrayed their family and friends and businesses, and destroyed their own and everyone else's lives. One by one they would look at me with tears running down their faces and say, 'Stevie, don't do this to your life.' They all helped me to make the most important resolution of my life: that I will not be sixty-five years old and be in Betty Ford."

About Christine, she was almost reverential. "She has always been a very strong mother figure to me," she confided. "A tiny bit older and a lot wiser. I respect her very much. She took me under her wing. And if she ever felt envy or jealousy because of me, she never showed it." I'd sat listening to almost identical words from her before. Who was she trying to convince?

*

Tango in the Night was recorded at Rumbo Recorders in Canoga Park, LA, and in Lindsey's own home studio.[1] From the off, the project was fraught with issues. Without formal collective management, they lacked guidance and had lost direction. It was hardly surprising. They'd barely played together for the past four years. True to form, their personal lives were again in turmoil, and everyone was angst-ridden. History had shown this to be a good sign—their creativity was fueled by drama—but there were additional obstacles. Lindsey assumed control of the project, and threw his weight around as usual, but some of the problems he faced he simply couldn't overcome. His biggest problem was Stevie, specifically her lack of availability. Given that she wasn't free to record with them until January 1987, the others had to crack on without her. Mick would later remark that the "Tango experience" had been like pulling teeth. But this stop-start, problem-infused album that took a year and a half to finish brims with gems. Many fans rate *Tango in the Night* as the true successor to *Rumours*. Had their magnum opus been a double album, several *Tango* tracks would have fitted perfectly.

The opener is Buckingham's explicit "Big Love," a galloping trip with a ripping riff. His vocal smolders, while Stevie's panting and gasps are suitably orgasmic. "There's a line in there about 'Looking out for love,' and it wasn't about looking for love, it was about guarding *against* love," reflected Lindsey down the line. "I had seen a lot of people that I knew who were spouses and parents, and they were not there for their families during that time. I didn't want to be one of those people." It took him a while to figure that side of things out. He was in no rush at all for commitment or parenthood. He would eventually become a father 1998, at the age of forty-nine. He married two years later during his fifty-first year, and welcomed two more children.

The title track, too, is Lindsey's. "Tango in the Night" is a cheeky trick, with strange, oriental overtones and aggressive undertones. Menacing guitar, tribal drumming and cinematic chorals build the tapestry. The breakout climax showcases Lindsey in superlative rock-god mode. As the solo superstar, in fact, that he never quite became.

There is compensation. Christine and Lindsey emerge here as the definitive strong, dynamic songwriting partnership. This development bodes well for the future. They turned out three collaborations for this album: "Mystified," a lush, hypnotic listen defined by Chris's ethereal, echo-y vocal and Lindsey's melodic guitar; "Isn't it Midnight," also sung by Christine, is raw, guitar-driven, and rocks; and "You and I Part II," which twinkles and floats in the manner of a "Christmas song," featuring epic harmonies and a gentler, brighter Lindsey, keeping his heart open and his eyes shut tight.

Of Stevie's triplet on *Tango*, "Welcome to the Room…Sara" stands out for the way it diminishes the brilliance of "Sara," its predecessor. Christine's "Everywhere" and "Little Lies" became smash hits, and are still played everywhere today. The album zapped to No. 1 in the UK, to No. 7 on the U.S. Billboard 200. It became, no surprise, the second biggest-selling album of their career.

Its further distinction is that when it was finished, Lindsey walked. He did so on the eve of the Mac's Shake the Cage tour to promote it, which was set to open on 30 September 1987 at the Kemper Arena, Kansas City, take in forty-five dates across America and wrap on 17 December at the Seattle Memorial Coliseum before transferring, after a four-and-a-half-month break, to Europe: kicking off at the Edinburgh Playhouse on 10 May 1988, delivering three nights at the Birmingham National Exhibition Centre (where I would review them), six nights at London's Wembley Arena, then Sweden, Germany, the Netherlands, back to Wembley that June for three further nights, a hop to Dublin, then finishing at Manchester City FC's Maine Road stadium. No way could the band pull a whole tour of that magnitude. The promoters would have sued them to the bone. Was Lindsey having them on? Was his list of conditions for the upcoming tour just a big tease?

"He said he wanted two, maybe three, other guitar players, percussion players, all sorts of interesting things. So, now we were over a barrel," Fleetwood recalled, as recounted by *Ultimate Classic Rock*. "'Whatever you want,' we said, 'just let's get out there.' For a while he looked as if he was going to do it—but he changed his mind after we booked the tour. It was not amusing."

Perhaps it did begin as a tease, because no way would they be able to go on without him. He was the heart and soul of the band. Right? Utterly indispensable. But the bluff was called. They did hit the road minus Lindsey, because they had no choice.

They replaced their lead guitarist with not one but two fine pluckers: Rick Vito and Billy Burnette. Both were dynamite. The tour was electric—despite the cancellation of the Australia leg and the reduction/rescheduling of European dates after Stevie lost her voice. Without Lindsey's resentful sulking to dampen things, without his superiority complex so casually splashed, the band's energy and positivity soared.

Accounts vary as to what actually happened that day at Christine's house when the band convened to discuss why Lindsey had pulled out, and to see whether they could find a way of talking him round. After months of negotiations and planning, initiated only after he had agreed to the tour, everything was ready to roll. How could he do this? Stevie's frustration and anger got the better of her. She lost her rag and flew at him, prompting Lindsey to scream, "Get this bitch out of my way! And fuck the lot of you!" before he assaulted her. In her defense, Stevie was at that point hooked hopelessly on the tranquilizer Klonopin. The most addictive of benzodiazepines had been prescribed by a psychiatrist following her sojourn at the Betty Ford, to prevent a relapse. Her dosage was increased gradually over the ensuing eight years, until she became heavily overweight, dazed, confused and unable to think straight, let alone write. While Lindsey downplayed the incident in virtually every interview thereafter, the other four have always contradicted him. They revisited it during the 1990s for "The Fleetwood Mac Story": an episode of the television series *Rock Family Trees* narrated by broadcaster John Peel and based on *Sounds* magazine contributor Pete Frame's intricate drawings of how musicians connect and cross-fertilize across bands and decades. For all the doubters, there was the proof, right there, in the Mac's own words.

"He ended up chasing me all the way out of Christine's maze-like house and down the street," said Stevie. "...and back up the street...and he threw me against the car...and I screamed horrible obscenities at him…and I thought he was going to kill me…and I think he probably thought he was going to kill me too…and I said to him…if the rest of the people in the band don't get you… my family will…my dad and my brother will kill you."

"It got ugly…physically ugly," affirmed John McVie. Who then mimed strangling someone. "And I said to Lindsey…why don't you just leave…he left…but what I *meant* was, why don't you just leave the *room*!"

According to Mick, Lindsey slapped Stevie then bent her over the bonnet of a car, before storming off shouting, "You're a bunch of selfish bastards!"

Said Christine, "That was in the courtyard of my house. There was a bit of a physical fight, and she wasn't beating him up. It wasn't nice."[2]

Lindsey later sidestepped the drama and violence to explain his defection. "I needed to get on with the next phase of my creative growth and my emotional growth," he said. "When you break up with someone and then for the next ten years you have to be around them and do for them and watch them move away from you, it's not easy." Would there ever come a time when he would stop playing the victim, blaming Stevie for all that had befallen him? No one held their breath.

*

The year 1988 was a turning point for some of them. Mick and Sara married that April at their home in Malibu, in the presence of a superstar throng. Mick's loyal compadre John served as best man. George Harrison, Bob Dylan, Jeff Lynne and the other Macs were present. Even Lindsey turned up. During a live musical interlude performed by the LA Philharmonic Players with the bridegroom, naturally, on the kit, Chubby Checker stepped up to give his signature, "The Twist." He also dragged Stevie on stage to sing a duet with him. She was dressed—gasp—in a gorgeous long white satin gown, and a pinned-back floppy hat festooned with blooms. She also sported a large silver crucifix and an air of demure, wide-eyed innocence. Everything about her screamed "bridal." If she was trying to tell persons there present "It shoulda been me," they would have got the message. What the actual bride thought of her former best friend's demeanor and get-up that day is not on record. Stevie later took to the mic alongside Ray Kennedy, Dave Mason, a gang of songsters, and Jeff Healey on guitar, to improvise the Sam Cooke classic "Bring It On Home to Me."

Marital bliss for Mick and Sara was short-lived. Their shared taste for the bottle didn't help. Mick, as was his wont, met another woman, only a year after that lavish, feelgood wedding. In 1995, he divorced Sara and married Lynn Frankel. The couple would be blessed with twin girls, but not for seven years. By which time, Mick was fifty-five. His marriage to Lynn lasted longer than most: by the time they divorced in 2013, they had been Mr. and Mrs. for eighteen years.

In February 1989, Mick's then forty-three-year-old best man, John, who had relinquished the booze following an alcohol-induced seizure, welcomed his first child, a daughter, with his second wife Julie Ann. No ifs, no buts, his former wife had to be godmother. "I was the *fairy* godmother," Christine said with a wry smile. "The one who could make anything come true for anyone, but never for myself."

*

Time was when the greatest hits album was the tried and tested label executive's wheeze, cynically designed to wring as much money as possible out of an artist's most popular tracks, the ones that had already banked them a bundle; also, to fleece completionist collectors who had to own every single thing in every format released by their idols. Little thought goes into the curation and sequencing of the majority of such compilations. Downloads, streaming and personal playlists have lately reduced demand for them.

Bands and artists have not always been thrilled by their record companies' dependence on greatest hits packages. The Beatles were famously furious when Allen Klein, the outgoing manager of John, George and Ringo (Paul was at that point managed by his father-in-law and brother-in-law) released the "Red" (*1962–1966*) and the "Blue" (*1967–1970*) albums, from which he alone stood to make a killing. Didn't that backfire.

The biggest-selling greatest hits release to date is *The Very Best of... The Eagles* (2003), a two-disc compilation comprising all the tracks on their two previous greatest hits albums plus other album tracks and a brand-new composition. The band were incensed when WEA released it. They switched to thanking their lucky stars when the checks rolled in.

With only three further studio albums left to make, not that they knew this at the time, Fleetwood Mac entered the realm of the retrospective. Aware that the glory days of the Buckingham-Nicks dynasty were behind them, they saw sense in bringing out a best-of that would not only earn a tidy bob or two as it showcased their wares, but would also serve as a concise introduction, for those previously not yet born, too young or as yet uninitiated, to the full diversity and impressiveness of their legacy. If nothing else, it should stretch their reputation and keep the band afloat for a few more years. This celebration of the *Rumours* Five era with two bonus tracks, both of them new songs, was received enthusiastically on its release in November 1988. The U.S. and European/Australasian track listings differ slightly, NB. The album climbed to No. 14 on the U.S. Billboard 200 and made it to No. 3 in the UK on release. It has often returned to the charts, and has sold consistently.

*

Recording work on the next Mac album, *Behind the Mask*, commenced at the Complex in Los Angeles during 1989 for an April 1990 release. Although Lindsey was the cat pissing in the corners, marking out "his" territory with an acoustic cameo on the title track, that's Rick Vito and Billy Burnette on guitars on the rest. They are the reason why *Mask* bears no true audio resemblance to a Fleetwood Mac album. Production was also under new management, Richard Dashut having departed and Greg Ladanyi (Don Henley, Toto, Jackson Browne) having crept into his blue suedes.[3]

The pervading tone is pop-chart newcomers do Fleetwood-Mac-lite. Where's the substance? The single memorable song? Never mind, up it went to No. 1 in Britain, No. 18 in America. Stevie's contribution, the slightly lazy "Love is Dangerous," was penned with Vito. Christine's "Do You Know," the fourth track on side one and on which she duets with Billy Burnette, is a country-infused lament with clear, moreish harmonies and a clever, accomplished guitar solo. "Skies the Limit" (sic) and "Save Me," co-written by Mr. and Mrs. Quintela, as she was then, leave this Mac fan scratching. The former is a snappy breeze elevated by Christine's melodic vocal. The latter is all too eighties, too pacy. It ticks boxes, sure. But it is, like the album itself, a bit too good and a bit so-what.

"But [Lindsey's] departure brought about a real commitment by the rest of us to what we're doing," insisted Mick. Christine was on the same page: "I like the fact that we really did pull it off," she divulged to *Rolling Stone*. "The record was well-arranged and well thought-out, despite the fact that Lindsey wasn't there." Mick buckled with praise for and pride in Christine, for stepping up to offer leadership in Lindsey's absence. "Christine really took the bull by the horns this time," he told the *Boston Globe*. "And with Lindsey gone, the older members of the band enjoyed getting back to how we used to make albums. It was very much a team effort…No offense to Lindsey, but he was becoming obsessive in the studio, and we were beginning to take a backseat." Can't have that.

While *Rolling Stone* were hailing the band's newest members as the best thing ever to happen to Fleetwood Mac, plenty of others were hissing "Next!" They got less than they bargained for. Following their 101-date, 13-territory tour between March and December 1990, Christine, Stevie and Rick Vito would stand down. That outing commenced in Brisbane on 23 March, advanced across Australia before moving on to Japan, then spent June, July and two days in August satisfying the U.S. market. It was then off to Belgium, the Netherlands and the UK, Sweden, Germany, Austria, Switzerland and Italy. October, November and early December were spent back in North America. On 6 and 7 December in Oakland and Inglewood, the last nights of the U.S. tour, Lindsey put in an appearance and was rewarded with tsunamic adulation. Because rock fans are the most nostalgic people on this planet. They always crave what they had before. Lindsey performed "Landslide" with Stevie, joined the band in their closing "Go Your Own Way," and even skipped back on with them for their encore, don't mind if I do, for "Tear It Up." He just couldn't resist it, could he: giving Vito and Burnette what-for by cornering them into guitar duels. Up you grow, Buckingham. Before it's too late.

"And then," said Christine. "And then. When every flight and hotel room blur into one, when every landscape looks the same as the one the day before, when all the colors start draining and your eyes glaze everything gray, when every language and accent sound identical, when touring becomes so much going through the motions and you just want to get off, go home and go to sleep for a really long time, you know it's time to stop. If only you can remember where and why 'home' is. It's that feeling you get when your existence begins to feel like a work of fiction, the kind of novel that no one would find plausible. If they could be bothered to read it in the first place. When each day feels like a dull, hollow ache, a case of, 'Oh no, here we go again, I must get up and go and do it because I have no choice,' and you only feel alive when you are actually on stage, you find yourself dreading everything else—that has got to be the time to stop. My sudden fear of flying wasn't for nothing. It was telling me something. Don't stop. I wrote the song, didn't I? But boy, was it time to."

What did she want most at that point? She sat silently for a couple of minutes. "I wanted time with my thoughts," she responded eventually. "I wanted a relationship with myself. I no longer wanted to feel like I did, the urchin outside the window, peering in and wondering what it would be like to live like that. I knew I needed to kill the pattern of trying to live my life through some chosen, magical man who would somehow wave a magic wand and make it all right, because that's just bollocks, and focus on what I meant to *me*."

His death turned out to be the most meaningful gift her father ever gave her, she said. "In dying, he showed me how to live. That probably sounds odd, but it's true. Time was running out, I realized. I was hurtling toward fifty and in many ways I felt as though my life hadn't even started yet. I needed to take myself in hand. To do something about that."

*

Fleetwood Mac released another greatest hits package in November 1992: *25 years—The Chain* was a four-disc box set (variations were also available) encompassing the band in all its incarnations from 1967 to 1992. The popular release would be dusted off and brought out again for its twentieth anniversary in 2012, when it reached No. 9 on the British chart. Public taste for the Mac had never really waned.

Two months after the box set's original release—great timing—on 19 January 1993, the *Rumours* Five reconvened against all conceivable odds for a historic live performance, at the request of newly elected Bill Clinton: the 42nd President of the United States. He had expressed desperation to have *that specific line-up* perform his unofficial election campaign theme, their 1977 hit written by Christine, "Don't Stop," at his Inaugural Gala. He had chosen the song because it appealed to his fellow baby boomers. This would involve performing live at the Capital Centre basketball and hockey arena in Landover, Washington, DC. It was not so much about the venue as the implication. The most recent previous outing of the full *Rumours* Five had been eleven years earlier, on the brief, disappointing Mirage tour back in 1982. Which, in rock'n'roll terms, is an eternity. The world would be watching. It could make or break them, both as a band and as artists. Could they still do it? They thought they were off the hook, anyway, because no way would Lindsey ever agree to it. Then he did, with persuasion from Stevie. Mick would later recall a moment backstage before they went on, when he looked down and saw that Christine and John were holding hands…and so were Stevie and Lindsey. "And that really did get to me," Mick said. "That was quite a moment, it really was."

And just like that, as if they had never been away, they were Fleetwood Mac again. Chris, who would turn fifty that July, arrived with hair neatly-bobbed and looking elegant in dark red sequins. Her former husband John, now forty-eight, was by contrast still a couldn't-care-less, I've-always-looked-like-this-so-get-off-my-case. Mick, forty-six, had shed most of his hair, but was otherwise reliably rock-tramp. Forty-five-year-old Stevie glowed center-stage in sheeny black chiffon, lobe-ripping chandelier earrings and her trademark silk top hat, her blonde locks flowing to the waist, her tambourine tied with white ribbons. At forty-four and still the youngest, Lindsey looked handsome, tanned and slim, and boasted a full head of glossy dark hair. Of the five, not that he would admit it, he seemed the most thrilled to be there. He did that crossed-legged, need-a-wee stage-hop as he wowed the crowd with his guitar solos.

He issued emphatic denials afterward. The performance, he insisted, was a one-off. This was not the prelude to any permanent reunion. Despite which, it did reignite interest in the band, who had been going their own ways for several years. Stevie had quit in 1990 to focus fully on her solo career. Chris was refusing to tour further because of her aviophobia. Only the diehard rhythm section remained. Mick and John's excursions as the last Mackers standing, plus stand-ins, had been well-intentioned but feeble. But lo, the magic was back! There was something about the chemistry of the *Rumours* Five that none of them could resist. Which was the problem.

"At the inauguration, I just realized I wanted it to be back the way it was, or I don't want to be in it anymore," Stevie told the *Houston Press*. "For me, it made me realize that it had to be *that* five, or it couldn't be. I couldn't continue to be in a Fleetwood Mac that didn't have Lindsey in it." Even though he had almost throttled the life out of her over the bonnet of a car six years earlier.

For Christine's big birthday six months after the Billary Ball,[4] her husband Eddy threw a glamorous party. To which he did not invite Mick, John, Stevie or Lindsey. Enough with the Fleetwood Mac shit, he seemed to be saying. That's all over now.

"She was done with the band, and he was trying to have her to himself," observes Richard Hughes. "Which seems reasonable. We have to remember that when he and Christine met, she was working on a solo album. To all intents and purposes, she was out of the band. And you don't want to go marrying the band. If Fleetwood Mac had a huge resurgence at that point, it would have created big tabloid interest. He didn't want his wife to be defined by the band at that stage in her life, which I find rather endearing. If anything, he was being protective of her. With hindsight, that does look a bit controlling and unnecessary, but we should extend him the benefit of the doubt."

Christine didn't want to be controlled. She sometimes went along with it for the sake of a quiet life, but compliant wifeliness was wearing thin. She paid the bills, so she would call the shots. She grew, she agreed, less meek and more disagreeable in middle age. When she purchased her manor house in Wickhambreaux, Kent, in 1990, she knew that she would be moving there alone. Work commenced at the estate several years before she relocated to live in it.

Meanwhile, in March 1997, the *Rumours* Five—including Lindsey and Stevie—were invited to film an MTV Unplugged Special. That gig was recorded, and both audio and footage were released as a CD/DVD package entitled *The Dance*. The first album by The Five for ten years, released on 19 August, exceeded all expectations. An instant No. 1 on the U.S. Billboard 200— a feat they hadn't achieved since 1982, with *Mirage*—it would become the fifth best-selling live album ever in the U.S., shifting more than a million copies in the first eight weeks. It lingered for seven months on the Top 40 there, hit No. 15 in the UK, and went on to sell more than 6 million copies worldwide. It wasn't even a debut live recording. They had released *Live* seventeen years earlier in 1980. But that was a collection of live recordings cherry-picked from more than sixty different performances and pasted together. *The Dance* was recorded all on one night, methodically, making space as they proceeded for subsequent overdubs. The Marching Band of the University of California, who had graced the original recording of "Tusk," performed for that track and also on "Don't Stop."

Essentially another Greatest Hits offering, *The Dance* also included new compositions and some of the band's favorite album tracks. Its title was inspired by the painting *La Danse* by French artist Henri Matisse—"an ode to life, joy and physical abandonment, and an emblem of modern art"[5]—the Mac having decided to use an image of the painting as their cover art. After they failed to secure permission, they chose to pose for something based on it. Mick's stance in the photograph draws the mind way back to the *Rumours* sleeve. Nine of Christine's best songs were deployed across the compilation: "The Chain" (as co-writer), "Everywhere," "Say You Love Me," "You Make Loving Fun," "Don't Stop," "You Make Loving Fun," "Over My Head," "Temporary One" (with Eddy Quintela) and, of course, "Songbird."

How many lives were left to them? They could never have predicted this one, though they seized it all the same. A forty-four-date September-through-November arena tour then ensued, which became one of their highest-grossing ever. It was during that jaunt that Lindsey settled, found his feet and gelled again with his bandmates. He would remain part of the line-up until 2018, when they would fire him during yet another disagreement.

They disbanded for Christmas, then gathered with ghosts just over a week into the New Year at New York's Waldorf Astoria hotel, for their induction into the Rock & Roll Hall of Fame. Every major musician in the band's history had been named to the Hall: Peter Green, Jeremy Spencer, Mick Fleetwood, John McVie, Danny Kirwan, Christine, Lindsey and Stevie. Bob Welch was ignored—for the simple reason that he and Mick were estranged at the time. There was no mystery to it. That has never stopped the conspiracy theorists raging.

"They were the sound of the times, and of the times to come," stated Sheryl Crow during her induction speech. "They were, and are, the reason I got into music. They became the backdrop of so many people's lives…they were challenging all of us to look at the sensual, mystical and spiritual sides of ourselves without us even knowing it. I think what is most interesting is that, at a time in our history when we are all evaluating our vitality on the planet, that a band that truly went through its own changes personally, creatively and emotionally has found its way back into our lives in a very prevalent way. They wrote of relationships, glorious and crumbling. Of believing, of hoping, of despairing, of hurting. They introduced us to the darker sides of our being without us even knowing, and we joined the dance.

"Their story," she concluded, "is indisputably one of the most incredible stories ever told in rock'n'roll. And it began with the wizardry of a guitar guru named Peter Green..." who got up with the band to accept his share of the award, and who was also coaxed into returning to the stage with Carlos Santana to perform his own song, "Black Magic Woman."

A month later, they landed at Heathrow to attend the eighteenth annual BRIT Awards at the London Arena on the Isle of Dogs. In a year that belonged to the Verve, Prodigy, Radiohead and Stereophonics ("British Breakthrough Act"), they were honored with the Outstanding Contribution to Music award. They performed a medley of "Rhiannon," "Go Your Own Way" and "Don't Stop," closing the televised show. And they were on fire. Lindsey milked it to the hilt. Manic Mick spilled enough sweat to flood the building. Stevie, Christine and John cracked on big-time, showing them how it's done. The ecstatic throng leapt to their feet, grabbed every available bottle and swilled as they rocked themselves stupid. It was mayhem. What was this, New Year's Eve? Cool cats and designer-clad execs threw caution, their arms in the air and anything spare around each other. They swayed, sang and wept their way through the Mac's sensational nostalgia-fest. Who remembered next day the antics of Chumbawamba singer Danbert Nobacon, who had attempted to steal the night by emptying a jug of water over serving Deputy Prime Minister John Prescott with the retort, "This is for the Liverpool dockers"?

Back in the U.S., they presented, swishly-clad, at New York's Radio City Music Hall on 25 February, for the 40th Annual Grammy Awards. They were nominees in two categories:

Best Pop Album for *The Dance*, and Best Pop Performance by a Duo or Group with Vocal for *two* songs, "Silver Springs" and "The Chain." The former went to James Taylor, the latter to Jamiroquai. Oh well. The Mac beamed their way onto the stage anyway, and thrashed that medley to bits. Christine might have given it extra welly. Who could blame her? This was her final performance with the band she had lived for, at times almost died for, been one of the principal writers and composers for, the mother of, the gatekeeper of, the heart and soul of, for twenty-eight exhausting, life-changing years. The others were shattered by her withdrawal. As far as they knew that enervating night, The Five were finished forever.

CHAPTER 14

WICKHAMBREAUX

"I sold everything and moved back to the old place in England. Selling the house and the car, giving up my green card (well, I let it run out—it's redundant now) make it much harder to go back. I left everything behind. Friends too, unfortunately. I still stay in touch. It was the thing to do. I felt it was right. The moment I landed at Heathrow Airport, I knew this is it. I was home. It was this weight lifted off me. I never really wanted to leave England. When we left to try and hack out a career in the States, John and Mick assured me it would only be for six months. We never came back. Twenty-eight years later…I have always loved England, but one thing led to another and I didn't manage to come home any sooner. I wish I had…Once I have made up my mind, it's like my relationships. Once they are over, that is it. They are history."[1]

Christine had longed for freedom. She had dreamed of the day when she could quit the rock'n'roll madness and reinvent herself as a lady of the manor: clad in Barbour and Hunter wellies, tramping the fields with her small, blond, fringy Lhasa apsos, Dougal and George; wielding a mud-caked Range Rover through country lanes; welcoming friends to her bucolic paradise for long weekends, lighting blazing log fires, preparing and serving rustic feasts and throwing open her wine cellar. She spent her early years back in England doing all of these things and more, while commissioning replacement beams, fixing roofs, and converting outhouses into a small studio and snug guest accommodation. She took her time over her interiors, designing the perfect kitchen and selecting just the right drapes, furnishings and rugs to make the place home. She also supervised the planning and planting of her fine gardens. She was literally putting down roots, digging herself into the soil, and creating a safe haven. Her forever home had to be the nest that she would never want to leave. That was the idea.

Why did she choose the county of Kent to retire to? It wasn't as if she had Kentish roots. She was a Midlander, with strong ancestral connections to the south London suburbs, as well as tenuous links to Yorkshire. She explained that she'd purchased on impulse in 1990 following the death of her father, because "I felt I hadn't spent any time with my brother." He lived a few miles from Wickhambreaux. She panicked, in other words. Her sense of guilt at not having spent enough time with her dad transmuted into a burning need to be with her elder brother. But those whom we need the most might not always be available at weekends.

Christine's dream was short-lived. Once the conversion, renovation and decoration works were complete, the appeal of the location began to wear off. She had thrown herself into the all-encompassing project, but began to feel unsettled when all was done. She felt isolated. She filled her days signing up for cookery courses, perfecting an impressive culinary repertoire, particularly in Italian food, and welcoming family and friends to feast-like Sunday lunches. She loved to cook epic roasts with all the trimmings, spaghetti seafood, risottos. There was often an Italian edge to her dishes, but she couldn't get excited about desserts. She could turn out a pandoro, panna cotta or zabaglione to feed the best of them, but found puds a fiddle and was more inclined to reach for a tub of ice cream. She talked about opening her own restaurant. She never got round to it. She resumed drawing and painting for a while, and thought about taking up sculpting again, but…she never got round to it. She still wrote songs, she said, but never with any intention of recording them. She wrote the way Stevie had always journaled: as therapy.

Friends flagged a bit. She was OK with that, she said. People had their own lives to lead. She relished the solitude, she said. She could do what she wanted when she wanted. There was no schedule, no particular place to go. She walked a lot, read a lot—mainly fantasy novels—and watched television a lot, favoring crime dramas, sitcoms and cookery programs. She was partial to *Have I Got News for You*, had a soft spot for televised tennis during Wimbledon fortnight, fell madly for *ER*, and liked to relax in front of the TV of an evening with a flute of champagne in hand. Which soon became a top-up, which in turn became might-as-well-finish-the-bottle. Without even noticing, she was suddenly drinking heavily again. She started to rely on medication to help her sleep.

"There was disillusionment," observes Richard Hughes. "The relocation from Los Angeles to Kent, the fresh start, the creation of a grand home, the comfort derived from being surrounded by cherished objects: sometimes that all fails to 'bring us home.' It can have the opposite effect, making us feel even more detached and alienated. Freud explained the concept well. Sometimes, such a sanctuary exists only in our minds and in our memories, no matter how much time, money and effort we invest in recreating it. Because 'home' is not necessarily about stuff, about the physical aspect. Christine went to extreme lengths to achieve what she thought she wanted. It didn't live up to expectations. She was deeply disappointed all over again." Despite which, she dug in her heels. She remained at The Quaives for the best part of seventeen years.

Hence the booze and the pharmaceuticals. She weaned herself off in the end, following a fall down the stairs that prompted a shock realization: that there was no one to hear her scream. She could have been badly injured or even killed, and she might not have been found for days. The realization knocked some sense into her. She picked herself up, quit smoking while she was at it, and took to the nicotine gum. The former owl evolved into a lark, getting up early to take the dogs out. She drove sometimes to Birmingham to visit "the other Perfects." During "retail therapy" wanders around London, she would comfort-purchase trinkets and antique perfume bottles. She lunched and dined with a small circle of very close old friends, including Mick's double ex-wife Jenny Boyd and Sandra Elsdon Vigon: a former fashion model who had dated both Peter Green and John McVie, and who trained and was in practice as a Jungian psychotherapist in Los Angeles for twenty-plus years, before relocating to London.[2] She also hung with her manager, former Warners executive Martin Wyatt: "one of the nicest men in the music business," many say.

One thing she didn't do was spend much time at her desk. She owned a state-of-the-art computer system, but couldn't be bothered typing, she said. Which was surprising. You would think it would come naturally to a keyboard player. Pianists tend to type faster and more accurately than non-pianists, studies have shown.[3] They are able to "play words" as quickly as any administrative expert can type them. She would drag herself to the screen now and then. She and Mick exchanged emails. She and Stevie would correspond occasionally.

Recording with her nephew Dan Perfect came about quite by accident. When they began working together, he was thirty-eight and she was sixty. She described him as gifted guitarist who was very good with Pro Tools: a type of software used to create music.

"I have a little converted barn which we call the Saloon," she said. (She also said that her bar was called "Swallows": just a party room to begin with, a garage that became a sitting room with a bar, then the instruments and the equipment arrived and it became a studio.) "It has a mock-up of a bar in there, and some gear in the corner and a computer. A lot of people said, 'This is sounding really good, why don't you make a record?' I balked at the thought of having to do this again. This is the bit—no, I lie—this is not the bit that really gets me. It is the touring and the live performances. That is out. I got persuaded into releasing this, and the proviso was that nobody expected me to do live performances anymore. I have retired."[4]

While all she really cared about was the songwriting, she was proud of the album she and Dan made together. Without a deadline, pressure from a record company, a Lindsey breathing down her neck, and without the need to create a commercial product, it was music for music's sake. She felt liberated. She described the result, *In the Meantime*, as "completely self-indulgent." She did virtually nothing to promote it. It failed to chart.

Christine owned up in the end, that a man had been behind the new songs. Not Eddy, she insisted. That marriage had "been and gone." Besides, she didn't write about him. Which was telling. Ah, so there had been someone new. Who? "Anonymous." "Someone" had walked into her life at the turn of the millennium when she was hurtling toward sixty and felt vulnerable, yet just about still in with a chance. "Sod it," she said, and went for it. But as always seemed to happen with Chris, the romance didn't work out. Some of the songs were "working the thing out, working the demons out," she said. She felt angry and frustrated with herself, for having fallen for the fantasy yet again. When would she learn? She resolved, this time, that she never would again.

"I've had my good times," she said with a shrug. "No, both Stevie and I, we were married to Fleetwood Mac. That was what we did, and it was a harsh marriage. During those years, there was no time for anything else, and we used to moan about how we were married to the band. During our thirties and forties, that is what we did. There was no time for relationships of our own." Huh? The list of rock stars that Stevie plowed through could have made an entire rock orchestra all by itself. Chris had had her crew moments, her marriages and her ultimate bad boy, Dennis: the love of her life. What were all of those if not relationships?

When writer and broadcaster Mark Ellen asked to interview her for *The Word* in July 2004, she invited him to her eclectic London pad: as he remembers it, "an unimaginably costly box-of-glass apartment on the south bank of the Thames, its gold-leafed books and rolled hand towels suggesting hotel suite more than home."

"She's that rare breed of musician who can enter a room without you noticing," he reported. "She's not a member of the frontline, the preserve of attention-seeking singers and garrulous guitarists, nor really a member of the backline, characterized by I've-had-a-drink-me drummers. She occupied a dimly-lit middle ground, stationary, almost anonymous, just the way she liked it." In Fleetwood Mac she had been, concluded Ellen, "this dark-eyed and dependable Brummie stoking the engine and the keyboard."

How much, Mark wondered, did she have to hate the life around music to give up the music itself? "For some people that is their life, to get on those boards and have the light shining on them," Chris responded. "And some people never even reach that point. But for me, the day had come. I hated the LA earthquake, I hated living out of a suitcase, I hated flying—I mean, how many paranoias do you want? There were tiny moments on stage when you'd get that feeling of magic, but otherwise you were just going through the motions. I just started to feel a little dizzy under the lights, to be honest. The vibration of the boards, the volume and the heat, they started to make me feel a little unwell! I'd just had enough. I just didn't want to have any of that noise anymore."

*

Stevie and Lindsey continued to record. She very successfully, he less so. His solo album *Gift of Screws* was rejected by Warner Bros. They put it to him that he could redeploy a few of its tracks for another Fleetwood Mac album. Which infuriated him, but he agreed to try, getting together with Mick and John in LA. Stevie dipped in when she was available. There was even the ghost of Christine. Although she had declined to be part of it, she had already contributed keys to a couple of Lindsey's tracks before she left the band. The result was *Say You Will*, released in 2003. It hit No. 3 in the U.S., No. 6 back home. Then, what else, they took it on tour. Another sixteen months traveling the world and it was 2004, the year that Stevie, Lindsey, the Mick Fleetwood Band and Chris all had albums out.

Then there was no further Mac project for the next five years. Mick's finances collapsed again. Having squandered most of his fortune on ex-wives, booze and drugs, he was the only one who desperately needed to keep at it. So, in 2009, The Four hit the road again on yet another world tour, even though they were without a new album to flog. "All" they had was a re-release of *Rumours*, as an expanded CD/DVD box set with studio outtakes, footage and photos. Making this outing a nostalgia-fest, milking the goodwill of their fans. Just as she had six years earlier, Chris joined the Wembley Arena throng to cheer them on. As on previous occasions she was spotted, and was honored with a standing ovation by the crowd.

She would have liked to travel further afield. Not only to witness her old band's performances and share in the magic in other territories, but also to visit countries she had never seen, such as Vietnam and China. She wanted to take herself on a big, proper African safari. "All of them feasibly accessible only by plane," observed Mick. "She came back to herself through a deep desire to travel, and only by confronting her fear was she able to find herself again." Her extreme aviophobia had made air travel impossible for close to twenty years. Everywhere she had had to go, she had gone by rail and sea. Could anything be done for her? Therapy was suggested, which she was willing to try. She consulted Dr. Richard Wolman, a psychiatrist in Wilton Crescent, Belgravia. He and his wife Astrid Kolf soon became her close friends.

"I had long been intrigued as to whether she ever submitted to psychoanalysis," says psychotherapist Richard Hughes, "because she was such an introspective person. We knew that she sought help for her fear of flying. It's fascinating that she saw that kind of specialist. Did she see him in a hypnotherapy frame, about the aviophobia, or was she was looking for something more, something deeper?" Given that he's a psychiatrist who is interested in human systems, the developmental side, and aspects of class, patriarchy and trans-cultural psychology, I'd say she was looking for more.

"During that *Desert Island Discs* interview, the question of ego arose quite significantly. It felt as though the presenter Kirsty Young was really pushing her on the subject: did she leave her ego behind when she quit the band, what was it like having it stoked for so many years then walking away, and so on. Christine was firm on the subject. She said she was aware of who she was, and of her status within the band. There was something there in her responses that strongly suggested she had done therapy, and not 'just' to overcome her fear of flying."

It was Richard Wolman who projected her into a future in which she would be able to board a plane again. He asked her, during one session, where she might like to visit first, when she was ready to take to the skies again. Maui, she said. She wanted to visit Mick and John. Wolman instructed her to book herself on a flight six months hence. She even told Mick what she was planning. He wasn't holding his breath. Then in 2013, just ahead of her deadline, Mick arrived in London for a week of press junkets ahead of the band's gigs at the 02 Arena. When he and Chris got together, Mick suggested that it might make sense for her to travel back to Hawaii with him, so that he could look after her during the flight. To his astonishment, she took him up on it. It was her first flight anywhere for fifteen years.

She had the best time in Hawaii, he said. She lodged at a fabulous hotel, spent time with Mick on his farm, sat in on his own band's rehearsals ahead of a fundraising gig, and appeared relaxed throughout. Mick started to hope that she might even get up with them and perform on the night. In the end, she agreed to. They didn't announce her in advance, just in case she changed her mind. But she did it, old numbers and new, and "Don't Stop.""She'd flown 6,000 miles and got on stage for the first time in seventeen years and she wasn't fucking frightened, in fact, she was amazing," said Mick. They sat and talked about it together afterward. Everything she did musically beyond that night "hinged on that moment," he said. "It literally all started there. I've known Chris a long time and played with her for over forty years, so I can say without a doubt that the timbre of her voice expressed just how tentatively she took that first step."[5]

*

Rock'n'roll nights blur into sameness. If you can remember it, they say, you weren't there. But I remember very clearly the Thames Clipper that conveyed my friend James Irving and me from the London Eye to North Greenwich Pier and the 02 Arena on Wednesday, 25 September 2013. They poured us champagne on the boat as we chugged our way east, unsure as to how the night and the gig would unfold. Just in after two shows in Dublin, Fleetwood Mac were in the middle of their London dates,

24, 25 and 27, before progressing to Birmingham, Manchester and Glasgow. Rumour had it that Christine was in town, and that she would be getting on stage with them. When she failed to appear the previous night, fans scoffed and forgot about it.

On the evening we went, tribute was paid to Peter Green, who was seated somewhere in the audience. Stevie dedicated their performance of "Landslide" to him. We assumed it to be the surprise of the night. We were wrong. On came Chris toward the end of the gig, to a roar and tumultuous applause. The woman who had celebrated her seventieth birthday two months earlier looked slim and chic in black leather and skinny jeans. There was nothing "seventy" about her. She and Stevie fell on each other. Lindsey budged in for a clumsy group hug. Then, standing at her piano, bouncing at the knees, pounding the keys and harmonizing with the others as sharply as ever, she banged out "Don't Stop." She and John hugged and kissed. She even joined in the whole-band bow. Her former husband then took her by the arm and escorted her safely off the stage. It was a more poignant moment than anything the audience had just seen. O-o-h, don't you look back.

Her many years in the wilderness had taught her a lesson. Her instincts served her. She had long been aware that nothing matters more than family. She had abandoned the rock fantasy to go back in search of a time, a place, a clan, even a childhood, that no longer existed. She was orphaned, but still had a sibling, and half-siblings. They had children of their own, who themselves were her flesh and blood. There would be great-grandchildren. But she had long been detached from them. The band had consumed her for more than forty years. The life she had left behind was no longer there for her in quite the same shape or way. She had tried to walk, leave the band to it, start a new life. She had removed herself to the other side of the world, and had mostly kept her distance. In the end, she couldn't stay away any longer.

"Because it was about something that only the band could give her," affirms Richard Hughes. "*They* were her family. She *had* to go back to them. She had no choice."

But the days were numbered. Christine was into her eighth decade. The others weren't far behind. People pointed at the Stones, the Who, McCartney, what about those guys? If wizened octogenarians can still be out there, croaking and thrashing it, why not the Mac, who for one thing can still sing? The band agreed. What they wanted to know was whether she was coming back for good. They had plans. Commitments for the next three years. Was she in or out? As for Chris, she couldn't be sure that they wanted her.

What the public didn't know was that she had joined them during rehearsals in Ireland before the 02 gig, just to make sure they were still on the same page. Although they rehearsed several songs together, all agreed that less was more. She then went along with them on various European dates. "Watching her and Lindsey reactivated as a creative pair was invigorating," said Mick. "We started talking about getting into the studio and working on a new record, and discussing how we would—and should—give it another go together."[6]

"McVie reluctantly acknowledged," reported Adrian Deevoy in the *Daily Mail*, "that her voice, piano and presence make the band somehow complete. Without her, Fleetwood Mac serve up a satisfying set of ingredients, but she is the sauce that unifies them. 'The gravy?' she suggests. 'I think we all sensed that.'"

During early November, some six weeks after her surprise pop-up appearance at the 02, she received journalists at her glamorous apartment overlooking the Thames to talk about the experience. She "enjoyed it immensely," she said. "Not quite to the point of being tearful, but it felt really good and completely natural." There were other things on her mind that day. The band had just been forced to wipe their Australia and New Zealand dates, because John McVie was receiving urgent treatment for cancer of the colon.

*

In January 2014 came the official announcement: Chris was back with the Mac. In her interview with the *Sunday Times*, she admitted to feeling as though she had just surfaced from years of isolation and "mud, and gray days, where your life is dark, your heart is dark, your brain is dark." Cue spotlight.

By the time she rejoined the band in LA the following spring, installing herself in the Santa Monica house that she, John and Mick would be sharing during studio sessions for a planned new album, she had been on her safari and had game-spotted in tiny prop planes. She had also booked a holiday in South Africa for the end of the tour. She told the others more than once that it all felt like a dream.

Their predictably named On With the Show world tour kicked off in Minneapolis that September, ran for 120 gigs, and caught up with Australia and New Zealand, having been forced to cancel their appearances there while John was going through treatment. They even played that year's Isle of Wight Festival on June 2015: their only UK festival appearance. "Show 90!" exclaimed Stevie, addressing the vast gathering, a sizable proportion of whom had come as her. "Welcome back, Mrs. Christine McVie...She's *ba-a-a-ack!*" And there she was. Looking cozy yet statuesque behind her Yamaha and sounding better than ever. Her voice did catch here and there, but so what. Stevie was no longer hitting the high ones, or that might have been the chill in the air that had her reaching for fingerless gloves and a knitted black beret. Chris, too, had swathed her neck in a black cashmere scarf. There were a few bum notes, but the harmonies worked. Lindsey postured a lot less, seemed subdued and sounded raspy. Dependable John and Mick were on it, solid. "Dreams," "Little Lies" and "Go Your Own Way" and they were done. Lindsey high-fived his ex just before the bow. The footage doesn't live up to the experience on the night. Festival footage never does.

Christine put The Quaives on the market that September. She had poured her heart, soul and wealth into the place that did not deliver her the long-term peace and fulfillment she had believed she would need to survive. She had offered it at £3.5 million, but let it go for significantly less that the asking price. The shortfall represented how badly she wanted to sell it. She spent three days prior to her final departure hugging the trees she had planted in memory of loved ones. She offloaded most of her furniture, belongings and personal effects and headed for London without a backward glance. Within two years, she would upgrade her Thameside flat for a more superior dwelling: a large penthouse apartment in Eaton Place, Belgravia. The roof garden must have sold it to her. She had soon installed further trees, albeit in giant pots. What price, the Perfect London abode? £7.5 million.

*

As for the pending album; nothing was going to happen while Stevie was still out there flogging her solo career. Chris had returned with a bag of new songs. Lindsey met her in the middle with stock to match them. It occurred to Mick that they might as well get on and do a duets album together. He was only weighing up the possibility when he alluded to it to *Classic Rock*. Well, another self-fulfilling prophecy. John and Mick would stand up as the rhythm section, naturally. They began recording toward the close of 2016, more than four years after the original sessions and over two years since Chris rejoined them.

Lindsey Buckingham Christine McVie, their "almost Fleetwood Mac record" according to Chris, saw the light of day on 9 June

2017. It hoisted to No. 5 in Britain and No. 17 in the U.S. The fans had been starved of new Mac material for fourteen years: no wonder copies scudded out of the shops. "It's that invisible chain, it's that alchemy," explained Christine in an interview for *Uncut* magazine. "It's what I want to invest my time and my future in from now on, so I won't leave again." The decades of living out of suitcases, losing the will to live on aircraft and her mind in press interviews, never knowing what day of the week it was or what country she was in, the fearful thoughts that had haunted her when she quit the band in 1998, seemed all but forgotten.

Chris and Lindsey hit the road on a brief promotional U.S. tour that July, showcasing classic Mac tunes as well as their new music. It was so successful and they were so in demand that the outing was extended into November. Stevie, John and Mick were so excited by the reaction to their bandmates that they swiftly arranged a new world tour for the following year.

Storm clouds gathered. Skittish Lindsey demanded that they hold back, to give his latest solo album a chance. Stevie, infuriated, stood firm. They must stick to the plan. An unfortunate occurrence ensued at the MusiCares Person of the Year Awards in New York in January 2018. When they could have chosen any Mac song to introduce the band as they headed for the stage, the organizers selected Stevie's "Rhiannon." Lindsey was incensed. Stevie swore she caught him sneering at her as she delivered her long-winded acceptance speech. Lindsey scoffed, protesting his innocence. Camel, straw. Nicks declared that she would never again share a stage with Buckingham. Who to choose? The band fired Lindsey.

That was when Tom Petty's guitarist Mike Campbell and Crowded House's Neil Finn joined the line-up for what turned out to be the final Mac tour; and when Lindsey went all-out and sued the band for lost earnings ... to the tune of more than U.S.$12 million. They settled. He suffered a heart attack the following year, and underwent life-saving surgery. His former bandmates kept their distance. His wife of twenty-one years walked out on him. Fleetwood Mac, at long last, were over the finishing line.

*

Although he would forever hold out hope that the others would come to their senses and that they would somehow ride again, Mick conceded with a swansong. On 25 February 2020, getting it in quite by chance before the pandemic locked us down, he hosted a star-studded tribute to the musician who had started it all, in support of the Teenage Cancer Trust. Peter Green was invited, but didn't turn up. He did not witness the lively performances in his honor by the Mac, Pete Townshend, John Mayall, Noel Gallagher and the rest. He managed to miss Christine's step back into the blues, too, with her fond homage: an interpretation of his 1968 number "Stop Messin' Round." Not that anyone knew it at the time, but this would be her last ever live performance. No one would ever see Greenie again, either. Five months later to the day, the seventy-three-year-old man behind the Mac died peacefully in his sleep.

*

In a deal brokered by her personal manager, Martin Wyatt, her Colony Group business manager, Paul Glass, and lawyer Mario González in August 2021, Christine became the fourth member of Fleetwood Mac to offload the rights to her songs. These were acquired by Hipgnosis: according to *Variety,* the fast-growing music company that had spent more than U.S.$2 billion over three intense years snapping up the rights to some of the world's most popular songs. Chris's deal included rights to her pre-Mac work with Chicken Shack, and also songs on her three solo albums.

Lindsey had been the first to sell to Hipgnosis. Stevie struck a U.S.$100 million deal with a rival, Primary Wave, while Mick had agreed a lucrative payday with BMG.

"I am so excited to belong to the Hipgnosis family, and thrilled that you all regard my songs worthy of merit," said Christine in a statement. "I'd like to thank you all for your faith in me, and I'll do all I can to continue this new relationship and help in any way I can! Thank you so much!"

"Christine McVie is one of the greatest songwriters of all time, having guided Fleetwood Mac to almost 150 million albums sold and making them one of the best-selling bands of all time globally," said Hipgnosis co-founder Merck Mercuriadis. "In the last forty-six years, the band have had three distinct writers and vocalists, but Christine's importance is amply demonstrated by the fact that eight of the sixteen songs on the band's Greatest Hits albums are from [her]. It's wonderful for us to welcome Christine to the Hipgnosis family, and particularly wonderful to reunite her once again…with Lindsey Buckingham. Between Christine and Lindsey we now have forty-eight of sixty-eight songs on the band's most successful albums."

She didn't need the money. What was this about?

If anyone stood a chance at getting near the truth, it was Johnnie Walker, revered presenter of BBC Radio 2's long-running show *Sounds of the '70s*. He had interviewed Christine on his Sunday, 7 February 2021 show, but had found her, he remarked, to be "closed," and their chat "inconclusive." The seasoned professional did ask her the inevitable: would Fleetwood Mac ever tour again? Her disjointed response left him wondering. "If we do, it'll be without John and without Stevie, I think," she said. "John is feeling a little bit frail. You know he was ill. He's fine, but he just hasn't got the heart for it anymore. He wants to get on his boat. You reach a certain age where you go, 'Hey, I'm not going to bust a gut doing this anymore. I think I'm getting a bit too old for it now, especially having had a year off. I don't know if I can get myself back into it again.'"

In May 2022, Christine granted an extensive interview to Michael Bonner, the editor of *Uncut*, just ahead of the release of her compilation *Songbird (A Solo Collection),* an album of remixes of songs from her 1984 album *Christine McVie,* five tracks from her 2004 album *In the Meantime,* and previously unreleased recordings. Its stand-out is an orchestral interpretation of "Songbird." The lovely cover painting is by Hong Kong-born British artist Fiona Rae. The insert booklet features a career-spanning Q&A with Chris by Johnnie Walker.

"Mentally, I'm still sixteen," she told the writer, while acknowledging the severe back pain that was preventing her from getting around or doing much, painful cortisone injections into her spine notwithstanding. There were days when she could barely stand, hence the interviews at home. "Looking back at the young Christine," she said, "I admire her sense of humor. I hope I've never lost it. The ability to laugh, especially at oneself, to be self-deprecating, is super precious, a real quality to have. Because you can join in with everyone and see the funny side of yourself."

At that time, she kept up regularly with Mick and John. "Not Stevie very much, and not Lindsey, for sure," she told Bonner. "There are no hard feelings between he and I. But since he left, we haven't really been in touch."

Songbird was her last release during her lifetime.

*

Christine died at Charing Cross Hospital, Fulham, on Wednesday, 30 November 2022. She was seventy-nine. The causes of her death were listed as bilateral renal infarction and ischaemic stroke, large atrial thrombus and atrial fibrillation.[7] Although family members were well aware that she was gravely ill, and some of them were with her when she died, the outside world was none the wiser until the news broke in the media. Not even her fellow band members had been informed. Stevie said she'd had no idea that Chris was ill until late on the Saturday night, a few days earlier. She had wanted to fly to London immediately to be with her friend, she said, but was told to wait. They were all confused. Hadn't Christine seemed good for another decade at least? She had looked fit and well the last time Mick, John and Stevie had seen her. After all the years, and after everything they had been through together, they were devastated at having been left out. Maybe someone assumed they would hijack it, dramatize it, give interviews left, right and center and make it all about them? Whatever, they never got the chance to say goodbye.

Grief ran around the world. Effusive were the outpourings. Loud was her music. Silent were her family. If a formal funeral was held, it was conducted in the strictest privacy. The last thing she would have wanted was a circus. Her cremated remains were retained by her relatives. What they did with them is unknown. There is no grave, no headstone, no monument at which fans might pay their respects. Not yet, anyway, and perhaps there never will be. One thing's for sure, Christine would have been horrified by the thought of a statue. She would have chortled like a drain at the mention of a mausoleum. Sanctification in death was the kind of thing she loathed. Her music says more, in a universal language, than a chunk of stone ever could.

I'm sure she would have enjoyed the laidback, emotion-driven Celebration of Life memorial service held in her honor on Monday, 9 January 2023 at Malibu's Little Beach House: an exclusive branch of the Soho House private members' club group accessible only to the elite on their local "Malibu Plus" deal. Situated just off the Pacific Coast Highway in a part of the world she adored, the chic wood and glass structure with far-reaching views across the ocean sits high on stilts on the sand. Supported by his bandmates and Fleetwood Mac's extended family, Mick gave a moving eulogy which began with the words "Part of my heart has flown away today."

He continued: "When we first learned that we might be losing Christine, there was an immediate coming together of everyone in the band and the Fleetwood Mac family, with the hope and possibility that we would not lose Chris," he said. "And now…we are all still trying to come to terms with the fact she has really flown away."

She would have been astonished by all the attention and celebration of her music all over the world, Mick added. She would also have been "in total disbelief at the fact they were closing down sporting events to pay tribute to her. But that was our Christine—she was a North Country girl from beginning to end, never caring about the fluff…again, it was our Christine who gifted so much to millions around the world…Just as her song says, 'I want to be with you everywhere.' And she is."

CHAPTER 15

A SLUMBER

I have never found rock pilgrimages appealing. I wouldn't board a flight to visit Elvis's Graceland, though I might pop in if I found myself nearby. I'd never go specially, but if I'm passing through Kensington, I'll take a detour down Logan Place to pause for a moment outside Garden Lodge, where Freddie Mercury once lived. When in Montreux for filming or to do an interview, I'll always visit his statue on the edge of Lac Leman before repairing to the bar of the Montreux Palace hotel to order one of his favorite tipples, a Stoli and tonic or a bottle of Cristal. In New York, I'll usually cross town to the Strawberry Fields memorial in Central Park, to pay my respects to John Lennon. On Barnes Common, I take the long way round to visit the shrine of Marc Bolan. Cutting through Beckenham, as I often do en route to my mother's house, I'll salute the High Street restaurant that was once the Three Tuns pub, where David Bowie played and hosted his Arts Labs. And up on Southend Road, I slow down beside the place where Haddon Hall once stood, David's home in early days. Local kids including this one used to doorstep him there.

There is no such place for Christine. No obvious spot at which to stop, think and remember. The house in which she was born, in Greenodd village, Cumbria, is a private residence the best part of 300 miles from London. But there is nothing to see there, not even an English Heritage blue plaque on the wall. She will not become eligible for one of those for nearly eighteen more years, and only then if they decide to put one up there.

So now and again, if I'm in the vicinity with time to spare, I go back to Wickhambreaux, to the house that she owned for a quarter of a century. I went there last on Bonfire Night day, Sunday, 5 November 2023. Her newly re-available 1984 second solo album had dropped through my letterbox that morning. I fancied a drive through sodden country lanes to listen to it. Eric Clapton, Steve Winwood, Mick Fleetwood and Lindsey Buckingham are on it. Two of its tracks, "Love Will Show Us How" and "Got a Hold on Me," were hit singles almost forty years ago now. This is Christine at her best. Tuning in again to her cheerful, upbeat melodies and vocals countered by despondent lyrics, I felt profoundly sad. Melody and melancholy. As she said, it always came back to the blues.

Later that day, I pulled up on my desktop the strange official video for the former (what were they thinking?) and the softer, more pleasing promotional piece for the latter: a black and white drama featuring Chris playing a Bösendorfer Grand, on which is set a crystal flute containing a single scarlet rose. The symbols of love being never distant. She was forty-one years old in these films. She had separated from Dennis Wilson a couple of years earlier, and had learned of his death only weeks before the videos were shot. Another track, "Ask Anybody," she had written at the height of their relationship. A melody had eluded her. Her old friend Steve Winwood got it, when they spent time together at his home studio. That song is here, too. She was still in a Dennis state of mind when she met Eddy Quintela during the recording of this album. She would marry him two years after its release. So Chris was drawing on love spent and passion brewing.

I remembered Andrew Loog Oldham's words: "Success is nothing without someone you love to share it with."

My thoughts returned to what she had said about Dennis. "He was my child," she remarked, "my lover and my child. What would the psychiatrists make of that! But honestly, he exhausted me. He used me up. I was wrung-out and used in the end. So I settled, for something that seemed safe. But Eddy didn't make me happy. It was Dennis, really, and that was that. I thought I could fix him. He was beyond fixing. His hurt went back to long before us. It would have taken an archeologist to dig him out and put him back together again. I couldn't do it, I was too damaged myself. From childhood, from my mother dying, which I never really processed, and then losing Pop, and from the fear of winding up alone."

He awakened things in her, she agreed, that she'd been scared to experience, and made her feel the extremes of every emotion. "*I* needed saving, never mind him," she said. "Had we stayed together, we would have destroyed each other. But I still fantasize about him. I still write about him. Subliminally. I always will. He was The One."

Was he? Or was he the fantasy? Haven't we all been there, with The One who caused us nothing but pain. Who bled us dry, wiped the floor with our heart, took us for granted, squandered our dough, totaled our car, drove us demented, and left us as good as dead. Haven't we all had a Dennis.

*

I hung about for a while outside her old house, kicking through leaves. I took a picture of the two songbirds etched on the shields that are still fixed to the tall wrought-iron gates. They reminded me of the tiny silver "songbird" charm that she wore on a chain around her neck. Her symbol. Her logo. Her "penguin." She wore it at her throat so she could always feel it on her skin, would always see it in the mirror. Those images of the songbird at the entrance to her castle were a subtle clue to the world.

*

Twenty minutes or so ticked by before it occurred to me that I was loitering. I crossed the road, climbed the wooden stile, ambled over the field for a bit then clambered back, for a last glimpse of something that is barely visible. This wonderful house—on which she engraved her personality and in which she invested her wealth and love, but which she had to relinquish in the end as an impossible dream—and also because it had become a virtual prison, and because she had other things to do—remains well-hidden. Only the rooftops and the back of one of the outhouses are visible if you take a chance and lean right through the gate spindles. I recalled the times when I was invited inside. The day we paced her gardens, sipped tea and revisited memories at her table. Only yesterday. Only moons ago. Only now, as Mick said, beyond her death, is Christine everywhere. I flick on the car radio. There she is.

A lilac tint seeps across the sky. Shadows lengthen. I turn my car in the lane and head back to the edge of the village, parking up across the road from the old Mill House. I trudge the green and go and sit in the Rose.

Hunched over a half of dry cider at "her" table, I find myself thinking about Steve Kalinich, Dennis Wilson's curious best friend. We'd been speaking again over Zoom the night before. I forget now which of the Beach Boys' songs we discussed, but it was one of those for which he'd written the lyrics. Steve alluded to Dennis having been the "angel and the devil in Chrissie's life." He returned to the time when Dennis slept with Stevie Nicks. That unfathomable betrayal put distance between the two women for the first time in their history, puncturing their bond and dissolving the magic. I remembered Stevie's stricken comments about her friend after her death, her quotes in the press, the snaps on Instagram and elsewhere of her handwritten letters. Grief can sound hollow in unstarry, off-grid places. Chris knew they'd done it, Steve said. If the scales fell in that moment, the recovery took years.

Christine escaped Fleetwood Mac's septic Camelot. Never the type to rip ivy from turrets or confront fire-spurting dragons, she withdrew quietly. She took herself as far from Stevie, Hollywood and the circus of myth and madness as she could. She returned to England, though not all the way home to Smethwick. The move, ultimately, proved futile. That drastic, life-changing relocation emptied and silenced her. It made her invisible. But she would re-emerge. Enough. Enough. *Enough.*

There came a time, long though it took, when she felt that she didn't exist without Fleetwood Mac. How to overcome that? She could only go back. There was mileage still in the tank. She forgave Stevie, then, by giving in and returning cap in hand after sixteen years? One could interpret the volte-face as subliminal punishment of the younger woman; a variation on the theme of killing with kindness. It was as though she were saying, "Look at me, Bitch, I'm back. To remind you. You took him. He was mine." Even though Chris knew in her heart that he wasn't worth keeping. So did Stevie do her a favor, then? It's one way of looking at it.

"Unlucky in love." What does she know, she who exists for crumbs tossed by heartbreakers? That she will never win? Because she knows that life is only about winning and losing, and only those who have never loved can't ever lose?

Chris was the first to admit, down the line, that her life had been spent in thrall to the falsity of One True Love. Hoping for it, dreaming about it, writing about it, singing about it. Chasing it, finding it, losing it, mourning it. "The greater the success, the more money, the more opportunities, the bigger our world became," she said to me, "the more I found myself shrinking inside. Reducing. Becoming…less. Less confident. I needed—I thought I needed—a man to validate me. I needed coke and booze to fortify me to go on [stage]. It was easier somehow to live in that permanent haze than to face reality. Those things made me who I was. Until they made me who I wasn't."

Until she awoke to the realization that the only One worth having was herself. Without the Greatest Love of All, as per Whitney, is the suggestion, we are nothing. Chris's quest for The One consumed her. Hollywood, Hallmark and Disney conditioned her to crave it; to fear that her life would have been for nothing if she failed to find her "other half." Being who she was, and given the kind of songs she wrote—about love, relationships and romantic despair—legions of people all over this orb desperately seeking the same thing believed that she and her bandmates had the answers.

Oh, boy. Why did we think that? We had only to listen to *Rumours* a few more times once we knew a bit more about life for the pennies to drop; to twig that Fleetwood Mac had fewer answers than we did. To recognize them as a collective relationships car crash. They showed us how little they knew about having, holding and cherishing; that they'd got it wrong; that they'd broken hearts, got broken, snorted feelings and guzzled pride, vomiting love freely shared and heat-seeking the resistant. They had wrecked families and lives with impunity. Maybe that is the Mac's secret, the lesson behind rock's quintessential soap opera and career-defining LP. Did their disintegration comfort us—in the sense that, however badly we screwed up, we would never get it *that* wrong, and at least our lives would never be *that* desperate—?

I think now that many of us got the wrong end of the stick about *Rumours*. "The divorce album" was exclusively introspective. All it did was expose their own relationship, character and personality problems. They didn't give a toss about ours.

Only in her seventies, long after she had stopped expecting her prince on his charger to rock up and save her, could Christine accept that the *quest* had been futile...but not her whole life. She knew folk who had found what she hadn't. Maybe she looked at Paul and Linda, at John and Yoko, at Charlie and Shirley Watts in awe. She must have known that they were rarities, those Beatles and Stones marriages; that there are few lifelong love matches in rock'n'roll.

Love, they tell us, those who reckon they know, is about compromise. There's not a lot of that in this game. Rockstars tend not to bend or defer. It's their spouses, managers and minions who do that. As for the obsession with The One, that's a trap based on fear—of loving and losing again.

We grow old. We wear the bottoms of our trousers rolled.[1] We regret the years, the goneness, the half-lived life, to the dying of our days. We cast back now and then to The One, the ones, who got away. Wasn't it *we* who got away? We know. In the end, we know.

Christine knew. It's in the songs. Though her lyrics were lucid, there were always hidden meanings. It all makes sense to me now.

Ghost-hunter Mrs. Beatrice Perfect and her White Eagle

Left: Who you gonna call? Christine's mother, psychic, medium and faith healer Beatrice Perfect, who died when her daughter was only 25. *(The Birmingham Gazette)*

Below right: Smethwick Baths, West Midlands, once of the UK's top music venues. The Beatles played here, and Beatrice Perfect led ghost walks. *(Wikimedia Commons)*

Balsall Heath College of Art, Birmingham. Christine enrolled at Moseley Junior Art School here in 1956, when she was 13. *(Wikimedia Commons)*

Right: Lashings of lashes: Christine in 1969, aged 26.

(© Evening Standard/Hulton Archive/Getty Images)

Below: I'm choosing the cherub. Chicken Shack singer and keyboardist, Christine Perfect, with Fleetwood Mac bassist and husband-to-be, John McVie, in February 1969.

(© Associated Press/Alamy)

Top: *The Rumours* Five: Mick Fleetwood, Stevie Nicks, Lindsey Buckingham, Christine and John in 1975.

(© GAB Archive/Redferns/Getty Images)

Above right: Window or aisle? Christine and Stevie taking the bus in 1976.

(© Michael Ochs Archives/Getty Images)

Left: Only over you: Christine with Beach Boy Dennis Wilson, her dangerous obsession.

(Photographer unknown)

'"Eponymous", let me spell it
for you ...' Christine at the
MTV TV studios in New York,
6 March 1984, giving an
interview to promote her
second self-titled album.

(© Gary Gershoff/Getty Images)

Getting the hang of hair
and make-up: Christine
in 1987.

(© Aaron Rapoport/Corbis/Getty Images)

Together forever … if not quite. Lindsey, Christine and Mick backstage at the then Brendan Byrne Arena (now Meadowlands), East Rutherford, New Jersey, on Tuesday 14 September 1982, during their two-month-long Mirage US tour. This was the band's last live outing with Lindsey until he returned for The Dance in 1997. *(© Mario Ruiz/Zuma Press/Alamy)*

Chris performing with the Mac at Bloomington's Met Center, Minnesota, 30 June 1990, on the band's 'Behind the Mask' world tour. Her father died while she was on the road, prompting her withdrawal from live touring.

(© Jim Steinfeldt/Michael Ochs Archives/ Getty Images)

Amor com amor se apaga – only a new love can get over an old love. Christine with Portuguese musician Eddy Quintela, who became her second husband in 1986.

(Photographer unknown)

Friends for life: Mick Fleetwood and Christine pose for posterity in London, c. 1995.

(© Steve Speller/Alamy)

Eat to the beat: Christine's kitchen at her Kentish home The Quaives.

(© Strut Parker/Bournemouth News/ Shutterstock)

Refuge at the Rose, Wickhambreaux.

(Courtesy of the author's collection)

Top: Only the lonely: Grade II listed The Quaives, Wickhambreaux, Kent, where Christine took up residence in 1998.

(© Strut Parker/Bournemouth News/Shutterstock)

Above right: Only the name remains. *(Courtesy of the author's collection)*

Left: It's been ages! Christine and the author at the Savoy, London, for the BASCA 40th Annual Gold Badge Awards, 16 October 2013. Chris had been awarded her own Gold Badge in 2006.

(Courtesy of the author's collection)

She's back! Christine makes a triumphant return to the line-up after a 16-year absence. Seen here at the Viejas Arena San Diego, California, 2 December 2014, during Fleetwood Mac's 'On with the Show' world tour.

(© Daniel Knighton/FilmMagic/ Getty Images)

Mick, Christine, Stevie, Lindsey and John at Radio City Music Hall, New York on 26 January 2018 for the MusiCares Person of the Year awards, at which they are honoured.

(© Kevin Mazur/Getty Images)

Dragonfly: her years plagued by aviophobia now behind her, Christine took to the skies with Mick Fleetwood on a Hawaii-bound flight in 2013.

(Photographer unknown)

APPENDICES

OVER AND OVER: A TIMELINE

1943
12 July: Christine born Anne Christine Perfect in Greenodd village, Furness.

Late 1940s
Family relocates to Bearwood, Smethwick, near Birmingham.

1947
Aged four, she is introduced to the piano.

1954
From age eleven, she studies classical piano, reintroduced to the instrument by a friend of her brother, John.

1956
Enrolls at Moseley Junior Art School, Birmingham.

1958
At fifteen, she awakens to rock'n'roll after happening upon a book of Fats Domino sheet music brought home by her brother; she also discovers the Everly Brothers.

1959

Leaves Moseley Junior Art School, enrolls at Birmingham Art College, where she studies sculpture and plans to train as an art teacher. Falls in with other musicians, starts playing in duos and bands.

1967

Peter Green forms Fleetwood Mac, naming the band after his drummer Mick Fleetwood and bassist John McVie.
Chris joins Stan Webb, Andy Silvester and Alan Morley in white blues outfit Chicken Shack.

1968

February, the Mac release debut album *Fleetwood Mac/Peter Green's Fleetwood Mac*.
Chris gets to know the band on the circuit, is enchanted by Green, and contributes keys to their second album *Mr. Wonderful*, released that August.

1969

Thanks to the popularity of her lead vocal on a Chicken Shack cover of "I'd Rather Go Blind," Chris is voted Top Female Singer on the *Melody Maker*'s Readers' Poll.
Marries Fleetwood Mac bassist John McVie.
August: she leaves Chicken Shack to launch her solo career on Blue Horizon Records.
September: the Mac release album *Then Play On*.
December: they follow it with *Fleetwood Mac in Chicago*.

1970

Peter Green quits Fleetwood Mac during a period of mental instability.

18 September: the day Jimi Hendrix is found dead, they release new album *Kiln House*, for which Chris creates the cover art.

Early 1970s

March: the Fleetwood Mac family move together into remote six-bedroom Kiln House.

20 June: Fleetwood marries girlfriend Jenny Boyd there.

Chris's involvement with the Mac escalates from session player to permanent member. She aids their transition from sixties blues purists to more rock-oriented project.

1971

As the Kiln House lease is about to expire, band members club together to buy Victorian mansion Benifold in East Hampshire. It will be their collective home, rehearsal space and recording studio—with the help of the Rolling Stones' mobile recording unit—for the next three-plus years.

Band release album *Future Games*.

1972

March: they release their album *Bare Trees*.

1973

March: they release their album *Penguin*.

October: they follow it with *Mystery to Me*.

1974

Confusion over the attempted launch of an alternative
Fleetwood Mac. Speculation as to what actually happens persists
to this day.
The real band relocate to the U.S.
September: they release the album *Heroes Are Hard to Find*.
New Year's Eve 1974: Mick invites American musicians Lindsey
Buckingham and Stevie Nicks to join the band.

1975

With Buckingham and Nicks on board, the Mac sound
crystallizes.
July: the new quintet's first album (also confusingly called)
Fleetwood Mac released. A huge success. Three of Chris's four
songs for the album become hit singles. But John McVie is
drinking heavily, and their marriage is in trouble. Chris indulges
in affairs with record producer Martin Birch and their lighting
director Curry Grant.

1976

John and Christine divorce.

1977

February: the band's magnum opus *Rumours,* driven by
collapsing relationships within the band, is released to global
acclaim. It becomes one of the biggest-selling in history, and
remains the world's top seller until Michael Jackson's *Thriller* in
1982.
August: Beach Boys drummer Dennis Wilson, prolific
songwriter and the only active surfer in the surf-music group,
releases his only solo studio album: the belatedly acclaimed, now
cult recording *Pacific Ocean Blue*. He declares that he has left his
family band.

1979

Chris begins a relationship with Dennis Wilson.
October: the Mac release their controversially punk-infused
album *Tusk*.

1981

Stevie Nicks, the focal point of the band, launches her
immediately successful solo career.
May: band reconvene to record, for the first time in eight years
away from the U.S.—at the Château d'Hérouville outside Paris,
the studio of Elton John/Honky Château fame.

1982

Chris and Dennis separate.
July: the band release the album *Mirage*.

1983

28 December: thirty-nine-year-old Dennis, five times married,
father of four, homeless hell-raiser, in and out of rehab, drowns
at Marina del Rey, Los Angeles. He is buried at sea in January
1984. When Christine hears of his death, she refuses to believe
it, insisting he was "indestructible." Her song about him, "Only
Over You," appears on Fleetwood Mac album *Mirage*.

1984

Records second solo album *Christine McVie*, featuring a freshly
assembled band and special guests: Lindsey Buckingham, Mick
Fleetwood, Eric Clapton, Elton John and Steve Winwood. It
spawns a pair of hits, "Got a Hold on Me" and "Love Will Show
Us How."

1986
18 October: she marries Portuguese musician Eddy Quintela, and records a cover of the Elvis Presley hit "Can't help Falling in Love" for the soundtrack of the movie *A Fine Mess*.

1987
April: they release the album *Tango in the Night*, featuring Chris's "Little Lies" and "Anyway." Lindsey Buckingham leaves the band to launch a solo career.

1990
The band reform with singer/guitarist Billy Burnette and guitarist Rick Vito as Lindsey's replacements.
April: they release the album *Behind the Mask*. While she is on the Behind the Mask tour, Christine's father dies.
Stevie and Chris stand down from the band.

1992
Box set *25 Years—The Chain* released, featuring a new song by Chris, "Love Shines."

1993
The *Rumours* Five line-up reunites to perform at U.S. President Bill Clinton's inauguration gala.

1995
October: the album *Time* featuring five songs by Christine is released.

1998
Christine decides to quit the band, sells her house, packs up and moves back to England. The band will be without Chris for sixteen years.

She is among the eight members of Fleetwood Mac inducted into the Rock & Roll Hall of Fame. She also receives the BRIT Award for Outstanding Contribution to Music.

2003
April: the Mac release album *Say You Will*.
Chris and Eddy Quintela divorce.

2004
Releases her third solo album *In the Meantime*.

2006
Receives her Gold Badge of Merit Award from BASCA, now the Ivors Academy.

2013
Makes her first appearance in fifteen years with Fleetwood Mac, during a one-night-only reunion at London's 02 Arena.
Receives Ivor Novello Lifetime Achievement Award from BASCA.

2014
January: she rejoins Fleetwood Mac.

2017
Appears on BBC Radio 4's *Desert Island Discs*. Releases duets album with Lindsey Buckingham.

2018
9 April: the band fire Lindsey, replacing him with Mike Campbell and Neil Finn.

2019

February: Lindsey suffers heart attack. Undergoes open-heart surgery and triple bypass.

2021

Chris receives UK Americana Awards Trailblazer award.

2022

30 November: following a brief illness, seventy-nine-year-old Christine dies.

SOMETHING TO REMEMBER ME BY: A SELECTION OF CHRISTINE MCVIE'S BEST SONGS

"I'd Rather Go Blind"—with Chicken Shack, 1969

"Remember Me"—from *Penguin*, Fleetwood Mac, 1973

"The Way I Feel"—from *Mystery to Me*, Fleetwood Mac, 1973

"Why"—from *Mystery to Me*, Fleetwood Mac, 1973

"Come a Little Bit Closer"—from *Heroes Are Hard to Find*, 1974

"Say You Love Me"—from *Fleetwood Mac*, Fleetwood Mac, 1975

"Over my Head"—from *Fleetwood Mac*, 1975

"Sugar Daddy"—from *Fleetwood Mac*, 1975

"Songbird"—from *Rumours*, Fleetwood Mac, 1977

"You Make Loving Fun"—from *Rumours*, 1977

"Don't Stop"—from *Rumours*, 1977

"Oh Daddy"—from *Rumours*, 1977

"The Chain" (co-writer)—from *Rumours*, 1977

"Brown Eyes"—from *Tusk*, Fleetwood Mac, 1979

"Think About Me"—from *Tusk*, 1979

"Over and Over"—from Tusk, 1979

"Love in Store"—from *Mirage*, Fleetwood Mac, 1982

"Hold Me"—from *Mirage*, 1982

"The Challenge (featuring Eric Clapton)"—from *Christine McVie* (solo album), 1984

"Little Lies"—from *Tango in the Night*, Fleetwood Mac, 1987

"Everywhere"—from *Tango in the Night*, 1987

"Isn't It Midnight"—from *Tango in the Night*, 1987

"Temporary One"—from *The Dance*, Fleetwood Mac (live album) 1997

"Friend"—from *In the Meantime* (solo album) 2004

"Northern Star"—from *In the Meantime*, 2004

"Feel About You"—from *Lindsey Buckingham Christine McVie*, 2017

"Game of Pretend"—from *Lindsey Buckingham Christine McVie*, 2017

THE BEST OF "RUMOURS FIVE" FLEETWOOD MAC'S LIVE ALBUMS:

The Dance (August 1997)

In Concert (March 2016)

Rumours Live (September 2023)

The best compilation by that line-up is *The Collection* (June 1987).

CHAPTER NOTES

CHAPTER 1

1—Michael Ralph "Mo" Foster, 22 December 1944–3 July 2023, was a Wolverhampton-born musician, composer, producer, artist, author and raconteur. As a recording session musician and live performance sideman he worked with many artists, including Ringo Starr, Cliff Richard, Van Morrison, Eric Clapton, Sting and Jeff Beck. He taught himself musical notation, released several albums of his own, and founded the UK's first ever bass guitar course at Goldsmith's College, the University of London in 1975. Mo died of liver and bile duct cancer at the age of seventy-eight. His maxim was adapted from an old African proverb: "When an old man dies, a library burns to the ground. And when an old woman dies, I say, a school burns to the ground. And when a child dies, well: a church, a synagogue, a mosque, all burn down to the ground."

2—There is no definitive explanation of the name "Quaives." It could be the plural form of *Quaife*, an anglicized version of the Gaelic *Ó Caoimh*, which in Irish and Manx is O'Keefe. It may also be of Norman origin, a nickname derived from *coif*:

a close-fitting cap, or a maker or wearer of such caps. Compare modern French *coiffe*, a cap, and *coiffure*, the styling of hair. The name also appeared as *Coyf* and *Coyfe*. The family name *Quaife* existed in England, particularly in East Sussex and West Kent, in Scotland and in North America, between 1840 and 1920. The variations *Quave* and *Quaves* also exist, but are rare. As the originally Tudor house was extended and remodeled in the Flemish style during the 1600s, there may also be Flemish, Dutch or German origins to the name.

3—Miss Havisham is the sour, jilted bride in Charles Dickens's 1861 novel *Great Expectations*, who lives among the ruins of her own aborted wedding celebration.

4—Interview with Johnny Black for the late American music magazine *Blender*, May 2005. Although Stevie Nicks's song "Dreams" was about, and was produced by, her former lover and fellow bandmate Lindsey Buckingham, she was by that time already involved with the Eagles' drummer and vocalist Don Henley.

5—Mick Fleetwood confessed to having stolen his legendary pair of wooden balls from a pub in which one of the earlier bands he performed with, John Mayall's Bluesbreakers, were playing. The balls, attached by chains, served as the flushing levers of lavatories. Many toilets around Britain had these at the time. Until that night, he had "never seen them as rhythm instruments until…I pulled them down, tucked them through my belt and started beating them with my sticks once I got back on stage. They sounded pretty good," he recounted in his 2014 memoir *Play On*. "…and there they were, right on my belt —my pair of wooden bollocks." The balls would inspire all the drum solos that he had previously been too terrified to play. "In truth, I started off as a blues player," Fleetwood told *Maui Time* in 2009. "The whole ethic of a lot of blues music is slightly suggestive…I walked out on stage with these two lavatory chains with these wooden balls hanging down, and after that it just stuck."

The balls became Fleetwood Mac's good luck charm. He used them during nearly all Fleetwood Mac's performances, but then lost them somewhere along the road. He had replicas made. They were not the only suggestive item that Fleetwood Mac traveled with. For many years, Mick kept a dildo on top of his bass drum. Nicknamed "Harold," it became the group's mascot. It once nearly got the band arrested, during a show at a U.S. Southern Baptist College.

Mick auctioned the replacement wooden balls for charity in January 2023, following Christine's death. Who knows what became of Harold.

6—The Children of God are now the Family International. Jeremy Spencer is still involved.

CHAPTER 2

1—Analyzed by the *BMJ*, Phosferine was later shown to consist of alcohol, quinine, phosphoric acid and a little sulfuric acid. Phosphoric acid, which can cause chronic kidney disease, bronchitis, shortness of breath and dermatitis, is a component of cola drinks. Sulfuric acid is a corrosive that causes harm to human skin, eyes, teeth and lungs, and can be deadly in high doses.

2—Perfect from the Latin *perfectus*, meaning "to finish or accomplish." In France, it arose as "Pierrefitte" ("pierre" meaning "stone"), the name of various villages and communes there, such as Pierrefitte-sur-Seine and Pierrefitte-en-Auge. The Norman Conquest of England in 1066 delivered it to Middle English (c.1100–1500) as "Parfit." In England, the name was first recorded in Hampshire in 1115; in Somerset as "Parfet" in 1196; and in Herefordshire in 1383. The most usual forms of the name today are Parfit and Parfett. Perfect is also quite common, arising from the reconstructed, learned spelling of the adjective. The name also became popular as a nickname, applied to, say, an apprentice who showed promise on completion of his training. Later Perfects (various spellings) migrated to Canada and the U.S.

The second middle name of Christine's father, Absell, is of western Scottish (Argyllshire) origin, derived from the Gaelic form of the Biblical name Absolom, meaning "peace." Members of the ancient Absell (various versions and spellings) clan migrated to Ireland and the American east coast.

3—The name of Kingston Upon Thames was hyphenated until 1965. The ancient market town was once classed as part of the County of Surrey, but later became a London borough. It is one of only three Royal boroughs in London, the other two being Kensington & Chelsea and Greenwich. The latter received its Royal Charter the most recently, from Her Majesty Queen Elizabeth II in 2012. There are four others in England —Windsor & Maidenhead, Leamington Spa, Tunbridge Wells and Wootton Bassett; and one in Wales, Caernarfon. Royal status is bestowed upon places closely related to the history of the British Monarchy. Kingston had been unofficially royal since the Middle Ages, Queen Mary Tudor having conferred a charter for the town to hold extra market days. King George V formalized its status in 1927. Kingston is situated south-west of central London, ten miles from Charing Cross.

4—Given that Beatrice was more than likely pregnant with John when she and Cyril married, she was fortunate that he was honorable. Christine might never have been born otherwise, and Beatrice's fate could have been grim. As late as the 1970s, unmarried mothers were regarded as "sinful," and were routinely thrown out by their families and abandoned to mother-and-baby homes. Frequently forced to relinquish their infants for adoption, the mothers were often confined to mental asylums. It was never "simply" a case of them becoming "socially unacceptable." The stigma of illegitimacy and the many couples desperate to adopt (before fertility treatment became available) led to the establishment of many mother-and-baby homes between the wars. These were usually run by the church or the Salvation Army. Adopting parents contributed toward the running of them. Beatrice Reece was lucky to have been saved from such a fate.

5—Interviewed by *Harper's Bazaar* in March 2019.

6—*The New Yorker*, February 2022.

7—Ulverston was the birthplace of Arthur Stanley Jefferson (1890–1965). As Stan Laurel he performed with American partner Oliver Hardy as Laurel and Hardy. The comic duo starred in many popular pictures throughout the 1940s. On 19 April 2009, Liverpudlian comedian and singer Ken Dodd unveiled sculptor Graham Ibbeson's bronze statue of the duo outside Coronation Hall in County Square. Nine days later, Ulverston was rocked by an earthquake measuring 3.7 on the Richter scale: the strongest seismic event in the region since a 4.4 quake struck Lancaster in 1835. The statue was unshaken. A museum commemorating the pair stands on Ulverston's Brook Street.

8—A bonded warehouse is a secure space in which goods that are liable to import duty and other taxes are stored. Customs duty on such commodities are deferred until the goods are sold or removed from the bonded warehouse. Source: The Customs People.

9—Beatrix Potter threw her energies into farming, was elected the first woman president of the Herdwick Sheep Breeders Association, and became a keen conservationist and a strong supporter of the National Trust. She left a legacy of 14 farms, 8 cottages and 4,000 acres of land to the Trust after her death. Her home, Hill Top Farm, has become a place of pilgrimage for Potter fans from all over the world. Source: *Westmorland Gazette*.

10—*Guardian*, "The reader interview," as told to Dave Simpson, 9 June 2022.

CHAPTER 3

1—William Mitchell, established 1825, is still based in Smethwick, and is today a famous name in the art of calligraphy.

2—J. R. R. Tolkien and his brother Hilary briefly attended St. Philip's Grammar School; and Dr. Joseph Spence, Master of Dulwich College, London since 2009, was a pupil there.

3—*Birmingham Mail*.

4—The 11-plus was the competitive exam imposed under the Education Act between primary and secondary school at around age eleven. Children were tested in General English,

Comprehension, Arithmetic and General Intelligence/
Knowledge. The exam was established in 1944 to determine
which school a child should progress to: grammar, technical or
secondary modern. Some areas still operate the same or a similar
selection process, but the 11-plus was largely phased out during
the 1970s. Source: www.the11pluswebsite.co.uk

5—*Birmingham Gazette*, Saturday, 2 January 1954. This provincial
title, launched as a weekly in 1741, was one of Birmingham's
earliest newspapers. It published daily from 1862 after paper duty
was abolished and it was able to drop its price to one penny per
copy. The *BG* merged with the *Birmingham Post* in 1956.

6—Ariosophy, "wisdom of the Aryans," was the ideological
system that arose and grew in Austria between 1890 and 1930.
Alongside Armanism, the pursuit was part of an Austria- and
Germany-wide occult revival during the late nineteenth and
early twentieth centuries. Adolf Josef Lanz, aka fascist agitator
Jörg Lanz von Liebenfels, coined the term "Ariosophy" in 1915.
It became the name of his doctrine during the 1920s. The
former Cistercian monk, political and racial theorist and
occultist developed the theories of "blue-blond Aryanism" and
the "lower races" that helped lead to the rise of Adolf Hitler, the
Austrian-born German politician who became leader of the
Nazi Party, dictator of Nazi Germany in 1933, and who caused
the breakout of World War II when he invaded Poland in
September 1939.

7—Monica Black quoted by writer Tim Gebhart, *Exploring
History*, 30 June 2021.

8—Royal Navy battleship HMS *Barham* survived several
German attacks during World War II and lived to tell the

tale. On 24 November 1941, she and other vessels departed Alexandria, Egypt to hunt Italian convoys in the Mediterranean, where *Barham* was torpedoed and sunk the next day by German submarine *U-331*: 862 officers and ratings were killed, including two who died after having been rescued; 487 others were rescued. Captain Geoffrey Clement Cooke, fifty-one, went down with his ship. Source: www.uboat.net

9—Robin Eggar's 2004 interview with Christine was commissioned by *Sunday Express* supplement *S* magazine. His entire transcript, much of it previously unpublished, was included in *Fleetwood Mac on Fleetwood Mac*, a volume of interviews and encounters edited by Sean Egan (author's edition, Omnibus Press, 2016).

10—Architect William Henry Bidlake also designed two of Birmingham's eighteen Grade I listed buildings, both of them churches: St. Agatha's Church, Sparkbrook, and St. Andrew's Church, Handsworth.

11—American pianist Albert Ammons (1907–49), the "The Boogie Woogie Man," was the founding father of the boogie-woogie genre as well as its best-known and foremost exponent.

12—A recording of Ralph Vaughan Williams's "The Lark Ascending" was played at the funeral of the author's father Ken Jones in October 2019.

CHAPTER 4

1—Music journalism lost Ray Coleman in 1996. Chris Welch, Michael Watts, who earlier went by "Mick" Watts, and Richard Williams are still going strong.

2—Jazz musician Johnny Smith's 1954 composition "Walk, Don't Run" was re-recorded in 1956 by Chet Atkins. This was probably the version that Christine and Theresa knew. When the Ventures reworked and re-recorded it in 1960, it earned them stardom and a massive hit. They recorded it again in 1964, and became the first group to have two Top 10 hits with two versions of the same tune. Many other artists have recorded the piece, including Count Basie, Glen Campbell, Led Zeppelin, the Shadows and Jeff Beck.

3—Professor Rose authored the excellent book *Working Against the Grain: Women Sculptors in Britain c.1885–1950.*

4—This according to Richard Hamilton's 1957 letter outlining pop art to his friends, architects Peter and Alison Smithson. Source: Tate Modern.

5—*Classic Rock* magazine (UK), James Halbert, August 2004.

6—Interviewed by Andrew Male for *Mojo* magazine, June 2017.

7—St. Cecilia, or Cecelia, is indeed the patroness of music and musicians. Her feast day is 22 November. She is said to have been a Roman noblewoman who was martyred under Emperor Alexander Severus; but is also said to have died in Sicily under Emperor Marcus Aurelius. The first recorded music festival in her honor took place at Evreux, Normandy, in 1570. She inspired compositions by Purcell, Haydn, Handel and Benjamin Britten, and by Paul Simon ("Cecilia" on the *Bridge Over Troubled Water* album, 1970), the Foo Fighters, Blue Oyster Cult, Brian Eno and David Byrne and various others.

8—In *Metamorphoses, Book X*, Roman poet Ovid told the tale of a sculptor called Pygmalion who created his ideal woman in ivory, and fell in love with the statue. He named her Galatea, then begged the goddess Venus to bring her to life. She did so, and their child Paphos was born, after whom Paphos in Cyprus is named. Ancient Greek and Roman artists strove to simulate nature as far as humanly possible. The pursuit of realistic perfection became Pygmalion's obsession. As Ovid wrote of the sculptor, "His art concealed his art." Pygmalion succeeded in deceiving even himself.

9—Mick Fleetwood talking to the *Daily Express*, March 2014.

CHAPTER 5

1—*Chronicles: Volume One,* Bob Dylan, Simon & Schuster, 2004.

2—The 1930s Golden Eagle pub, birthplace of legends, closed for good in January 1984. It was demolished soon afterward. They paved paradise and put up a parking lot. Don't it always seem to go. Chapeau, Joni Mitchell.

3—By the 1980s, Spencer was living on the West Coast, still performing and touring. He died of pneumonia in 2020, aged eighty-one.

4—Chris Wood quit The Sounds of Blue before they evolved into Chicken Shack, and teamed up with Jim Simpson's jazz-based Kansas City Seven. In 1967 he co-founded rock band Traffic with Jim Capaldi, Dave Mason and Steve Winwood, the latter leaving two years later to co-found supergroup Blind Faith. Traffic reformed in 1970 as a major prog rock outfit that lasted around four years, until Winwood embarked on a successful solo career. Wood continued as a session musician until his death in 1983. Jim Capaldi died in 2005. Guitarist Dave Mason, who, seventy-seven at the time of writing, is still performing, worked with Fleetwood Mac during the mid-1990s during Lindsey Buckingham's absence, recording with them for their album *Time* and touring with them 1994–95.

5—*Mojo*, June 2017.

6—The Music Aficionado blog, June 2017, quoted from *Uncut*.

7—The other two being Albert King and B. B. King.

8—"I'd Rather Go Blind," written by American artist Ellington "Fugi" Jordan during a spell in prison, and credited to Billy Foster and Etta James. It has been covered to death, by everyone from Rod Stewart to B. B. King to Beyoncé.

CHAPTER 6

1—Mick Fleetwood speaking in *How to be a Rock Star* by David Ambrose with Lesley-Ann Jones, Little Wing, 2020.

2—John McVie's Fender bass "got ripped off (stolen) in Redondo Beach," the musician revealed in an unpublished interview in 1997. "Serial number L12304. Yeah, it was all stripped down. Chris [McVie] had drawn a dragon on it, and I carved it out. Yeah, it's a shame. It was a nice bass. It used to be pink but it was a bit much. Eric [Clapton] had a stripped-down Strat. I stayed at John Mayall's house one night and [attacked it with] a bunch of newspapers and a scraper and a bunch of paint stripper. All night. It just took years [sic]. Have you ever tried stripping anything? Those Fenders are covered. They make them bullet-proof. But yes, it got ripped-off." In another interview, he stated: "My Fender, Reg. #L12304, was stolen from our van in Manhattan Beach. Many years ago. By then, it was scraped down to the bare wood and had a dragon carved in it. By Christine. Which tells you how long ago that was!"

3—The Bag O'Nails at 9 Kingly Street in London's Soho, near Regent Street and Carnaby Street, had begun as a 1930s jazz dance club called The Nest. Known during the 1960s as "the Bag" and run by two brothers, the pop agents and artist managers Rik and John Gunnell, it welcomed members of the Beatles, the Stones, the Animals, the Small Faces, the Who, and Jimmy Page, Jeff Beck and Lulu and more. In those years it had a parachute-silk-draped ceiling, small alcove tables and velvet-covered banquettes. It is said that Jimi Hendrix made his debut London performance there on 25 November 1966, although other sources give the date as 11 January 1967. It is also recorded that he first landed in London on 23 September 1966 and played his first London gig the following night at the Scotch of St. James club in Mason's Yard. On 15 May 1967, last remaining bachelor-Beatle Paul McCartney, 24, met and fell for 25-year-old American photographer Linda Eastman there. She would become his first wife and change his life.

CHAPTER 7

1—During the late 1960s, Tony Joe White wrote and recorded "Polk Salad Annie," made famous as a cover by Elvis Presley; and "Rainy Night in Georgia," recorded by Brook Benton, who had a more or less instant hit with it in 1970, and even more notably by Randy Crawford in 1981.

2—*Fleetwood Mac on Fleetwood Mac: Interviews and Encounters*, edited by Sean Regan, Omnibus Press, 2016.

CHAPTER 8

1—*Sense and Sensibility* (1811), *Pride and Prejudice* (1813), *Mansfield Park* (1814), *Emma* (1816), *Northanger Abbey* and *Persuasion* (both 1817). Austen died in 1817, aged forty-one, and is buried sixteen miles away in Winchester Cathedral.

2—*Play On: Now, Then and Fleetwood Mac*, Mick Fleetwood, Hodder & Stoughton, 2014.

3—Jeremy and Fiona Spencer had five children together. After they divorced, Fiona married an Italian known as "Andres," and gave birth to three more. Some of the children later formed a band together, called JYNXT, consisting of siblings Nat, Koa and Tally and non-relatives Blaine, DJ Dan Brown and Joe. Fiona later wrote about being a child bride and young mother, in context of her involvement with religious sect the Family International.

4—sweetlyrics.com

5—Michael Bonner, *Uncut*, 30 November 2022.

6—From the transcript of Robin Eggar's 2004 interview with Christine.

7—"Jennifer Juniper" was a song written by folk pop artist Donovan for Jenny Boyd, real name Helen May Boyd, a former model, who married Mick Fleetwood. Twice.

8—From "Goodbye Yellow Brick Road," Elton John and Bernie Taupin.

9—*Play On: Now, Then and Fleetwood Mac*, Mick Fleetwood, Hodder & Stoughton, 2014.

10—Lyric line from the Eagles' song "Hotel California."

11—*Play On: Now, Then and Fleetwood Mac*, Mick Fleetwood, Hodder & Stoughton, 2014.

12—*Mojo* magazine, 2017.

13—Oldham refers to the 29 September–3 November 1963 UK package tour that year featuring the Everlys as headliners until "the Dynamic Little Richard" joined them, the Rolling Stones, Bo Diddley and other acts on the outing that concluded at London's Hammersmith Odeon on Sunday, 3 November. *Neil Young: Heart of Gold* was directed by the late Jonathan Demme, who also directed *The Silence of the Lambs* (1991, won all five major Academy Award categories), *Philadelphia* (1993), *Southern Gothic Beloved* (1998), *The Manchurian Candidate* (2004) and *Rachel Getting Married* (2008). He also directed a string of concert films including *Heart of Gold* and *Justin Timberlake + the Tennessee Kids* (2016). He died aged seventy-three in 2017, of heart disease and cancer of the esophagus.

14—"Quivers down the membranes" is a lyric line from "Shakin' All Over," a British number-one hit for Johnny Kidd and the Pirates in August 1960. It was written by band leader Kidd, aka Frederick Albert Heath: one of the few pre-Fabs rockers to achieve international fame, mainly thanks to this record. On drums was the celebrated Clem Cattini, "Mr. 45 number-1 45s."

15—James Graydon also leads a group of in-demand session musicians known as California Dreaming. Inspired by the classic American West Coast songbook and interpreting songs by Fleetwood Mac in their repertoire, they perform around the globe and at corporate events.

CHAPTER 9

1—As documented by this author in *The Stone Age: 60 years of the Rolling Stones* (John Blake, 2022).

2—Johnny Winter released more than twenty-five further albums, and produced three Grammy Award-winning albums for his childhood idol Muddy Waters. The first non-African American artist to be inducted into the Blues Foundation Hall of Fame, he died in 2014 at the age of seventy. America's National Academy of Recording Arts and Sciences awarded him a posthumous Grammy in 2015, recognizing *Step Back* as the best blues album.

3—Robin Trower consolidated his career over the next fifty years, releasing twenty-three albums of his own, and numerous compilations and collaborations with bassist Jack Bruce. Seventy-nine at the time of writing, he is still making music. His latest album, *Joyful Sky*, featuring American blues rock artist Sari Beth Schorr, appeared in October 2023.

4—Bonnie Raitt spent years crafting countless albums but never quite breaking through, until she did. Her ten Grammy Awards and her inductions into both the Rock & Roll Hall of Fame and the Blues Hall of Fame say it all. Her 1974 interpretation of John Prine's 1971 sublime encapsulation of wasted life and longing, "Angel from Montgomery," included by Bonnie on her fourth album *Streetlights*, is by far the best version of all.

5—As told to Canada-based rock writer and blogger Dmitry M. Epstein for dmme.net

6—"Riot house" was an accurately ironic variation on the hotel's real name. The original hotel on that site had been actor Gene Autry's Hotel Continental. In 1966, when the establishment was leased to the Hyatt Hotels Corporation, its name was changed to the Continental Hyatt House. Ten years later it became the Hyatt on Sunset; in 1997, the Hyatt West Hollywood; and in 2009 it relaunched as the Andaz West Hollywood. Its proximity to the bars and live venues of Sunset Boulevard has ensured its perennial popularity. Its restaurant is now officially named the Riot House. Legend has it that rock stars, namely Keith Richards, lobbed televisions from its balconies, specifically that of room 1015. Said balconies have since been preserved for posterity as glass-paneled sun terraces. Scenes for rock'n'roll films *Almost Famous* and *This Is Spinal Tap* were shot here.

7—Lyle Tuttle (1931–2019) was a legendary tattoo artist and historian of the art form, who inked many a rocker in his time, not least Cher, Janis Joplin, actor Peter Fonda, the Allman Brothers and KISS star Paul Stanley, as well as John McVie.

8—Asked to leave Fleetwood Mac in 1973 during the recording of their next album *Mystery to Me*, because his attitude and vocal style did not fit in with the band's, Dave Walker joined forces with former Mac-er Danny Kirwan in the short-lived, musically directionless outfit Hungry Fighter. But Kirwan was already on the way down. In October 1974, Walker moved to the U.S. with his American wife and co-founded another short-lived band, Mistress. His "cocaine years" put paid to its potential. His marriage collapsed after a year, and he returned to the UK to lend his talent, briefly, to Black Sabbath. Back in the States, he became a "shiftless hippie," working on building sites, in kitchens and doing manual jobs. He launched the David Walker Band in 1981. Their only album was never released. The reason? "Drugs." Walker spent the next eleven years in Gallup, New Mexico, and rejoined Savoy Brown six years later. He released a solo blues album, *Walking Underwater*, in 2007.

9—After he was dismissed by Fleetwood Mac, Martin Birch returned to the Deep Purple fold, having collaborated with them on five albums previously. He built a solid reputation in the industry, recording another six for them, and also from working both as engineer and producer with Black Sabbath, Rainbow and Iron Maiden. He also produced and/or engineered Jeff Beck, Canned Heat, the Faces, Gary Moore, Cozy Powell, the Michael Schenker Group and more. He retired from the business in 1992 at the early age of forty-four, after producing his tenth and final album with Iron Maiden. He died on 9 August 2020, aged seventy. He was followed to the grave just over nine weeks later, on 16 October, by Christine's second husband Eddy Quintela.

10—Tim Fraser at www.songcentre.co.uk

11—"Fern bars," so called during the 1970s, flourished to serve U.S. city-dwelling singles, particularly young women, who found the standard seedy saloon bar too masculine and intimidating to drink in. They were designed to attract young ladies into a soft and welcoming atmosphere festooned with reproduction Tiffany lamps, pot plants and sitting-room furniture. Single men and women could sup cocktails—Harvey Wallbangers, Screwdrivers—or white wine spritzers among likeminded folk while waiting for their friends without fear of being pestered by undesirables. Fleetwood Mac made precisely the kind of music favored by such establishments. TGI Fridays, Houlihan's and Bennigan's were typical fern-bar franchises. They were replaced during the 1980s, says the *New Yorker*, by "cocaine, Cosmopolitans and Californian wine."

12—"A Change is Gonna Come," Sam Cooke, 1964.

13—*Jennifer Juniper: A journey beyond the music* by Jenny Boyd, Urbane Publications Ltd, 2020.

14—*Play On: Now, Then and Fleetwood Mac*, Mick Fleetwood, Hodder & Stoughton, 2014.

15—Ibid.

16—"I Am…I Said," Neil Diamond, 1971.

17—*The Guardian*, December 2013

18—Ninety percent of the population are right-handed. "Handedness re-learning" (in which left-handers were forced to write with the right hand) was common in British schools until the 1980s, though this left-handed author was never subjected to it. The practice has now been banned. But desks, stationery, implements (rulers, scissors, etc.) and even handwriting in schools (and shorthand) are still designed around the right-hander. Younger pupils, for example, experience difficulties when learning letter-formation. Some regard left-handedness as a special educational need, and call for greater awareness and adjustment, for repositioning left-handed children in class to prevent constant elbow-banging with right-handed pupils, and for better teaching of effective pen grip. Equipment such as left-handed guitars, golf clubs, etc. could also be provided. But plenty of southpaws have done all right for themselves: Mozart, Bill Gates, Barack Obama, Rafael Nadal, Oprah Winfrey, Gordon Ramsay, Paul McCartney...

19—Interviewed in *Fleetwood Mac's Songbird—Christine McVie*, a documentary aired on BBC Four television after her death in November 2022.

CHAPTER 10

1—Caillat, Ken and Stiefel, Steven, *Making Rumours: The Inside Story of the Classic Fleetwood Mac Album*, Trade Paper Press/Turner Publishing Company, Nashville, Tennessee, 2012.

2—The *Guardian*, 2016.

3—Stevie interviewed in *Crawdaddy*, 1976.

CHAPTER 11

1—*Play On: Now, Then and Fleetwood Mac*, Mick Fleetwood, Hodder & Stoughton, 2014.

2—The Rainbow Theatre closed in early 1982. Granted Grade II Listed status, it could not be demolished, and sat mostly idle for the next fourteen years. The Universal Church of the Kingdom of God took it over in 1995.

3—*Play On*, Mick Fleetwood.

4—In 1979, after his relationship with Stevie had ended, Henley was charged for contributing to the delinquency of a minor after a naked sixteen-year-old prostitute suffered a drug overdose during a party at his LA home. Cocaine, marijuana and quaaludes were seized. The musician pled no contest, and was sentenced to probation.

5—Stevie Nicks had many lovers, including fellow rock stars Joe Walsh and Tom Petty, and record producers Rupert Hine and Jimmy Iovine.

6—Dave Marsh for *Rolling Stone*, January 1978.

7—Hal Blaine was one of the most recorded session drummers in music history. He appears on 150 U.S. Top 10 hits, 40 of those No. 1s. He played for Elvis Presley, Frank Sinatra, the Byrds, Neil Diamond and many more; drummed innovatively on the Ronettes' "Be My Baby"; famously on Simon & Garfunkel's *Bridge Over Troubled Water* album, creating the crashing crescendo that draws the title track to its conclusion; and on the Beach Boys' *Pet Sounds* and "Good Vibrations." He was honored with a Grammy Lifetime Achievement Award in 2018, and died aged ninety on 11 March 2019.

8—The age of consent in Arizona is eighteen. Had it been proved that Wilson had engaged in sexual activity with a sixteen-year-old, he would have committed a class 66 felony and could have faced imprisonment.

9—Dennis Wilson's 50-foot twin-mast ketch *The Harmony* was built in Japan in 1950 by the Azuma Boat Company for New Englander George T. Folster. She started life not as *Watadori* (Bird of Passage) as has been reported, but as *Wataridori* (which does translate into English as "migratory bird"/"bird of passage"). A beautiful wooden carving of a bird sat under the boat's bowsprit. There were also birds etched into the cabinets below deck. Various types of wood were used to build her, including mahogany from the Philippines, Burmese teak and Formosan camphor. Her brass furniture was Scottish and her sails English. Dennis bought his beloved boat in 1976. He made it his home, decking it out with fat cushions, fur rugs, a drumkit, an electric piano, a collection of percussion instruments and recording equipment. He sailed her to Santa Catalina Island in Southern California, a get-away-from-it-all destination where he loved to hang out in its quaint towns, Two Harbors and Avalon; and down to the Baja California peninsula in northwest Mexico. The yacht was repossessed in 1980, and sold the following year to cover debts. Dennis Wilson died in 1983. At the time of publication, it has not been possible to ascertain whether the craft still exists.

10—Mike Love vehemently denied the claim. Although he refused to accept paternity, he settled a 1965 suit against him out of court, conceding to child support and to Shawn using his surname once she reached her eighteenth birthday. Thanks to her alleged father's many liaisons, Shawn had at least five half-sisters and three half-brothers.

11—Most of the tracks destined for Dennis Wilson's second solo album *Bamboo* gathered dust on shelves until thirty-four years after his death. In 2017, they were retrieved, the mixes were completed, and his debut *Pacific Ocean Blue* was re-released as a two-CD set that included out-takes and songs from the never finished or released *Bamboo*.

12—Jon Stebbins authored the 2000 memoir: *Dennis Wilson: The Real Beach Boy*, ECW Press, Canada, 2000.

CHAPTER 12

1—The Golem effect is a psychological phenomenon in which the more one expects the worst of a partner, the more that partner is likely to live down to expectations, until extreme disappointment and heartache are caused.

2—*Uncut*, May 2003.

3—*Play On: Now, Then and Fleetwood Mac*, Mick Fleetwood, Hodder & Stoughton, 2014.

4—*Uncut*, May 2003.

5—*Play On*, Mick Fleetwood.

6—Ibid.

7—Musician and sound engineer Laurent Thibault took over management of the studio at Château d'Hérouville in June 1974. Legal and financial disputes occurred during its sale a decade later. The studio closed its doors for good in July 1985. Thibault and his team were ejected, and the château fell dormant for many years. It was then acquired for development as a "major studio facility" set for relaunch in 2013 with, according to publicity, "a waiting list of artists seeking to compose and record in this venue so steeped in rock history." But digital technology and modern recording methods had rendered redundant the traditional large, residential recording studio. The château and studio as they were during the 1970s and early '80s can be seen in the DVD of the making of Elton John's album *Goodbye Yellow Brick Road.* http://www.lechateaudherouville.com/

8—*Play On*, Mick Fleetwood.

9—In 2001, French group Barrière acquired and refurbished the Montreux Casino. Mountain Studios relocated to Attalens nearby. In December 2013, weeks before he died, fifty-seven-year-old Richards attended the casino with Queen stars Roger Taylor and Brian May to unveil a replica of his world-famous studio. The permanent exhibition, *Queen: The Studio Experience*, was also installed, to display Queen costumes, instruments, lyrics and other memorabilia, including Freddie Mercury's own studio chair. Montreux is today synonymous with Freddie Mercury. Millions of fans flock there every year to pay their respects at Irena Sedlecká's statue of him at the water's edge.

10—Chris quoted in her own press kit for *Christine McVie*.

11—American record producer and songwriter Russ Titelman bagged a Grammy for Steve Winwood's hit "Higher Love," and two more for Eric Clapton's albums *Journeyman* and *Unplugged*. He has worked with an extensive roster of artists, from Dion DiMucci to the Monkees, Nancy Sinatra to George Harrison, the Allman Brothers Band to James Taylor and Neil Young to Paul Simon.

12—From Chris's aforementioned press kit.

13—*Nashville Scene*, a weekly local newspaper in Music City, Tennessee.

CHAPTER 13

1—Rumbo Recorders was a studio complex in LA founded in 1977 by Daryl Dragon, a former keyboard player for the Beach

Boys, and his then wife, Toni Tennille—also a keyboardist, who also played with the Beach Boys. She toured with them for a year, affording her the distinction of having been the only "Beach *Girl*" in the band's long history. The couple, who later married, achieved chart success as the duo The Captain and Tennille. Daryl acquired his nickname thanks to his penchant for wearing a ship's captain hat while performing on stage. Their first hit single, "Love Will Keep Us Together," was a cover of a Neil Sedaka song. It sold more than a million copies, earned them a number one, and also a Grammy for Record of the Year. In 1976, they performed live in the presence of Her Majesty Queen Elizabeth II, having been invited by the then First Lady Betty Ford to the White House as part of the U.S. Bicentennial celebrations. Their other best-known hit is their second number one, "Do That to Me One More Time" (1979), written by Toni. She also worked as a session vocalist, contributing backing vocals to some highly celebrated recordings: not least the Elton John albums *Caribou, Blue Moves* and *21 at 33*, and notably to his smash hit "Don't Let the Sun Go Down on Me," as well as various Beach Boys and Art Garfunkel recordings. She also famously sang backing vocals on Pink Floyd's *The Wall*.

2—*Daily Mail*, December 2013.

3—Sixteen times Grammy-nominated record producer Greg Ladanyi—he won in 1982 for best engineered non-classical recording (Toto's *Toto IV*) and was up for Producer of the Year for Don Henley's single "The Boys of Summer"—died in a freak stage accident at Nicosia's GSP Stadium, Cyprus, on 29 September 2009. Fifteen minutes before the start of a performance by Greek Cypriot singer-songwriter Anna Vassi, the fifty-seven-year-old slipped and fell thirteen feet from a ramp, sustaining fatal head injuries.

4—"Billary" was a joint media nickname for President Bill Clinton and his wife, First Lady Hillary Rodham Clinton.

5—*Artsper* magazine, 2019.

CHAPTER 14

1—Christine interviewed by journalist Robin Eggar for *S* magazine.

2—It was for Sandra Elsdon that Peter Green wrote "Black Magic Woman." His nickname for her was "Magic Mamma."

3—Research by the German Max Planck Institute of Informatics. "Pianists type at a rate of 120 words per minute, compared to just 50 words per minute for non-pianists," found a study published in 2019. "When you play the piano, you have an increased feedback loop, an analytical process that is intrinsically yours, and you utilize all ten of your fingers equally."

4—*Play On: Now, Then and Fleetwood Mac*, Mick Fleetwood, Hodder & Stoughton, 2014.

5—Ibid.

6—Ibid.

7—Bilateral renal infarction denotes failure of both kidneys. This is often suffered by patients with other life-threatening conditions, such as atrial fibrillation—which can lead to blood clots, stroke, heart failure and other heart-related complications. The large atrial thrombus is a clot that impedes blood flow. Ischaemic stroke is the most common type of stroke, which occurs when a clot blocks the flow of blood and oxygen to the brain. The secondary cause of Christine's death was cancer, previously diagnosed. The location of the original tumor was unknown or not disclosed. Metastatic malignancy describes a spreading of cancer cells to other parts of the body. When tested and observed microscopically, metastatic cancer cells have features in common with the primary cancer, and are not like the cells in the tissues that the metastatic cancer has invaded. This is how specialists are able to determine that the cancer has spread from another part of the body. Metastatic cancer does not always cause symptoms, but these can include pain and fractures, seizures, headaches and dizziness, shortness of breath, and jaundice or abdominal swelling.

CHAPTER 15

1—"The Love Song of J. Alfred Prufrock," T. S. Eliot.

EVERY TIME THOSE WORDS: QUOTES

Well, when I met Chris her name was Perfect. And then she married me.

But "Songbird," for years we used to close the show with it and every time, stand in the wings and Mick would stand with me and we'd both get a tear. Uh, whether it's 'cause it's a beautiful song or because it evokes memories, I don't know...

When Christine played "Songbird," grown men would weep. I did every night.

She's my oldest friend.

—John McVie

You're Christine fucking McVie, and don't you forget it!

Christine McVie's sudden passing is profoundly heart-breaking. Not only were she and I part of the magical family of Fleetwood Mac, to me Christine was a musical comrade, a friend, a soul mate, a sister...for over four decades, we helped each other create a beautiful body of work and a lasting legacy that continues to resonate today. I feel very lucky to have known her. Though she will be deeply missed, her spirit will live on through that body of work and that legacy.

—**Lindsey Buckingham**

See you on the other side, my love. Don't forget me.

—**Stevie Nicks**

This is a day where my dear sweet Friend Christine McVie has taken to flight, and left us earthbound folks to listen with bated breath to the sounds of that "song bird"...reminding one and all that love is all around us to reach for and touch in this precious life that is gifted to us.

I will miss everything about you, Christine McVie. Memories abound...they fly to me.

—**Mick Fleetwood**

[We'd say] "Let's pretend to be Fleetwood Mac!" There's a song on *Abbey Road*, the "Sun King," that tried that. At the same time, "Albatross" was out, with all the reverb on guitar...So we said, "Let's be Fleetwood Mac doing albatross, just to get things going." It never really sounded like Fleetwood Mac...but they were the point of origin.

—**George Harrison**

Christine McVie—she radiated both purity and sass in equal measure, bringing light to the music of the '70s.

—**John Taylor, Duran Duran**

I'm so sad to lose Christine McVie. She was a unique and soulful musician, supremely gifted songwriter and a warm and wonderful friend, and I am so grateful to have shared some hours in her beautiful presence.

—Neil Finn

I am so sad to hear of Christine McVie going on to heaven. The world feels weird without her here. What a legend and an icon and an amazing human being.

—Sheryl Crow

Such a great songwriter, singer, and a beautiful presence in Fleetwood Mac. A truly sad loss.

—Rosanne Cash

Christine McVie has left us. What memories, what joy, and what a legacy.

—Bette Midler

I'm saddened by the passing of Christine McVie. "Don't Stop" was my '92 campaign theme song—it perfectly captured the mood of a nation eager for better days.

I'm grateful to Christine & Fleetwood Mac for entrusting us with such a meaningful song. I will miss her.

—Bill Clinton (aged 76, alongside a video featuring the 1977 single and footage from his campaign as well as the reunion performance)

Christine was a gem. Soulful, classy and a beautiful songwriter. "Over My Head" was always my sultry, angelic favorite. Bon voyage sweet soul!

—**Ann Wilson**

Well, this is some pretty sad shitty news. Always loved her. Always loved her songs. Sing in power Christine.

—**Diane Warren**

Rest in peace rock'n'roll icon Christine McVie, singer and songwriter for Fleetwood Mac. McVie helped shape the sound of the '70s alongside her counterparts in Fleetwood Mac.

—**The Doors**

We are deeply saddened by the news of the passing of Christine McVie. Hers was a vibrant, soulful spirit, and her music was, and will remain, a gift to the world. We had the utmost admiration and respect for Christine. We send our heartfelt condolences to her family, her bandmates, and her legions of fans.

—**The Eagles**

Christine McVie of Fleetwood Mac has passed today. Our hearts and prayers go out to her family and friends. RIP Christine.

—**Scorpions**

If you were a kid in the '70s, approximately 32 percent of your childhood was Christine McVie singing the lines *"I never did believe in the ways of magic...but I'm beginning to wonder why"* with that unmistakable, melancholy/joyous smoky voice. RIP goddess.

—**Mo Ryan**

Peace and love, Christine McVie.

—**Susanna Hoffs**

I'm at a loss for words...I would listen to Fleetwood Mac with my best friend Sammi Kane Kraft constantly. I wrote my verse to "hallelujah" to try to help me heal after she had passed. Seeing Stevie and Christine together changed my life forever and made me want to play music. I'm speechless. I love you so much Stevie, RIP beautiful songbird.

—**Alana Haim**

What joy and depth she brought; what stories. RIP beautiful Songbird.

—**Gary Kemp**

Sad to hear of Christine McVie's passing. In honor of her I'm playing *Rumours* full blast. I was just reminded that this album was released well before Brickwall mastering came into practice. And the songs, OMG! What a great writer McVie was. These songs are Classic Classics!

—**Tony Visconti**

Shocked and saddened by Christine's passing. We'll miss you Christine.

—**Mike Love**

I would rather go blind…Christine Perfect RIP.

—**Midge Ure**

Oh no. The voice of an angel. RIP Christine McVie. Forever loved.

—**Belinda Carlisle**

With love and respect. RIP Christine McVie.

—**Carole King**

On my first trip to Paris, I…bumped into Christine as I was coming back to my hotel. Her limo was parked out front, and she rolled down the window and asked me, "Don't you love Paris?!" I confessed, I hadn't seen anything. My record company had kept me sequestered in a room doing interviews every day. She looked shocked and asked, "Did you at least see the Eiffel Tower? Or Notre Dame?" I answered, "Nothing." She said, "Get in." I got in her car and she drove me all around Paris, pointing out all the sights. I'll never forget that act of kindness. I still can't look at Paris without smiling.

Later on, I would go see her on stage being a rock star in Fleetwood Mac, but I always felt I had seen a glimpse of who she really was. She was a wonderful woman. I miss her.

—**Chris Isaak**

We adored her. The funniest moment for me has to be back in
'67, '68, when Ricky [Parfitt] and Francis [Rossi, Status Quo
guitarists] tried chatting her up and she told them point-blank
to "piss off, boys"…they were then "totally in love." You didn't
mess with her, for sure. Years later, whenever they saw each
other, they would all laugh about it. But the boys were never
quite sure she wouldn't shout at them again. She kept them on
their toes.
Smart lady.

—**Patty Parfitt**

She was a huge figure for the teenage me, *40 Blue Fingers*
(*Freshly-Packed and Ready to Serve*, 1968 studio album by
Chicken Shack) [was] the first album I ever bought. I was
besotted with her. There were tons of British girl pop singers
—Sandie Shaw, Dusty, Cilla, etc.—but they didn't seem part
of real life somehow. Whereas the only two British girl rock
stars, Christine and Julie Driscoll, did. You read about them in
Melody Maker and imagined them in vans full of guitars and
amps in a world scented with patchouli oil, booze and tobacco,
which seemed unimaginably thrilling and romantic. I loved
her mod clothes and her dark eyeliner. She was a real pioneer.
It must have been tough being a girl in that almost exclusively
male world.

It was about 2005 when I met her, I think. But you always
carry a torch for the people who made that kind of impression.
I told her she'd been a big hero when I was 14, but didn't reveal
the extent of my besottedness. I suspect she guessed, though!
She seemed impossibly cool and experienced in her gorgeous
glass-box apartment beside the Thames.

—**Mark Ellen**

Christine McVie. You left this place better than you found it, for sure. Your music and voice will live on forever. I will never forget the opportunity you offered me and the confidence you instilled in me. I will never forget your beautiful soul, your grace, friendship and generosity. I wish I could have had the chance to tell you that one more time. Perhaps I will one day when we get together to write more songs and laugh again. Today, I am heartbroken.

—**Todd Sharp**

For me, growing up listening to their music, you had three incredible vocalists. You had Lindsey Buckingham, who brought this kind of punk, angular ethos to the whole thing, and you had Stevie Nicks, whose voice was just angelic, other-worldly. And then you had Christine, who for me was the maternal, soulful, heartbeat vocal of the band. I just wanna sing a few of her songs tonight.

—**Keith Urban**

Fleetwood Mac's evolution from British blues band with quite possibly the greatest electric blues guitarist (Peter Green—check out the live version of "Jumpin' at Shadows," one of the greatest pieces of blues guitar I have ever heard) to quintessential West Coast soft rock sound of the '70s is the key to their success. Every character during their classic *Rumours* period was unique. Each was essential to the endurance of the music from generation to generation. Mick was not a writer, but his belief and determination kept the band going no matter how bad their inter-band relationships got. John was happy to sit at the bar, observe the unfolding chaos and simply play the bass, with no strong views regarding musical direction. Someone needed to be the foot soldier in a band of generals.

Lindsey was viewed as the mad genius who led the band. But he would never have been able to write as well as he did without Stevie. Great music/art never comes from a comfortable place. Strife and tension are what bring out the true emotions that connect with your audience.

But Fleetwood Mac's secret weapon, who never gets the credit she deserves, was Christine. She had a true gift for writing perfect pop heartbreak and longing. She was always overshadowed by Lindsey and Stevie, but her songs were some of the best. *Tango in the Night* was one of her finest moments. The lead single "Looking out for Love" was Buckingham's, but the real radio staples were Christine's. "Everywhere" and "Little Lies" are still all over the airwaves. Technically, they are not hard to play. But the ability to write a perfect three-and-a-half-minute tune to which everyone can sing along and that touches hearts universally is something very few artists are blessed with. To have three members of your band who are able to do this is an absolute miracle. Add to that the amazing blend of their voices and the never-ending soap opera of their lives that was the source material for their hits, and it's easy to see how special they were.

—**James Nisbet**

SELECT BIBLIOGRAPHY

Ambrose, David, and Jones, Lesley-Ann, *How to be a Rock Star*, Little Wing/Mango Books, 2020

Boyd, Dr. Jenny, *It's Not Only Rock N Roll: In Their Own Words*, John Blake, 2013

Boyd, Jenny, *Jennifer Juniper: A Journey Beyond the Muse*, Sandstone Press, 2023

Caillat, Ken, *Making Rumours: The Inside Story of the Classic Fleetwood Mac Album*, John Wiley & Sons, 2013

Chrisp, Pete, *Don't Stop: 55 Years of Fleetwood Mac*, Sona Books, 2022

Cox, Ryan T., *Fleetwood Mac Biography Book: The Complete Story of the Legendary Band*, independently published, 2023

Davis, Stephen, *Gold Dust Woman: The Biography of Stevie Nicks*, St. Martin's Press New York, 2017

Docherty, Geoff, *A Promoter's Tale: Rock at the Sharp End*, Omnibus Press, 2002

Fleetwood, Mick and Bozza, Anthony, *Play On: Now, Then and Fleetwood Mac*, Hodder & Stoughton, 2015

Goodrick-Clarke, Nicholas, *The Occult Roots of Nazism: The Ariosophists of Austria and Germany*, 1890–1955, The Aquarian Press, 1985.

Rose, Professor Pauline, *Working Against the Grain: women sculptors in Britain c.1885–1950*, Liverpool University Press, 2020

Santelli, Robert, *Pavilion Book of the Blues*, Pavilion, 1994

Spitzer, Michael, *The Musical Human: A History of Life on Earth*, Bloomsbury Publishing, 2021

Verny, Dr. Thomas R., *The Secret Life of the Unborn Child: A remarkable and controversial look at life before birth*, Sphere, 1982

ACKNOWLEDGMENTS

With thanks and love to:

Keith Altham
John Altman
David Ambrose
Jenny Boyd
Chris Charlesworth
David Courtney
Mark Ellen
Mick Fleetwood
Tim Fraser
James Graydon
Richard Hughes
Julia Jones
Ron McCreight
Stephen Kalinich
Nicola Meighan
David Mindel
The Revd Steve Morris
Jonathan Morrish

Peter Myers
Simon Napier-Bell
Stevie Nicks
James Nisbet
Andrew Loog Oldham
Andy Peebles
Edward Phillips
Patricia Phillips
Don Powell
David Stark
Johnnie Walker
Richard Williams

Black Country Living Museum, Dudley
The College of Psychic Studies, Kensington, London
The Four Seasons Hotel Los Angeles at Beverly Hills
The Quaives, Wickhambreaux, Kent
The Rose Inn, Wickhambreaux, Kent

The Imperial War Museum, London
The Society for Psychical Research, London

Thank you, Clare Hulton, James Hodgkinson, Joe Hallsworth and all the team at John Blake/Bonnier Books UK.
Thank you, Mum and Dad.
To Mia, Henry and Bridie; Adam and Matthew, Nick, Alex and Christian, Cleo and Jesse.
XXX

INDEX